# TOP DEAD CENTER 2

# TOP DEAD CENTER 2

Racing and Wrenching with *Cycle World*'s
# KEVIN CAMERON

## Foreword by Erik Buell

First published in 2009 by MBI Publishing Company and Motorbooks, an imprint of
MBI Publishing Company, 400 First Avenue North, Suite 300, Minneapolis, MN 55401 USA

The information in this book is true and complete to the best of our knowledge. All
recommendations are made without any guarantee on the part of the author or Publisher, who
also disclaims any liability incurred in connection with the use of this data or specific details.

We recognize, further, that some words, model names, and designations mentioned herein are the
property of the trademark holder. We use them for identification purposes only.

*Library of Congress Cataloging-in-Publication Data*

Cameron, Kevin, 1941–
  Top dead center 2 : racing and wrenching with Cycle world's Kevin Cameron / by Kevin
  Cameron;
  foreword by Erik Buell.
    p. cm.
  Includes index.
  ISBN 978-0-7603-3608-3 (hb w/ jkt)
  1. Motorcycles--Performance. 2. Motorcycles, Racing. 3. Motorcycle racing. 4. Motorcycling.
  I. Cycle world. II. Title. III. Title: Top dead center two.
  TL440.C292 2009
  –dc22

                            2009034499

Editors: Lee Klancher, James Manning Michels
Design Manager: Brenda C. Canales
Cover designed by: Matthew Simmons

**On the cover:** Three versions of Kevin Cameron's portrait have adorned his column during his
years with *Cycle World*.

**On the back cover:** Kevin in his natural element, in this case fettling a vintage Yamaha TD2 road
racer in his workshop. *John Owens*

Printed in United States of America

# Contents

# Part 3
## Gearhead Geniuses

# Part 4
## Racing Revealed

# *Foreword*
## *by Erik Buell*

Face it, this is really cool. Writing a foreword for Kevin Cameron's work is a big deal for me. Thirty years ago it would have been beyond my imagination.

Kevin was the guru, the guy who brought the best of racing right into my farmhouse bedroom. The real stuff, full of deep technical detail, and equally full of passion. The stories of the riders and tuners were up close and personal, like no one else told them. He built and modified the best privateer motorcycles, and he beat the factories. Kevin knew everyone and had their respect, so he was privy like no one else.

To make it even better, Kevin took writing to a totally different level because he was fueled by a desire to read, to learn. He portrayed amazing technical depth and heroic personalities. I was double saturated—no, triple saturated—with passion.

Not only could I read about campaigning an H1R, Kevin also included histories of the first engine designers and their challenges. There were stories of World War I and II engines and engineers. He told of those rebuilding postwar Europe with audacity and hope in the face of few resources, creating thrilling motorsports vehicles that celebrated life, freedom, and brilliance.

Kevin challenged me in his articles. He did not suffer fools gladly; his tolerances for the mundane, the bureaucratic, and the mediocre were as small as the tolerances in the machines he built. He spoke my language in every way.

His work inspired me—or perhaps fueled the insanity, who knows? But I built a Kawasaki 350 single roadracer as my first race bike because Kevin had built one. I battled my two demons: the desire to *be* a racer and the desire to *make* a racer.

Yes, every time I bought a factory racer it worked well (OK, not the RR250). But the demon Kevin awoke kept challenging me and taunting me to do more to make it better, to make myself better. Why not get more power out of the 900SS? What about a Yamaha engine in that H-D frame? Why did Irv make a new shorter and stiffer TZ750 chassis?

Well, some of you may know my history, but whether you do or not, I can add this: I would never have become who I am without Kevin's work.

So, read with pleasure and enjoy the ride.

And thank you, Kevin.

# Part 1

# MEMORABLE MACHINES

*John Owen*

*October 1974*

# The Honda CR-72:
# The Past as the Future

*Boston-area roadracer Andres Lascoutx came back from California with this Honda in 1967, but despite my intense interest in it, I wouldn't see it for several years. One story is that these larger twins were built by Honda for the use of its factory riders in the now-vanished non-championship events that were in those days essential to making a living on two wheels.*

In the last two seasons it has become obvious that the current four-stroke machines in American motorcycle roadracing have no chance against the two-strokes. Some people feel that an unfairness is being perpetrated, and this inequity should be corrected by new rules. But there's another viewpoint. The present one-sided affair in racing is not so much a result of inherent advantages of the two-stroke principle over the four-stroke one as it is of the financial or technological unwillingness of the four-stroke makers to build equipment on a par with the two-strokes.

A close examination of a high-quality four-stroke design confirms this view. The CR-72 Honda is one showcase for the innovation created in Honda's rapid rise to international racing glory in the 1960s. The machine is a Honda production racer. It is a 54 x 54mm, double-overhead cam (DOHC) 250cc twin, giving a claimed power of 40 brake horsepower (bhp) at 12,000 rpm.

It took Honda three years of trying before they won their first world championship (the 250 in 1961) in international roadracing. But after that, with a dizzying display of mechanical virtuosity, they won again and again with twins, fours, fives, and even a six-cylinder machine.

Traditional fans were horrified to see their Italian icons smashed by newcomers, and chauvinistic things were said to the effect that the Honda machines represented nothing new, that they were just refined copies of Gileras, MVs, or Guzzis.

At the same time, a new group of racing aficionados was growing up, who watched the Japanese successes with almost religious awe, who collected every scrap of information about the Honda machines, and who learned the novel magic phrases: *four valves per cylinder, eight-speed gearbox, 17,000 rpm.*

I was among those millions. I pored over catalogs and magazines, compiling notebooks full of statistics, measurements made from pictures, impressions by Honda team riders, anything at all that would help get me closer to knowing *how they did it.*

I even tried to race Honda street machines fashioned into racers, but learned, as so many did, that when Honda means a machine to be a street bike, they are usually right. Racing interested me more than brand loyalty, so I turned away from the Hondas to the new and available Yamaha production racers.

In the early 1960s, when Honda success was still new, the company made a number of high-rpm, DOHC 50 and 125cc production racers. These made a niche for themselves in club racing, but were well below standard for international racing.

*Lee Klancher*

11

Much smaller numbers of 250 and 305 twin-cylinder production racers were built, supposedly to provide rides for Honda teamsters in non-international events. These were sold to the riders at season's end, and they then filtered into the hands of the public. They weren't a great success. Handling was poor though power was considerable. Parts production for these models ceased in 1965, so it became necessary to "know the right people" to get spares. Gradually the machines dropped out of circulation.

Apart from this, the big CRs can be looked at in another way. Twelve-thousand rpm from a 54 x 54mm engine translates to 4,250 feet per minute (fpm) piston speed, a very high figure by any standard.

Forty horsepower from a 250 is ho-hum in this age of 50 bhp Yamaha twins, but consider this: double up this twin into a 500 four and you have 80 bhp, a figure that is almost competitive today. Treble it into a 750, and you have the staggering sum of 120 bhp, a number that our present day "Formula 750" machines have yet to reach.

Surely then, four-stroke technology is far from dead if a thought-experiment with a ten-year-old design can come up with horsepower that's competitive today.

A six-cylinder 750 would be costly, even if the new rule were adopted, requiring only 25 machines for AMA approval, but one should remember that Benelli is going ahead with plans to market a six-cylinder street machine.

Let's look at the numbers. The formula relating bhp, brake mean effective pressure (BMEP), rpm, and displacement is: bhp = (BMEP x rpm x displacement) / constant. If we have 40 bhp at 12,000 from a 250 engine, the BMEP must be 175 psi. This is a good figure today, but not an outstanding one. The apparent ceiling for unsupercharged four-strokes on gasoline is about 200 psi, the BMEP of the current Cosworth Grand Prix car engine (450–460 bhp @ 10,000 rpm from 3,000cc). This car engine is water-cooled, fuel injected, and CDI-sparked, all things that the CR-72 is not.

Therefore you can see that this is still a very refined piece of hardware, not to be scoffed at in any sense. Someone may point out that Norton's famous Manx engine could come very close to a 200 psi figure in a good example. That's true, but there was a sacrifice made to get it. The Manx has very pronounced "megaphonitis," that narrowness of powerband that comes from heavy dependence on wave action in the inlet and exhaust pipes, on long cam timings, and on large overlap.

The Manx has been around for a long time. Was Honda missing something, or were they working the compromises some other way? Honda's way was a very different one, as we shall see.

Among my notes from that period ten years ago are graphs showing the advances in BMEP made by each of the great racing companies, year by year. Honda's "progress report" is unique, because the figures rise, then actually fall! The rise takes place in Honda's early period, from the beginning until their first Grand Prix win, as the designers searched out the answers to basic engine problems. This we can understand, but why do the figures drop through the classic years, 1963–1966? Isn't progress supposed to be steady? This brings us to the central point, the basis of Honda's racing design philosophy.

When BMEP is raised to the highest possible level, through the use of strong pipe tuning and long valve timing, the torque curve shows the resonance peaks, and becomes steep. Instead of doing this, Honda settled for a somewhat lower BMEP in order to get the desirable flat torque curve that makes for a very rideable racing motorcycle. Then how did they get the horsepower back, after "throwing away" BMEP? By raising rpm through cylinder multiplication.

Since peak rpm is roughly limited by stroke length, then if the displacement is held constant and the number of cylinders is increased, the stroke of each will become shorter and rpm capability is raised. The final statement of this philosophy was the 250cc six-cylinder racer, capable of some 19,000 rpm and over 60 bhp.

It sounds easy. It wasn't.

Anyone who has worked with racing four-strokes is all too familiar with the problems of high rpm. Piston rings break. Rods stretch and snap. Bearings fail. Valves float and bend. Honda had their work cut out for them, but these were problems of machine design not gas flow.

Thinner rings, better materials and designs whittled away the peripheral problems, leaving a classic vicious circle as the outstanding and central problem—valve gear design.

The gas flow people want the valves to open and close as rapidly as possible, to reduce throttling and losses in the port throats. The mechanical engineers want to do it gradually, since rapid opening and closing means violent accelerations that bend and break parts, as well as tossing the valves right off the cam profile—the familiar phenomenon of valve float. Obviously, longer valve timings give more time in which to perform the required accelerations and decelerations of the valves; but these, in turn, make the engine dependent on pressure waves in the pipes, and the power curve gets steeper.

Up to the point that the parts are no longer strong enough to take it, stronger springs can be used to control float, but at a cost in cam and tappet wear.

The first choice was obviously overhead cam operation of the valves, since this did away at one stroke with heavy rocker arms and push rods, but this was by itself no guarantee of success. The MV 500 four of this period was a dohc motor of the latest design, but had only a 300-rpm safety band beyond the power peak, so that the rider had to be a genius with the throttle to prevent destructive valve float.

Constant trouble with valve gear no doubt motivated the Honda development team to look for a complete solution that would put these troubles behind them once and for all.

Airflow experts in England had proved that one large inlet valve could flow more air than two smaller ones, for a given cylinder size, so no one bothered about the archaic four-valve-per-cylinder idea any more.

This "proof," however, had come at a time when the chief limit to engine speed was crankshaft bearings and piston rings, so the Honda engineers, already having developed suitable rings and bearings, gave the four-valve idea another look in the light of their new requirements.

It turned out that the reciprocating weight of the two smaller valves was less in proportion to their airflow capacity than that of a single larger valve. A four-valve engine might suffer a small loss of breathing efficiency as compared to a highly refined two-valve design, but the extra rpm capability of the four-valve configuration would more than overcome this. The provision of a separate cam lobe and tappet for each valve alleviated the wear problem, so that proportionately heavier springs could be used.

Other benefits appeared along the way. There is no proper place in a two-valve head for the spark plug. To equalize flame paths to all parts of the cylinder and so safely use high compression without detonation, the plug must be in the center of the chamber in the way of the valves. The four-valve arrangement, however, has a nice little nest for the plug right in the exact center.

With the improved relationship between flow area and valve weight, the valve stem could be made much longer in proportion to the valve head. This made room for a long valve guide that would permit prolonged operation at high speed without developing excessive clearance, poor valve seating, and leakage. More importantly, it made room for the inlet pipe to make a much more gradual turn as it approached the valve throat. The abrupt turn before the valve is at the heart of many four-stroke engines' low BMEP problems, so this one benefit erased the last vestiges of truth from the old "proof" of two valves' superiority to four, and Honda was on its way to its "total solution" of the valve gear problem.

Of course, the other engine problems were being worked on at the same time, such as the correct relation of bore area to valve area, cam timings, port throat design, carburetion, and exhaust system design. The advantages of the four-valve layout were masked from public view by general lack of maturity of other design features, so that Honda's winning Mt. Asama racer of 1959 was regarded only as a curiosity in the western press. Its 35 bhp at 14,000 rpm was creditable, it was conceded, but the use of four valves per cylinder showed that the Japanese were still in the dark in engine design.

Two years later, the Hondas began to win repeatedly with four-valve racers and it was clear that the Western designers must be the ones in the dark. It wasn't long before they, too, were working with four valves. At this present day, most serious four-stroke racing engines designed as such use the four-valve concept.

Finally Honda refined the design to the point that they no longer needed very long cam timings and large overlap. The improved flow characteristics now allowed acceptably high BMEP without recourse to strong tuning of the pipes and resultant steep powerband.

By 1965, Honda engineers were ready to deliver a paper before a meeting of the Society of Automotive Engineers, in which they guardedly declared that Honda now had a "design manual" which enabled them to design confidently any size cylinder on paper, then build it and know that it would be close to optimum without development.

The CR-72 production racer was built with the benefit of all this new knowledge. It has four very long stemmed valves in each cylinder—two 23.6mm inlets and two 22.0mm exhausts. More than half of their 100mm length is supported by bronze valve guides. Each valve is urged to its seat by two nested springs, giving some 120 pounds at full lift, with 75 on the seat. Located above each valve is a cylindrical tappet which, although hollow, is closed on both ends. One end is the flat rubbing surface for the cam lobe to act on, while the other has a small projection that bears against the end of the valve stem. Operating clearance is adjusted by grinding this projection, or by selective assembly, since there are no adjusters to loosen, and no shims to drop out. These tappets are carried in pairs in bronze tappet guide blocks which are screwed in place after the valves and springs have been installed in the cavities below them. Spinning in four special close-clearance ball bearings, the cams are located directly over each set of four tappets, and are driven by a train of straight-cut gears from the crank center.

The valve timing is remarkably short, but there is ample valve area to make up for it. The ratio of piston area to inlet valve area is 2.62. After a 12-inch/sec clearance ramp about 20 degrees long, the inlet valve shows significant lift at about 50 degrees *BTDC*, shoots quickly to its full 7.0mm lift, then drops to the closing ramp at about 60 degrees *ABDC*.

Valve motion has two significant phases. As the valve is accelerated upward, the accelerating force is provided by the cam. When the valve has reached its maximum upward velocity, there is only the spring to provide the force to slow and stop it at the top of its lift, then start it downward, accelerating it to the maximum closing velocity. In this, the spring-controlled phase, the spring must supply enough excess pressure to keep the valve and its tappet pressed firmly against the cam lobe, preventing valve float. Finally, the cam-controlled phase takes over again to slow and ease the valve onto its seat.

Since the cam draws its power from the engine, while the spring is a fixed value, you can get quickest action without float by using a higher acceleration in the cam-controlled phase than in the spring-controlled phase. Usually, this is a ratio of two to one, but in this engine, it is three. The peak acceleration on the cam is 1,575 Gs, at peak rpm of 12,000, an incredibly high figure.

A typical maximum acceleration from automotive practice would be 600 Gs, while Mercedes-Benz used 1,200 Gs in the design of their desmo-dromic-valve Grand Prix car engine of 1954. This, then, is why Honda never bothered with desmo valves: They could get the same results without all the added complexity and bulk.

Feeding the inlet valves through an inlet tract of 255mm total length are a pair of the familiar sand-cast Keihin racing carbs, on rubber mounts. These 29mm instruments are built to stay together, as everything that turns is secured by lockwire or special tabwashers.

The exhaust valves speak into a pair of 520mm-long, 35mm ID head pipes that join long, straight-taper megaphones that enlarge to 90mm ID over 760mm. These gradual pipes were a Honda trademark, and are designed to exert a long, mild suction on the combustion chamber over a wide speed range, rather than a powerful and closely tuned one in a narrow range. The engine in fact has a powerband that begins at 8,000 and runs to the peak of 12,000, with a 1,800-rpm safety limit.

Sparks for the 10mm plug in each cylinder come from an energy transfer magneto. AC from a crank-mounted alternator is switched to the huge Kokusan racing coils by two sets of points whose cam is carried in its own bearings, geared to the crank on the left side of the engine.

The resulting pressure is converted to rotary motion by the exquisite full-skirted pistons and totally machined and polished con rod and crank assembly. Each piston carries two thin gas rings and one oil ring, and the crown is of simple pent-roof shape, matching that of the cylinder head.

Con rod big-ends are on caged needle bearings, while the crank runs in two ball and two roller bearings.

A straight-cut primary gear pair carries power to the dry clutch, which in turn feeds the very close–ratio six-speed gearbox. This is shifted in conventional manner by a rotating drum and three forks.

Following Honda design practice, both the engine and transmission parts are pressure-fed by the same oil pump, drawing cool oil from a detachable two-quart sump located beneath the horizontally split crankcase. The main oil gallery across the bottom of the engine supplies each of the four main bearings and two other oilways. From one pair of mains, oil is picked up to take care of the rods. Oil runs back to twin feeds to the gearbox shafts, and up into the bolted-up block of two cylinders, then tees and enters the head in two places. These two supplies are routed to the tappet guide blocks, lubricating the tappets and cam lobes. Splash takes care of the cam bearings, while returning oil flows downwards over the valve springs, cooling them before entering the central gear tower for the long drop back to the sump below. On the way, the oil must pass through small sieves, whose purpose is to trap the debris of any cylinder head disasters so it can't get into the rest of the engine.

This is a lot of machinery, and the weight of this engine is considerable at 132 pounds, which is four pounds more than the four-cylinder Grand Prix engine of the same period. Other Honda racers were much more successful, which is to be expected, since the CR's were a compromise between performance and simplicity, while the championship machines were built to win without regard for price.

However, the CR-72 and its more famous brothers were built on the same basis of engineering innovations and design philosophy; set the BMEP at a level that guarantees a flat torque curve without "tuning bumps" through the use of advanced valve gear, then select the number of cylinders that will permit the rpm necessary with that BMEP to give competitive horsepower.

The CR-72 and indeed all of the four-stroke racers Honda built in the 1960s are ready for the museums now, but they have left their mark, not only in the record books, but on current practice in high-output engine design. Then, too, they've left their mark on each of us who followed them through their career at a magazine's distance, or close enough to hear the unearthly "whoop-whoop-whoop" of the six warming up, or to see Mike Hailwood show his posterior to the competition.

As the rumors of new Honda participation in roadracing increase for the n-th time, I really want to see it happen. If and when it comes about, the machines will be full of new thought, whether two-stroke or four (or other), because they are very clever people at Honda. They hire only "A" engineers. And it will be fun.

### Honda CR-72 PRODUCTION RACER

**Engine type:** Four-stroke twin, 180° firing, DOHC with four valves per cylinder
**Bore & stroke:** 54 x 54mm
**Power @ rpm:** 40 bhp @ 12,000
**BMEP:** 175 psi
**Powerband:** 8,000–12,000 rpm, with a safety zone of 1,500 rpm extra
**Primary drive:** Spur gear, 19–63 (3.31:1)
**Transmission:** Six-speed constant mesh
**Gear ratios:** (1) 1.843 35/19, (2) 1.454 32/22, (3) 1.200 30/35, (4) 1.078 28/26, (5) 1.000 27/27, (6) .965 27/28
**Rpm drop @ upshift:** (1) 27%, (2) 21%, (3) 11%, (4) 8%, (5) 4%
**Ignition:** Energy transfer magneto, two sets of points, one spark plug per cylinder
**Carburetion:** Two Keihin 29mm smoothbore, dual-cable operated. Main jet #110, jet needle RH3, needle jet 2.6mm airbleed type, air jet #250, pilot jet #55, cutaway 2mm, float valve 2.5mm
**Oil pump:** Twin gear type, low volume, supplying engine and transmission
**Valve diameters:** Inlet 23.6mm, exhaust 22.0mm
**Port throat diameters:** Inlet 21.0mm, exhaust 18.7mm
**Valve lift:** Inlet 7.0mm, exhaust 6.0mm
**Valve springs:** Dual, 70–80 lbs on seat, 120–130 lbs open
**Valve overall length:** 100mm
**Valve guide length:** 55mm
**Valve weight:** 26.9 gm (with retainer, keepers, tappet, and 1/3 of spring weight 79.6 gm)

# Cosworth-Norton Technical Analysis

*Just as with the CR-72, I hoped that this engine (then owned by Robert Iannucci) would reveal more than it did. As Champion Spark Plug technician Bobby Strahlman once put it, "Good combustion occurs when the prevailing wind inside the combustion chamber carries the flame kernel in the right direction." Designer Keith Duckworth learned how to make that happen, but staring at parts tells us only so much.*

The 1960s were years when Norton had little unique to offer while the competition went from strength to strength. After feeble efforts at innovation such as the ill-fated Electra (can you build a British Honda?) the company collapsed and was reorganized as Norton-Villiers, Ltd. Now the old Norton technique of felicitously marrying tradition with something quite new again offered hope. The 500cc Dominator twin had been successively enlarged and redesigned; it was now a 750. Since both its pistons went up and down together (like all British vertical twins), its vibration was all in a single plane. If an engine mounting could be devised that was soft and compliant in this plane, yet stiff in all others, an acceptably smooth machine should result. And it did. The Norton Commando with its Isolastic engine suspension was a considerable success for a time.

Even the old Norton racing tradition began to revive a bit. A hotted-up Commando finished second in the 1970 750 Isle of Man TT, ridden by Peter Williams, who was now an important man in the development shop at NV. Little time passed before special racing Norton 750s were being built at a new Norton race shop, located appropriately at Thruxton race circuit. The men involved had no way of knowing that this would be the last try, that the trick of blending brilliant innovation with tradition would not see them through again.

For the 1972 Daytona race, Peter Williams created a special F750 racing Norton powered by the venerable pushrod twin, which gave slightly over 65-bhp with acceptable reliability. In a world of 85-bhp Triumphs and 100-bhp Kawasakis and Suzukis, it was hopeless but would have to do. Wind tunnel tests showed the way to a shape that should run 150 mph on the Daytona banking. Williams rolled through the big tri-oval at 149. Pretty good engineering, though of course the two-stroke giants weren't exactly shaking in their boots over this performance.

These people were clearly doing some things right. When I asked Peter Williams at Daytona what he could do with another 35 bhp he just grinned. Here is why.

As development of Norton's 1973 stainless sheet monocoque frame went forward, a radical new engine was discussed. Ford of Britain had in 1966 commissioned Cosworth, Ltd., to build a winning Formula 1 car engine and they had done just that. The Cosworth DFV had by 1973 won over 100 F1 events. It was a short-stroke water-cooled V-8. Two cylinders from that engine would total just 750cc. Two of those eight cylinders would also total 115 bhp!

*Lee Klancher*

Meanwhile, the monocoque Norton went off to Daytona with its ancient engine and talented development rider, Peter Williams. Under his arm were more tunnel data which now predicted that the monocoque should reach 175 mph at the speedway.

The Norton ran only 142 mph and the cause (choked flow to the carburetors) was not discovered until later. It was a setback.

Now Norton and Cosworth agreed to jointly design and build a new twin for motorcycles, based on the thoroughly proven moving parts and internal gas flow of the race car engine. A hugely ambitious plan, designated P86, required that the new engine be all things to all men. It had to meet an 86 db(A) noise criterion while making 75 street horsepower and running virtually without vibration. It must have a life before overhaul of 50,000 miles. It must meet any foreseeable air pollution standard without major redesign. Finally, it must also win international Formula 750 roadracing events.

How did they plan to do it? Why did they think it was all possible? A lot of noise would be killed by the water-cooling. More would disappear if a toothed rubber timing belt were used to drive the cams. The goal of 75 street horsepower was formidable, but remember, Cosworth, Ltd., was already the world leader in high-performance four-stroke design. Vibration? Counter-rotating balancer shafts could be incorporated in the design to take care of that. A 50,000-mile life? There were already plenty of street machines that old, and this one would have super-ample bearings with a modern, fully filtered oil supply. No problem. Emissions control would be simplified if the fuel were metered at a single point, so the new machine must be capable of running on one carburetor. That meant both pistons would have to go up and down together, just like all the vibrating Dominators, Atlases, and Commandos of the past. This is because a 180-degree twin has irregular firing intervals of 180 and 540 degrees, while the traditional big twins used the 360-degree crank. The 180-540 intake phasing would always make one cylinder rich and the other lean, an air pollution nightmare.

How, finally, did they think they could win F750 with the P86? Consider the opposition. Yamaha was running a 70 bhp 350, which was maneuverable but not blazingly fast. The TZ750 still lay in the future. Suzuki's entries were 400-pound triples with 110 bhp, real lumberwagons but very fast. The Kawasaki H2R was quick but brittle in the extreme. If everyone held still while Norton took aim with P86, they just might hit it right. The design went ahead.

*Lee Klancher*

And so the P86 emerged with both its 85.6mm pistons going up and down together. How do you make a big-twin idle? With a flywheel. Where do you put it? If it isn't to go outdoors it has to go between the cylinders. You say you'd like to put a center main bearing there? Forget it. Besides, look what happened when Matchless tried that back in 1952. The P86 began to look a lot like a traditional British big twin, and we have to suspect that people from Norton twisted Cosworth's collective arm a bit to achieve that conservative result.

Two balancer shafts, turning at crank speed, but in opposite directions, would generate an up-and-down imbalance equal to but opposite that of the pistons and rods. Instant smoothness but complicated.

While P86 plans were being made, the actual racing program went ahead slowly. Money was not coming in, so it was hard to spend. The 1974 chassis was light and clever, but the engine was the same old pushrod dinosaur. A test P86 chassis was also built—different but hardly revolutionary. The engine-gearbox would be a stressed member, with vestigial tube structures attaching the front and rear suspensions to it, rather like F1 car practice. The rear wheel would be braked by a disc *outboard* of the swingarm, on a common carrier with the drive sprocket. This allowed the rear wheel to be changed in less than a minute by withdrawing the axle, leaving chain line and brake caliper undisturbed. The axle would be live, turning in bearings pressed into the ends of the swingarm itself.

Money, money, money. The traditional design of the Norton Commando could not hold its own forever in the rapidly changing world of the Japanese mass-produced motorcycle. Norton's antique production equipment required hand labor and was expensive to operate, while the Japanese companies were using versatile automated factories that kept production costs low. Little by little, whatever Norton had had to offer in world markets was whittled away.

Every week in the British motoring press the controversy raged over whether it were nobler in the mind and pocketbook to buy British and endure the traditional deficiencies, or to yield to the seductions of a Japanese machine, as predictably efficient as a toaster. Stick in bread, get out toast.

By the end of 1974, Norton's race program had all but stopped. The plan now was to prove the P86 in racing first, then promote it to production as a roadster. As 1975 began, Cosworth predicted that horsepower goals would be reached and that 100 bhp was enough to deal with racing opposition. But there was no money!

Norton-Villiers-Triumph was petitioning the British government for 40 million pounds to revitalize the industry. A special team was researching world markets to determine the sales appeal of new Norton models. Together with the P86, Norton displayed an array of prototypes being readied for production. If the money were forthcoming, it would buy new production tooling that would cut costs and make the new line competitive.

In March the Commando-engined P86 test chassis weighed 325 pounds, no mean achievement. The real thing, complete with Norton-Cosworth engine, was to debut at Silverstone in August. A success would have enormous influence on the government's decision. The press vibrated with expectancy. August 30th came and went. They would try for Thruxton on September 28th. That date, too, passed with no Norton entry. Now the big moment would come at the Race of the South at Brands Hatch.

The bellowing P86 prototype came to the line at Brands, as promised. The flag dropped; machines streamed away toward Paddock Bend, 300 yards off. A Yamaha rider fell, bringing down eight others—including Dave Croxford on the prototype. It was a considerable blow to the project. Even though the Brands Superprang was a true accident, it damaged Norton; the company's financial condition was now very serious.

In December, Phil Read announced his willingness to test the new machine. Many times a world champion, Read had the prestige to carry the project ahead. In January he made a bid to take over the race effort, top to bottom, and required that everything be placed under his direct control. This was a sound move; only dictatorial powers could sort the good from the bad in P86, and only a real racer, as opposed to a bureaucrat, could do it.

By February Read had withdrawn his offer after consultations with the makers. His reasons were that the device could not win as it was, Cosworth was too busy with F1 commitments to make the needed changes, and it was not fair to the public to continue raising their hopes for a British renaissance. Read was out.

What had he discovered? What had he wanted? Right on the Cosworth drawings the weight of the race engine is given as 195 pounds. Of this large total, more than 75 pounds is rotating weight. This is doubly important, for during vehicle acceleration its mass must be accelerated not only in a straight line but also around its own axis. Competing brands' engines then weighed around 140 pounds, of which some 40 were rotating, and gave close to 125 bhp.

The power of the P86? The most the factory ever got was just over 100 bhp, achieved with an experimental fuel injection setup. With the standard Amal Concentric Mk II carbs, power fell into the mid-90s. And it was sluggish power because of the inertia of the heavy crank and balancers. This power, such as it was, was all on top.

What do you suppose Read asked Cosworth to do for him? Surely he asked that the engine be relieved of the 20 extra pounds of balancer shafts. Not so easy with the power passing through the front balancer. Surely, too, he asked that the huge center flywheel be dropped and a center bearing be substituted. With its support, Formula-car rpm would be no problem. He would also have insisted on a redesign of the gearbox, a constant source of trouble; insisted on fuel injection instead of money-saving carburetors; insisted on light metals where iron and steel had been used in the prototype.

Such a revised engine could have weighed under 150 pounds and might have given 110 bhp. That power peak combined with a four-stroke powerband and light vehicle weight might have been a good tool against the two-strokes with their bill-spike powerbands. Might have been worth a man's time.

But Cosworth could not do the impossible. Norton had no money and Cosworth had no time. A hastily organized public subscription netted 1,600 pounds to keep P86 alive, but it was only a gesture.

In April of 1976, Dave Croxford quit after a rash of mechanical failures. The project "cried out" for Peter Williams, now out of racing altogether owing to a bad accident. Croxford was a competition rider not a development engineer. It must have seemed to him that the Cosworth-Norton had been especially concocted to make a fool of him and his excellent reputation.

In August a major redesign of the chassis was begun, supposedly on the insistence of Cosworth's chief, Keith Duckworth, who felt that the machine's problems must stem from poor handling. The engine was relocated where he had wanted it in the first place, two inches lower and inclined forward. The live rear-axle scheme and forward-mounted Koni shocks were abandoned for more conventional parts. The machine was further lowered by shortening the steering head, which now had means of varying the wheelbase.

With this new chassis Croxford and Tony Smith went to open practice at the very fast Silverstone circuit. Mick Grant on the works Kawasaki lapped at 1:38 with apparent ease. The best the Norton riders could do was a 1:46.8. It was a catastrophe. Horsepower, please.

Cosworth and Norton had been partners in P86, but the division of labor was often paralyzingly complete. NVT people were under strict orders to touch nothing but the spark plugs. Any engine trouble required return of the complete unit to the makers (per Cosworth's F1 policy). Each party tended to see in the other's work the source of all current troubles. Norton had insisted on many traditional engine design features, and Cosworth had put its fingers into chassis matters. As money ran out, there was a constant speed-up of the schedule, and things done in haste are seldom right.

Everything had run out. The government rescue of NVT had fallen through. The skilled crew at Thruxton race shop were ordered to earn their keep by modifying batches of Russian sidecars, and many of them quit. That was that.

The prototype P86, numbered 002, made its way to NVT's California operations center just as the company's imminent demise made the whole thing into so much surplus property. And as such it came to the attention of a certain Robert Iannucci, a man who makes it his business to collect the unobtainable. Beginning years ago with an interest in the big racing singles, this extraordinary connoisseur has branched his interests in a number of directions. Time, the telephone, and stacks of correspondence summoned the P86 to him.

At the Bridgehampton fall AAMRR race in 1978 we were to hear it start and run with a blast of noise that nearly got us all jailed. The mechanical marvel was later ridden several laps in demonstration, retiring with a cracked waterpipe. Because of its unique place in British motorcycle history, there could be no real track test. Rider David Roper pronounced the machine "a blast," termed the brakes "good" and the power "OK—pretty good," and that was that. But we could disassemble, measure, and inspect.

The motorcycle is compact, incredibly dense. Even though it is low it gives an impression of ponderous weight. It has that indescribable development-department finish that says that the way it works is much, much more interesting than the way it looks.

The nice features abound, of course, as they always do on hand-built prototypes. The fork is a forward-axle design, allowing larger overlap of tube and slider for smoother action under braking. Five-spoke mags carry the weight; Lockheed aluminum calipers grip modest-sized iron discs floating on splined carriers. The swingarm is a bolted up fabrication of aluminum beams milled from solid into a complex pattern of reinforcing ribs and flanges. The section of the arm increases from front to back, the reverse of usual practice. By the old grab-the-tire-and-seat-and-pull test, this arm is not very stiff.

Flanking the engine at the front are the small water radiators. Below, in the center, are the oil radiator and filter. The power unit itself, squat, bulky, and complex, sits very low and forward. This is the modified frame, incorporating Duckworth's ideas. The left side of the engine is a maze of cam drive belt and pulleys; the ignition generator and trigger units. On the other side is only a vast featureless expanse of high-quality sand-cast primary drive cover.

The fuel tank, truncated at the front by the steering head subframe, sits tall and carries back to the very angular low seat. The two generously dimensioned header pipes emerge from the front of the near-vertical pillar of cylinder and head. The tubes join the collector at the back of the gearbox, and this large-bore pipe ends at the axle.

This engine cannot be removed from the frame. Rather, the frame must be removed from it—in pieces. The front subframe with fork and front wheel, once unbolted from the cylinder head and front of the main casting, can be wheeled away like some Buck Rogers shopping cart. The rear subframe, carrying rider and suspension loads, is clipped on at the gearbox and cylinder base areas. Footpeg plates originate at the back and bottom of the gearbox, jutting rearward to the rider's feet.

Really, the power unit is nearly all there is. A single 40-pound aluminum casting houses the crank and balancer shafts, the gearbox, the integral oil tank and the swingarm pivot bearings. The parts that fill all these spaces are not light. I knew as I helped load the engine in my van that I would need help to get it out again. I can lift and install a TZ750 engine as easily as the next fellow but this model was beyond my strength.

There was plenty of reason to be fascinated by this engine, success or failure. This monster twin was the little brother of the Cosworth DFV, the winningest four-stroke in recent F1 history. Right on my bench.

When the Cosworth F1 engine first appeared in 1967, its winning performance was a bit baffling to traditional analysts, but what Duckworth had done was to unify several concepts then current into a single workable engine. There had been plenty of oversquare engines before and there had been engines with four valves per cylinder. Duckworth, however, concentrated on the problem of getting rapid, efficient combustion.

In an ordinary two-valve engine with a so-called hemi chamber it could take a long time for the combustion flame to burn the whole charge. Hemi chambers had stopped being hemispherical as soon as compression ratios went over five or six to one; when that happened, the formerly flat piston top had to begin protruding up into the combustion chamber. It had become a dome. In modern two-valve designs, such as the Suzuki GS1000, if an 11:1 compression ratio is desired, the piston dome is so tall that the combustion space becomes very thin and arched, rather like the rind of half a cantaloupe. It is hard for hot, efficient combustion to occur in such a space—too much heat is constantly being lost to the nearby metal surfaces. In addition, the only place for the spark plug is over on one side, making the flame path long as well as narrow.

The early work with four valves, such as Hondas in the early 1960s, had concentrated on the rpm advantages of the layout. Piston domes remained tall and combustion thin.

All right then. I removed the huge Allen bolts retaining the head and lifted it off. There were no big surprises, no shocking innovations. There were the pistons, completely flat on top except for small valve clearance cut-outs. The combustion chambers in the head were like shallow V-shaped troughs, with the two sides and the valves in each of them at 32 degrees to each other. Because of this small included angle, the chambers are not very deep—10mm along their centerlines—but this is deceptive. Since the piston crowns are flat, the 10mm depth actually constitutes a strong concentration of mixture very near the spark plug, right in the center. This concentration of charge is the main feature of Duckworth's rapid-burn chamber. In the P86 there are two 34mm intakes and two 29mm exhausts per cylinder. These are equivalent in area to one 48mm intake and one 41mm exhaust, almost exactly the sizes used in the old 500 singles. Yet these cylinders are only 375cc each. The large valve area is needed for flow at the rpm peak of 10,500, whereas the old Manx pulled only to 6,800–7,200.

But how about this design? Could it have rescued the company, either on the track or on the sales floor?

The actual power of the race engine, some 95 bhp, was 20 percent down from the target 115 bhp figures. Where did the power go? Very likely several things account for this. First, the Grand Prix car was a fuel-injection design while the P86 has 40mm Amal Concentric Mk II carburetors. Fuel vaporization in a fuel-injected engine is assisted by the fairly high pressure forcing the fuel out of the spray nozzle. This is at least 500 times greater than the pressure difference which forces fuel out of a carburetor's needle jet.

It is customary when using carburetors to make the carburetor the largest part of the intake tract, then to progressively narrow the bore as it goes deeper toward the valve. This accelerates the flow. Carbureted mixture always includes a fair proportion of fuel in the form of large droplets, and the charge acceleration helps to keep them in the flow rather than on the walls of the duct.

The P86, which has the port dimensions of a fuel-injected car engine, has a constant cross-section through the carburetor and manifold right into the head. Once there, the section actually increases somewhat, finally necking a bit to approach the valve ports themselves. If the mixture flowing through this pipe has been mechanically produced by fuel injection, droplet size will be well controlled. However, anyone who has watched fuel streaming from the needle jet of a carburetor curing an engine test has seen the big globs of fuel which depart along with the mist. Without a port designed for this kind of mixture, the carburetion would have to be set very rich; many of these globs are not going to burn at all, simply getting hot, drawing valuable heat out of the combustion flame, contributing nothing.

In addition, the race car engine has a steep downdraft angle of 35 degrees where the intake pipe enters the head. In P86 this angle is zero, to allow the carburetor float bowls to work without an abnormal tilt. This means that the intake pipe and the mixture have to make that 35-degree turn inside the head in order to approach the valve ports as in the car engine. This turning is a further invitation to the fuel droplets: "Here, let us centrifuge you right out here on the wall. Drop out, droplets."

Another troublesome aspect is the cam drive system. Told that the engine had to be dead quiet, the designer knew that rigid drive by gears, as in the car engine, was out. To have the correct tooth spacing when hot, gears often have to be loose and rattly when cold. They require lots of precision machining and nice ball-bearing support. Good for the race car but not for P86. Chains were a possibility but still noisy and troublesome, always spitting their connecting links. They could be a development headache, too, requiring rubber-covered dampers to prevent vibration and irregular cam action. And they had to be in an oil bath. And they wore out and had to be adjusted. No good.

In the early 1970s toothed rubber timing belts were solving lots of automotive problems. They are quiet, need no lubrication, give a positive drive, and don't wear or require adjustment. These qualities made a timing belt the choice for P86. The 3/4-inch-wide, 3/8-inch-pitch belt chosen might have made a fine drive for the street bike's camshafts. The 75 bhp version was to have smaller valves and lighter springs than the race, and to turn fewer rpm. On the racer, however, the little belt didn't do well. It had to be replaced constantly. Better and better belts were tried. The belt on 002 bears the word "prototype." There was a bad torsional vibration at 4,000 rpm. Just tell the riders not to run the engine at 4,000 anymore—the power range is 7,000–10,000 anyway.

Even in development of the original Cosworth V-8 the cam drive had been a problem, giving rise to torque transients 10 times greater than expected. If this was a problem in an eight, with its overlapping valve events, wouldn't it be much worse in a twin? It was. The belt cannot have been a rigid drive. Valve events would occur according to the accident of belt action rather than designer's intent. Horsepower down, down, down

Belt life was also limited by having to drive the rear balancer shaft, a nearly eight-pound item which had to turn in exact lock step with the crankshaft. At a steady speed, there would be no problem, but in a clutchless upshift the heavy balancer would produce a violent torque transient.

Then there is crankcase pumping: The two pistons moving together produce a big change in crankcase volume every revolution. The pressure generated in its way is forced back and forth through the engine's internal passages much as oil is forced through the orifices of a shock absorber—absorbing power. Udo Guitl discovered how much power in his work with the BMW twin, and went to great lengths to eliminate it. On P86 there is only a 3/16-inch breather line with a check valve—not enough to make much difference.

Finally there is crank flexibility. Many are the engines which have gained power through stiffening of their bearing supports or rotating parts. Here in the Cosworth-Norton crank are two main bearings, one at each end, and suspended between them are the two rod journals and the huge flywheel. No center bearing. (After all, the 1952 Matchless twin had a center main bearing and it was a failure. We don't want that!)

Racing on short tracks is largely a matter of handling and acceleration. Here is the Cosworth-Norton with its 35-pound crank and 20 pounds of balancer shafts, a 12-pound steel clutch and an 8-pound gearbox, all rotating mass waiting to oppose vigorously any attempt to accelerate them.

Here is the basic layout, with facts and figures. The crank is carried in two 62mm plain bearing journals, copiously cooled and lubricated by pumped oil at 35 psi. The forged-steel, shot-peened rods are Formula 1 car parts and ride on 49mm-diameter plain bearing journals. The pistons are also from the car engine, beautifully made three-ring forgings made in Cosworth's own piston forge plant. The company was forced to buy their own to guarantee quality. The bore and stroke are 85.68 x 64.77mm for a bore/stroke ratio of 1.32.

A big gear pair takes the power from the left crank end to the front balancer shaft, which is a big iron bar of D-shaped cross-section, turning in plain bearings. Down its hollow center passes a quill shaft, taking the drive to the primary sprocket on the right side of the engine. This quill shaft is a torsion spring. Its job is to protect the primary drive and transmission from the whacking they would otherwise get from the big twin's power impulses. The rear balancer shaft, turning in ball bearings, is driven from the cam belt.

The primary drive is a 1-1/8-inch-wide Morse Hy-Vo silent chain at a ratio of 25:56 from the front sprocket on the balancer to the rear one cut on the outside of the clutch drum. No wear was expected from its drive, so there is no provision for adjustment.

The clutch is heavy but beautifully made. Four 140mm O.D. friction discs coated with sintered copper are confined with steel discs and top and bottom pressure plates, all compressed by a single diaphragm spring.

The gearbox is all indirect. Power from the clutch enters on the front shaft, then passes through one of the five gear pairs to the countershaft, whose left end bears the 5/8 x 3/8-inch final drive sprocket. The ratios are very wide by modern standards, with the minimum rev drop in an upshift being the 1,900 rpm between fourth and fifth. This is what four-stroke powerbands are all about. The gears are selected by conventional C-shaped shifter forks, actuated by a nicely finished drum cam and ratchet mechanism. The gears are also well-finished, and large enough for a medium-sized automobile.

Back to the crank. Outboard of the drive gear on the left end, isolated from lubricating oil by an intervening seal and casecover, is the cam belt drive pulley, and on top of that is the ignition trigger blade—a little tab of steel projecting from the rim. As the leading edge of this blade passes a magnetic pick-up, a positive signal is produced. As the trailing edge passes the pick-up, a negative signal results. For running, the leading edge signal is used to trigger the ignition sparks, but for starting, when a retarded spark would be nice, the rider thumbs a handlebar-mounted button and the ignition begins to trigger off the trailing edge signal. Instant retard. Clever. The ignition is the Lucas RITA CDI system. Running current is supplied from a small alternator mounted on the front balancer shaft, supplemented for starting only by a small NiCad battery. This battery, the output coils, and the ignition control box are all mounted in a box under the seat.

The hard-working timing belt finally arrives at the cam-drive pulley, which rides on a hardened-steel pin pressed into the head. The back of the pulley is a gear which engages the two camshaft's drive gears.

The short cams, each with four lobes, ride in pressure-fed, split-shell plain bearings in the head. Because of the narrow valve angle, a single cover spans both cams. Short, bucket-style tappets ride in the head material itself—there are no separate tappet guide blocks. Valve clearance is set with selective fit lash caps which socket down over the valve stems before the tappets are installed. There are thus no shims to be spit out. Reliable, strong, trouble-free.

The valves are rather short at 98.3mm and have 7.0mm stems. That part of the intake valves' that is in the port is necked down to 5.4mm to reduce airflow disturbance. There is no loss of tensile strength for this diameter is already present in the retainer collet grooves. Steel retainers transmit force from double coil springs.

The valves are opened to a lift of 10mm using a moderate (by the outlandish standards of United States drag racing) acceleration of some 1,600G at 10,000 rpm. The effective valve timing, measured at 1mm lift, totals 274 degrees, with the exhaust opening at 60 degrees BBDC and closing at 34 degrees ATDC. At the running clearance, these timings approximately increase seven degrees per side, becoming exhaust opening at 66 degrees BBDC and exhaust closing at 41 degrees ATDC, total duration 287 degrees.

The water pump is driven from the right-hand end of the head and circulates coolant through the head, the radiators, and around the wet cylinder liners in the main casting.

The oil pumps are driven from the back of the clutch. There is a scavenge section, whose pump volume is five times that of the pressure, or delivery, side. This is done, as in Formula car practice, to ensure that only a minimum of oil is ever present in the crankcase, where it can wrap around the crank at high speed to consume amazing amounts of power. The oil is sent to a separator, then to the integral holding tank behind the gearbox.

The engine is of dry-deck construction, rather than using a single head gasket which tries (often unsuccessfully) to seal everything. The cylinder head seals to each of the liners with a special metal ring and all oil and water passages are sealed by o-rings resting in counterbores.

The two Amal Concentric Mk II carburetors are flexibly mounted to short intake stubs and each is fitted with a lovely spun aluminum intake bell with a generous flaring shape. These are said to have added five horse-power in themselves.

In sum, here is a tool-room special—an engine clearly very expensive to make—which combines features proven in Grand Prix car racing with traditional design quirks taken from the most uninspired of street bikes. Although parts quality is high, and Duckworth's original design beyond reproach in its own field, the combining of features was done in such a way as to make this apparent: The designers ignored useful techniques current in Japanese design. Steeped in their years of tradition, they felt no need to look elsewhere. They had practically invented the motorcycle, after all, so why consult with anyone else? (Of course our frames handle—we're English.) NVT did not accept that the world had already turned.

Had the company readied this design in the late 1960s, when there was still a large following for English machines, things might have been different, at least in limited respects. As a racer, the P86 might well have done in the Triumphs and BSAs of the time, and through development it might have fended off the early, immature two-stroke racers as well. It could have had an honorable and successful career in racing and then faded quietly away, like Norton itself.

# Bimota
# Tesi 1D

*For a time, it seemed that* something *other than the* *venerable telescopic fork must provide enough advantage to justify its existence. It has yet to happen.*

OK, I give up. What is this? Doctor Dolittle's Pushmi-pullyu motorcycle? No, indeed. This is the Bimota Tesi 1D, the world's first hub-steered production bike. Without its clothes, you can't easily tell which way it goes because it has pivoted-fork suspension at both ends—not just at the back as conventional bikes do.

All the major companies have tested or shown forkless prototype bikes. Suzuki has shown its Nuda. Yamaha its Morpho. Honda hoards patents in the field, and has for years supported the famous Elf series of French-built forkless race bikes. So far, even after all this testing of the waters, none has taken the daring leap into production. Bimota, a tiny but influential Italian specialist company, has seized the initiative with the Tesi.

Bimotas are expensive, the Tesi especially so. List is $40,000. I hear you gasp, but consider what you get: the first production bike of its kind, powered by a Bimota-tuned version of Ducati's fuel-injected, desmodromic 851 V-twin, executed in superb fashion with beautiful welds, gorgeous paint, and many Grand Prix–style milled-from-billet parts.

On a conventional motorcycle, the steering pivot is located up high, in the bearings of the steering head. In hub-steering, the pivot is moved down into the center of the front wheel hub. The forward-projecting arms of the front swingarm are joined by an axle-bar. At its midpoint, a short, stiff kingpin is fitted. Tapered-roller bearings are pressed onto this kingpin, above and below the axle-bar.

A short piece of large-diameter tubing steers on these bearings: we'll call it a trunnion. When the wheel is pointed straight ahead, this trunnion tube is almost concentric with the axle-bar. The trunnion's steering lock is limited by contact between its inner diameter and the axle-bar—and by contact of the tire to the insides of the front swingarm. On the outside of the trunnion are two slim, large-diameter ball bearings—one on each end. These carry the front wheel, which has an appropriately large inner diameter to fit over the trunnion and its big ball bearings.

The brake discs bolt to the faces of the wheel hub, and the brake caliper carriers bolt to the faces of the trunnion tube. Brake torque is thus transmitted from calipers to trunnion, then through the steering bearings and kingpin, into the axle-bar. The ends of the axle-bar carry arms that, through links, transmit brake torque into the chassis itself—freeing the front suspension from all brake reaction.

Yes, but how do the rider's hands control the steering? A mechanical linkage of rods, levers, and ball-joints connects the rider's bars to the steering trunnion.

Why create all this? Why replace the telescopic fork? There are several tempting reasons. To start, the sliding bearings in even the best teleforks bind during braking, making suspension overly stiff, reducing front tire grip. A pivoted fork has only rotary motion, which does not bind. Second, a telescopic fork must be steered with the wheel; while in hub-steering, only half as much mass—the wheel alone—is steered. The lighter the steered mass, the greater the potential stability. For a third reason, look at the short, direct load path in this Tesi chassis. It runs almost straight from axle to axle, making no long, flex-prone detour up fork tubes, into a tall steering-head, and back down to the rear swing-arm pivot. There are just the two milled-aluminum plates, sandwiching the Ducati 851 engine between them. The swingarms attach to these plates. The final attraction of such a front end is novelty itself.

And what of the possible disadvantages? Telescopic forks are highly developed now—a mature technology. Although development may in time make forkless designs superior, the competition is tough. Plus, with telescopic forks, steering is direct—almost as though your hands were grasping the axle ends—so you can feel every nuance of front-wheel traction. This directness is difficult to provide in forkless designs. Lastly, all current engines were designed for tele-scopic-fork chassis, so many of them adapt poorly to alterna-tives such as the Tesi.

What's this future-bike like to ride? Different—very stable, yet quite responsive. So it should be; the steered mass is minimal. At speed, control resistance consists partly of wheel gyro reaction, and partly of steered-mass inertia. This bike has very little of the latter, and responds smartly to inputs.

The Tesi's front-end behavior is neutral under braking, not pro-dive as teleforks are, so our test riders found very little brake dive. This took some getting used to, as they normally use dive to

*Lee Klancher*

measure braking force. The Tesi's front suspension, lacking a telefork's sliding stiction, is extremely supple, and tracks small bumps well. This suppleness provides another advantage: Forkless bikes have phenomenal braking grip.

Every control innovation has two basic aspects: technical and social. Technically, the Tesi works well—outstandingly in certain respects. The social aspect is more difficult to assess. Riders today learned to ride on teleforks, so anything different automatically feels wrong. Does that mean it is wrong, or only that it takes getting used to? Now that a production run of 150 of these novel machines is under construction, many more riders can decide for themselves. For street machines, the Tesi is the first step in a direction that has long needed to be explored.

# Honda
# NR750

*Honda saw oval pistons as the means by which the four-stroke principle might yet prevail against two-strokes. Here was a fast-burning, ultra-high-revving engine, free of the usual ills of extremely large-bore, round, short-stroke cylinders. Flame travel was short, valve area large, and combustion-accelerating squish practicable (it's not in round cylinders with 5, 6, or 7 valves). High piston acceleration kept the NR500 from reaching design rpm, while two-stroke power soared out of sight. The NR750 production bike commemorated the attempt.*

It has taken more than 14 years, but production line reality has finally emerged from developmental fantasy. Honda's NR750, the first road bike to utilize the oval-piston technology initiated by that company way back in 1977, will go on sale to the public very soon.

This announcement, made recently to the European motorcycle press in Geneva, Switzerland, declared that these motorcycles, which embody "dynamism and elegance," will be produced only during the year 1992, and at the very limited rate of three per working day. In this sense, the company seems to be declaring that the NR will represent a high-water mark of motorcycle development at Honda, a statement that need never be repeated.

We shall see.

In evangelistic terms, Honda tells us that this machine will belong to the few true connoisseurs who recognize excellence on the highest level. But the NR750 buyer will first of all be distinguished by having approximately $60,000 of casual liquidity. And if a resident of the United States, he will have to procure his NR750 from Japan or select European countries; the bike will not visit the showrooms of this country. He'll also have to persuade himself that the uniqueness of the oval-cylindered engine is overwhelmingly desirable, for the 490-pound, 125-bhp NR750 will be neither the lightest nor the most powerful sportbike offered by its manufacturer in 1992. As to craftsmanship, the NR will surely be the equal of the well-detailed RC30, which it resembles in general chassis layout. It actually can aspire to the level of detail execution found in Honda's 500cc Grand Prix bikes—currently the finest in the world. All bodywork is in carbon-fiber-reinforced plastic (CFRP), and even the ignition key has a symbolic carbon-fiber insert.

Despite many well-publicized developmental troubles, the oval cylinder is workable. Gasoline and air find nothing sacred about round cylinders. They simply are convenient, for they can be bored, rebored, and honed using basic industrial machines. You may recall the English proposal, made some 25 years ago, to make *square* cylinders. They were to be "rebored" by simply unbolting one of the sides, grinding it flat and reassembling. Several square-cylinder, transparent engines are at work in research labs worldwide, supporting combustion studies.

Honda engineers, however, had ample reason to leap out of the deep groove that history has engraved in our collective engineering consciousness. In the late Seventies, they were assigned the formidable task of designing four-stroke engines that would win 500cc Grand Prix races during a period in which two-strokes were rocketing to final maturity.

At that time, Honda's last try at the 500 class had come in 1967, with the 85-bhp RC181 four-cylinder in the hands of Mike Hailwood. That powerful but unstable machine was defeated that year by a less-powerful but lighter and better-handling three-cylinder four-stroke MV Agusta ridden by Giacomo Agostini. MV four-strokes subsequently dominated the class until Yamaha and then Suzuki entered two-strokes. Just as Honda was considering the matter, MV gave up, its 98-bhp four-stroke having been defeated not by superior power but by the light weight and superior handling of the new Japanese two-strokes. Honda's attempts to overthrow that absolute domination by two-strokes were what forced its engineers to consider unconventional approaches to four-stroke engine design.

To understand the line of thinking that eventually led them to the oval piston, we have to examine the basic variables that make up horsepower: displacement, rpm, and stroke-averaged combustion pressure, commonly known as BMEP. Displacement tells us how big a boxful of fuel-air mixture we burn each cycle; rpm tells us how often we perform that cycle; and BMEP gives us a measure of how well we have filled the box and how efficiently we have burned its volatile contents.

Displacement, the first variable, is fixed at 500cc by the FIM's Grand Prix rules. The second variable, BMEP, is also largely fixed, but by physics, not by rule books. In an unsupercharged engine, only atmospheric pressure is available to fill the cylinders. Even taking maximum advantage of valves and ports specifically designed to optimize ram effect, engineers are consistently able to achieve only slightly more than atmospheric pressure in the cylinder. This 120 percent filling job, in concert with a decent, fast-burning combustion chamber, gives modern designs a BMEP in the 175-psi range, which further development usually can improve to perhaps as much as 190 psi. The big gains in BMEP were achieved in the 1950s; only the small scraps remain, so we can regard combustion pressure as hard to improve.

That left the Honda men with rpm as the only way of achieving their power goal. They would have to spin their new four-stroke engine at a remarkably high speed.

This was unfortunate in a sense; engineers since the beginning of motoring have disliked making power this way because of the enormous share taken by friction at higher rpm. They would have to fight this loss as recent sportbike engine designers do—by using light reciprocating parts to reduce bearing loads and by down-sizing bearings wherever safe to do so. Obtaining more gain than loss from ultra-high rpm is not an easy matter. But Honda's engineers had no choice; stratospheric rpm was the only avenue of development open to them.

How much power would it take to be competitive? At the time, 1977, 125 to 130 horsepower was the goal—*if* their four-stroke could be made as light as the competing two-strokes. Knowing the displacement, the likely beginning-of-development BMEP, and the desired power output, they could calculate the required rpm from this rough formula:

bhp = (displacement x rpm x BMEP) ÷ 793,000

(Note that displacement is measured in cubic inches and BMEP in psi.)

By plugging in the fixed numbers, the engineers could determine that the engine would need to deliver peak power at about 18,500 rpm. They also knew that piston speeds above 4,500 feet per minute lead quickly to parts failures; so, it was easy for them to determine the longest stroke they could use without exceeding this piston speed at 18,500 rpm. In round figures, that stroke was 36mm. Engineers Takeo Fukui, Ryosaku

Nishiyama, and Isao Satoh surely went through these same simple calculations as the program began.

At this point, history intervened. After the horsepower race of the early 1960s in which Grand Prix racing engines went from one cylinder to two, four, five, and six cylinders, the FIM decided to impose limits on complexity: Future 500s could have no more than four cylinders. This fixed the per-cylinder displacement of a four at 125cc. Using that information in conjunction with the 36mm stroke, Honda engineers were then able to compute the bore: 66mm.

Honda knew that an engine of these dimensions could not succeed. Back in the 1950s and 1960s, most engines were approximately "square"—their bore/stroke ratios were close to 1:1. As the search for more power pushed rpm higher, designers chose shorter strokes, to allow higher revs at the same piston speed. The bonus was bigger bores, which gave more room in which to locate valves. At the same time, the coming of higher-octane fuels in the post-war period allowed big increases in compression ratio. The combination of big bores, short strokes, and high compression drastically changed combustion-chamber shapes. What had been a roomy hemisphere in 1950 had become a wide, very thin disc by 1975.

This difference in combustion-chamber shape is significant. The flame speed of a motionless, correct fuel-air mixture isn't much—about one foot per second. But to complete its combustion in the short time available in an engine, the mixture must be made to burn far faster than this—two to three *hundred* times faster. This accelerated burning is accomplished by turbulence in the mixture, which speeds up the flame by wrinkling the flame front and increasing its area so vastly that it consumes mixture at a greatly accelerated rate. The turbulence comes mainly from the leftover energy of the intake flow, which persists through the compression and combustion cycles.

In the old, roomy chambers, there was little to stop this turbulent motion. But in the new, big-bore, high-compression chambers, the combustion space is so thin and wide that turbulence dies out quickly.

Slow combustion is the result, and it is manifested as a need for excessive ignition advance. A classic example is the 1990 OW01 Yamaha 750 race engine, with a bore/stroke ratio of 1.66:1. It uses 45 degrees of spark lead. With combustion taking this long, much of the charge is burned when the piston is far from the head, so the "effective compression ratio" at which it is burned is quite low. Long combustion also robs heat from the burning gases, reducing their push on the piston. As a consequence, such engines don't produce the high BMEP their designers would like.

This problem—how to make short-stroke, big-bore cylinders burn fast and efficiently—is the central problem in racing four-stroke engine designs today. Engineers want a short stroke so engines can rev to big numbers without exceeding the piston speed of reasonable reliability, and they want a big bore in which to locate the necessary large valve area. But they don't want the slow-burning, ugly, inefficient combustion chamber that results from extreme combinations of the two.

Honda has deep background in ultra-high-rpm combustion. Back in 1965, its engineers built a family of engines of various sizes with bore/stroke ratios of about 1.15:1, and they tested them to their limiting piston speeds (read about it in SAE Paper 700122, by S. Yagi et al., "Research and Development of High-Speed, High-Performance, Small-Displacement Honda Engines"). They found that combustion kept pace with rpm perfectly well all the way to 27,000 rpm; the test engines didn't need increasing spark lead as they revved up. This is because intake-generated charge motion and turbulence increase with rpm, carrying flame speed with them.

Fine, except that the FIM's four-cylinder rule and the need for a very short, 36mm stroke prevented Honda from making direct use of this knowledge. Those 1965 tests involved almost "square" engines, which had plenty of room above their pistons at TDC for charge turbulence.

Consider, for example, the following family of 500cc engines with square bore/stroke dimensions. This chart shows their power potentials when run to 4,500 feet-per-minute piston speed, with an early-development BMEP of 175 psi:

| no. of cylinders | bore & stroke | rpm at 4,500 fpm | bhp at 175 psi |
| --- | --- | --- | --- |
| 1 | 86 x 86 | 8,000 | 54 |
| 2 | 68 x 68 | 10,050 | 68 |
| 3 | 61 x 61 | 11,250 | 76 |
| 4 | 54 x 54 | 12,700 | 85 |
| 6 | 47 x 47 | 14,600 | 98 |
| 8 | 43 x 43 | 15,950 | 107 |
| 10 | 40 x 40 | 17,140 | 115 |
| 12 | 38 x 38 | 18,050 | 122 |

This was very discouraging. For Honda to get even *near* its horsepower goal with a square engine, it would have had to build a hideously complex, bulky, and surely very heavy V-12. Forget that.

But there still was hope. Keith Duckworth, in his Cosworth DFV Formula 1 auto-racing engine, showed how to maintain excellent combustion efficiency up to a bore/stroke ratio of 1.3:1 by using four valves set at a narrow included angle, with a central spark plug. This would allow a mere 500cc V-8 to have good, rapid combustion with bore/stroke dimensions of 47 x 36mm. Here's how the 500cc engine family looks with bore/stroke ratios of 1.3:1:

| no. of cylinders | bore & stroke | rpm at 4,500 fpm | bhp at 175 psi |
|---|---|---|---|
| 1 | 94 x 72 | 9,525 | 64 |
| 2 | 75 x 56.7 | 12,065 | 81 |
| 4 | 59 x 45.7 | 15,000 | 101 |
| 6 | 52 x 39 | 17,570 | 119 |
| 8 | 47 x 36 | 19,050 | 128 |

Note the data for the four-cylinder: They describe almost exactly the last engine tested but not raced by MV Agusta just as that marque gave up the game as lost in the middle 1970s. This table suggests that, by diligent development, the power goal might be reached with six or eight cylinders. But the FIM limit is four.

Now let's push on to the current "leading edge" in outrageous bore/stroke ratio: 1.5:1. Up in this region, Suzuki found the limit beyond which losses outweighed gains. Yamaha and Ducati are still struggling to achieve efficient combustion at or beyond a 1.5:1 bore/stroke ratio. Here is the 500cc family at 1.5:1:

| no. of cylinders | bore & stroke | rpm at 4,500 fpm | bhp at 175 psi |
|---|---|---|---|
| 1 | 98 x 65.5 | 10,435 | 70 |
| 2 | 78 x 52 | 13,165 | 89 |
| 4 | 62 x 41.3 | 16,600 | 112 |
| 6 | 54 x 36 | 19,050 | 128 |

Again, this is discouraging. Even with a design so oversquare as to invite proven combustion-efficiency problems, it would take six cylinders to do the job. How could the Honda engineers burn that awful, 66 x 36mm cylinder that FIM rules seemed to be forcing upon them? Its bore/stroke ratio was right off the deep end at 1.83:1!

One tempting possibility would be to speed up combustion by adding more spark plugs in each combustion chamber. After all, this had worked to perk up two-valve engines. But there is no place for more plugs with four valves. Would more plugs fit with more valves? Sadly, current experience shows that the more holes are put into a head, the more certain it is to deform or crack in operation. Four or five valves with a central plug seems optimum.

That put the engineers in a box. A central plug gave minimum flame-travel distance but not short enough.

Ah, but that's true only in a *round* cylinder. What about some other shape? What if they squeezed the cylinder into an oval, making it look awfully like two cylinders that had grown together. So, the engineers sketched just such a layout: Hmmm, put four valves in each "half" of this oblong chamber, and put one spark plug in the center of each group of valves. In that instant of unconventional thought, they achieved the short flame travel they sought—equivalent to the V-8 rejected earlier. That solved the combustion-efficiency problem.

Of course, this radical, oval-piston idea also created numerous other engineering challenges. The resulting pistons were so wide that they seemed to demand two con rods. And what about boring oval cylinders? Shouldn't be a problem: The people who make Wankel engines can make "cylinders" in any shape you want. How can we seal the pistons? Again, if they can seal up those unlikely Wankel contraptions, we ought to be able to seal oval cylinders.

Honda's engineers then began the tedious process of developing their idea. They first built a proof-of-concept top end on an XL250 crankcase, then built a special engine from the ground up to test the twin–con rod idea. Then came a series of 500cc racing engines, built as V-4s because the oval cylinders were too wide for an inline design. The pistons measured 93.4mm side-to-side and 41mm front-to-back, working through a 36mm stroke.

By July of 1979, the first of these engines, called the 0X, had reached the 100-bhp level. The NR500 motorcycle it powered, incorporating innovations such as 16-inch wheels, aluminum monocoque chassis, side radiators, and an inverted fork, was entered in Grand Prix racing.

The results were terrible. The bike was heavy, it had so little flywheel mass that it tended to stall in corners, it was hard to start, and its power was up high in the rpm band. At the British Grand Prix in August of 1979, veterans Mick Grant and Takazumi Katayama rode the machines, which were embarrassingly slow and did not finish. At the French Grand Prix three weeks later, they failed even to qualify.

Meanwhile, the 0X engine reached 115 bhp, and the next design iteration, the 1X, was begun. In January of 1980 it achieved 120 bhp. For reasons of practicality, the 16-inch wheels and monocoque chassis of the 1979 bike were replaced with conventional, Grand Prix–proven items.

Now the bike began to finish races, but far back. Honda was pushing development rapidly, but the two-stroke opposition was working equally hard, leaving the Honda equally far behind. The oval-piston machines were dense concentrations of the very finest industrial R&D; at European border crossings, their declared value was stated as one million dollars each.

At season's end, the 2X design was begun. By the end of yet another undistinguished season, this engine reached 130 bhp at 18,500 rpm. The NR500 was still heavy and smoky, but had a great sound—almost indistinguishable from that of its two-stroke competition.

This was no accident; with an engine firing half as often but turning almost twice as fast, the exhaust pulses reach the listener's ear at about the same frequency. At idle, it had the muscular growl of a Superbike, accompanied by a vast mechanical whirring and ticking.

By 1982, the NR500 had achieved much better reliability but remained uncompetitive, generally finishing out of the top 10. Freddie Spencer had pushed the bike to as high as fifth in the British Grand Prix only to suffer mechanical failure once again.

Nevertheless, this was not the disaster it appears. The early history of Honda's turbocharged Formula 1 V-6 auto racing motor was even worse; but persisting through seemingly endless failures, the engineers achieved success that turned shortly into complete dominance.

This is because mechanical systems are never easy to develop; it takes irrational persistence to make some things work. As company founder Soichiro Honda noted, there is no success for those who cannot tolerate failure. But in these efforts to make a four-stroke competitive in motorcycle Grand Prix racing, even mighty Honda had to admit it was swinging two bats in a game against strong opposition. The company therefore withdrew the NR500 and split its oval-piston development two ways: First, the NR250 turbocharged twin was initiated for a possible Grand Prix future; second, an NR750 was prepared for endurance racing. And the enormously innovative NS500 two-stroke was committed to Grand Prix racing in the NR's place. This motorcycle—underpowered but light and handy—was ridden to the World Championship by Freddie Spencer in 1983.

It's easy to dismiss the NR program as a loss, but it did provide one solution to the problem of how to efficiently burn a large-area combustion chamber at very high rpm. It also produced innovative work in sealing and friction reduction. Had Honda simply applied this technology at full strength to the endurance-racing NR750 project, the result might have been as much as 170 bhp up at 16,500 rpm. Instead, the engineers decided to trade away some of the all-out power potential (scaling it down to 156-160 bhp) to obtain unprecedented flexibility.

This meant shortening cam timings and reducing valve lift. The result had a quite different character from that of the 500. Whereas the 500 had its power up high, the 750 is described as having power everywhere and revving "seemingly forever." In an era when the highly developed, round-piston racing RC30 had become peaky and difficult to ride, oval-piston technology offered a new freedom to combine power and flexibility.

Honda did not expect much of the machine in endurance trim, however, sending it off to race at Le Mans in the hands of journalists. Even so, it qualified second before retiring in the race. So, in retrospect, the NR750 endurance-racing effort seems to have been a technological public-relations balloon rather than a serious racing program.

Since then, there have been constant rumors of production Hondas with oval cylinders. Now the moment has come. The bike introduced at Geneva is a road machine, detuned from the 160 bhp of the endurance-racing NR750 down to 125 at a "mere" 14,000 rpm.

These numbers are a testimony to what oval-piston technology has achieved. While recent RC30 round-piston racing engines (and their competition) strain to reach 14,000 rpm, the road-going NR750 is detuned *down* to this level. Built on an RC30-like chassis with all the expected features, it has a claimed dry weight of 490 pounds. Atop the V-4 engine sits a complex, eight-throttle-body electronic-fuel-injection system. A reminder of racing intentions and ambitions is the quickly removable, cassette-style six-speed gearbox.

Many industry observers had expected this technology to appear in high-end street motorcycles for low-volume mass production, and at a price of perhaps $15,000. But Honda has decided to offer it instead to the Bimota-class buyer—at the higher price and essentially hand-assembled.

Since the FIM has now decided that international racing will, in the near future, cater only to round-cylindered engines, the NR has become an expensive, historic and maximally exotic piece of R&D history—before it ever hits the streets.

Order now, while supplies last.

# Britten
# V-1100

*John Britten no sooner had an idea than he was at work implementing it in one of his five-week cycles of creation and very little sleep. He was brilliant at inspiring a group of largely volunteer craftsmen to put forth projects that would have done credit to any factory. This is the permanent contradiction in design: That creativity flourishes best outside organizations.*

Andrew Stroud sat in Pascal Picotte's draft, riding John Britten's unique, hand-built motorcycle. Any time Picotte's Ferracci Ducati would pull out a small lead, Stroud would promptly close the distance with a thunderous burst of acceleration.

Stroud clearly had power to spare. His 1,100cc Britten V-twin was the only machine at the Speedway—in any class, in any race—to wheelie repeatedly out of the infield horseshoe. Stroud was biding his time behind Picotte, just waiting for the last lap.

A typical March Florida rain shower brought the race to a brief halt, but on the restart, the same running order resumed—until, on lap 11, the Britten popped, lost power, and, a lap later, quit with a bad ignition battery. Up until that point, however, this semi-finished, homemade race bike, conceived and built in the few weeks before this Daytona SuperTwins race, had demonstrated a formidable performance advantage.

New Zealander John Britten created his first state-of-the-art racing motorcycle, the V-1000, four years ago from nothing but ideas and hard work. He likes, as he says, to "work from first principles" rather than to develop the designs of others. And despite having a shy and boyish manner, Britten, 41, is a man who makes a plan, then works at it with demonic energy until he has what he calls "a useful product."

Except for connecting rods, pistons, and gearbox, that first engine was entirely of Britten's own design and manufacture—casting patterns, castings, machining, and assembly. Chassis and swingarm used his "skin and bones" carbon-Kevlar fabrication technique, in which the high-strength filaments are wound, under tension, between grooved aluminum spools that bolt to engine and chassis hard-points. Once wetted-out with resin and heat-cured, this cat's cradle of filament bundles forms the "bones" of the structure, having immense compressive and tensile strength. This is then sheeted-in with a carbon-fiber fabric—the "skin." The result is an extremely rigid structure. Carbon supplies high tensile strength and the Kevlar's toughness compensates for the carbon's brittle nature.

By the time that original V-1000 was in its third year, Britten felt the bike needed updating. Its longish, 72mm stroke limited its rpm, and the Ducatis that already dominated the class had continually grown stronger. He wanted more than equality.

But where should his effort go? Into a new four-valve cylinder head? Or a five-valve? Or maybe he should develop a novel aerodynamic and cooling concept? Leading-link forks interested him; he felt none seen so far was much good, and he wanted to try ideas of his own. And Marvic mag wheels are expensive; perhaps he could save money and test some ideas by making his own wheels—in carbon fiber.

Any engineer would be proud to succeed in just one of these developments. Indeed, most of those concepts are clearly too much for entire factories, whose output of innovation is in detail improvement, not great leaps forward. John Britten decided to tackle them all: two new cylinder head designs, fresh aerodynamics, the fork, and the wheels.

They all worked.

Near Britten's house in Christchurch, New Zealand, there is an arrow-straight road about 20 miles long. Here, he had been annoyed to find that last year's machine, with its sleek-looking full fairing, was actually slower than a previous one with a half-fairing. What could be the reason?

Splitting the wind isn't the problem, of course. The hard thing is to put it back together—with minimum turbulence and loss—after you have passed. A full-faired machine leaves behind it a large low-pressure area because racing rules don't permit use of a full, tapering tail that would smoothly close the wake.

Britten's answer had two parts. One, by eliminating the wide lower fairing, he would reduce the area of the wake. Two, he would fill what wake there was with fast-moving air from two sources. The first source would be air passing between the rider's calves and the narrow engine-gearbox unit; the second source would be radiator-exit air, delivered from a fully ducted cooling system.

As a result of this approach, Britten's new race bike is built like a torpedo atop a knife blade. The torpedo is the windscreen and front fairing, the rider's body behind it, and the tapering seatback behind that. Below is the blade, consisting of the front and rear tires, plus the narrow engine. Small "boot fairings" provide coverage for the rider's feet.

Aircraft experience teaches that it costs more power to push air through a resistive radiator core than to flow that same air over the smooth outside of the machine. For lowest drag, then, radiator airflow must be reduced to the least possible. Bike radiators in the conventional position— between the front tire and the engine—work poorly because it's difficult to eject the heated air into a low-pressure area. Brute-force methods are used to compensate for this problem; radiators are simply made very large, fed by very large openings. This makes recent race bikes resemble clumsily faired, square-rigged ships. Drag is high.

Britten didn't want that. So, he located a very small cooler (about 5 x 14 inches) under the rider's seat, and forced air through it by taking air in at the highest-pressure zone (the front of the fairing) and ducting it back out into the lowest-pressure zone (the wake region behind the bike). With this maximum pressure difference across it, supplied through smooth ducting, the horizontal radiator gets adequate airflow at low power cost. Despite its small size, it holds the 1,100cc engine at 80 degrees Celsius, or 176 degrees Fahrenheit.

Britten was no less ingenious with the cylinder heads. Despite Yamaha's inconclusive results with its OX-series of five-valve auto-racing engines, he was intrigued with the extra valve area, which in his own flow-bench testing had delivered impressive amounts of air. First, however, he would develop an improved four-valve cylinder head to work with suitably altered bore/stroke dimensions.

A major source of impaired intake flow in cylinder heads is the masking of valves as a result of their closeness to the cylinder walls. Britten decided to scrap the idea of symmetry in favor of moving the intake valves closer to the roomy middle of the cylinder. This pushed the exhausts, and the spark plug with them, closer to the front wall. He chose a 99mm bore, partly because he could easily obtain a modern Omega three-ring piston of amazingly light weight in that size, designed originally for the Judd V-10 Formula 1 auto-racing engine. This bore, with the original 72mm stroke, would give 1,108cc of displacement, and with a 64.75mm stroke, a 1,000cc size.

Because Britten's resources are limited, he must always find ways to shorten development time—such as he did with the cylinder heads. He cut out an inch-thick plate of dimensions to match the cylinder bore. Into it he cut dummy valve seats and ports. At each of the cylinder-bolt locations, he placed spacers rising from the plate, serving to define space already needed by the bolts and therefore unavailable for use as port volume. Atop these spacers he located a second plate, into which cylindrical slugs were pressed at his chosen valve-stem angles, representing the volume to be taken up by valve guides, spring seats, and tappet bores. Each slug was bored to accept a valve stem. In this way, he defined the room left over for the construction of the ports themselves.

With this buck bolted to the flow bench, and with valves in each port, Britten began his port development. First, he measured the airflow of the bare seats with open valves, leading the flow to them with short bell-mouths made of clay. Then he built up the port lengths with clay, adjusting their dimensions as he worked so that no flow was lost as the ports grew longer and longer.

On the intakes, he led the port away from the valve stems at a 13-degree angle. Little by little, he built up the ducts until they reached the planned intake-flange location. He then filled the developed ports with a rubber casting compound to make a male mold, which was then used to make casting molds for the new heads. Aside from sanding to remove casting irregularities, no rework was done on the ports as cast.

The dyno did not disagree: It said 170 horsepower at 9,500 rpm.

Although the previous engine had its intake ports at the backs of the heads (like an H-D dirt tracker), the new Britten has both intakes repositioned in the Vee so they can be integrated into an airbox. Ram air to this airbox (itself an internal part of the fuel tank) is taken in by a pair of "nostrils" at the front center of the upper fairing.

On the exhaust side, separate pipes emerge from each valve port, bringing four pipes to the collector. The primary tubes are tapered, a design that Britten found no easy way to fabricate; as a consequence, there are 60 hours of work in the exhaust system.

Britten also chose new methods for developing the internal and external shapes of fairing, tank, and seat. The basic shape was defined using malleable aluminum welding wire, stuck in place on the mock-up using a hot-melt glue gun. Very quickly, a shape can be developed that resembles the wire-frame models used in computer finite-element analysis; and by bending the wire or relocating the joints, changes can easily be made. Once satisfied with the basic shape, Britten covered the wire frame with a foam that could be carved or sanded after hardening to make a plug on which a female mold was made. The resulting parts are of impressive complexity and smoothness.

Making his own wheels involved Britten first building up a strong hub-and-spoke structure using the previously described "bones" method. The rim was then formed by winding 27 turns of wet-out carbon tape onto this structure. The exact flange and safety-bead contour was defined after resin curing by turning on a lathe. Finally, molded shells were added, one on each side, to integrate the structure.

To measure strength and rigidity, Britten took one of his carbon wheels and a production magnesium wheel to a test center where calibrated loads could be applied and deflections measured. Load for load, Britten's carbon wheel had only 60 percent of the deflection of the metal wheel. Severe destruction tests followed, and the carbon wheel proved extremely rugged. Satisfied for the moment, he made up five fronts and five rears for use on the new bike.

Creating a new front suspension was more involved. Britten chose the basic girder concept—used by Fior and Hossack because of the versatility of its geometry. A pair of leading links projects forward from the front of the bike at steering-head height, each with a ball-joint at its forward end. Attached to the two ball-joints is a girder, each of whose two legs clamps to an end of the front wheel's 47mm tubular-aluminum axle. As the wheel and girder rise and fall over bumps, the leading links rise and fall, and the girder is steerable on the ball-joints. Steering control is through a scissors link from the girder to a set of handlebars pivoted in the usual location.

For Britten, the big question was, what geometry should he choose? Constant-wheelbase? Zero-dive? Antidive?

He rejected all of these—for special reasons. Riders are accustomed to the cues they get from conventional forks which, being set at an angle (the rake), are pro-dive. In other words, some of the braking force serves to compress the fork. The entire feel of a motorcycle entering a corner—its forward pitch and the changes this brings in rake and trail—depends on cues that come from this dive behavior. Take that away, and riders feel uncomfortable at the very least, and possibly in danger.

Britten therefore made his girder fork initially pro-dive, just like a telescopic fork. In the last 1.6 inches of the total 4.7 inches of front-wheel travel, this changes to a somewhat antidive behavior. Conceivably, when in the future more is known about the behavior of this type of fork, other geometries may prove to be better, and riders may become accustomed to their "feel."

Britten experimented on a computer with a linkage program to get the effects he wanted, and found that placement of the leading-link pivots had to be very accurate. Location of the lower pivot subsequently required setting the engine back a half-inch and integrating the pivot point into the engine's front-cylinder cambox. A conventional nitrogen-pressurized spring/damper unit acts on the lower link.

As with the previous bike, rear-suspension forces on the new Britten are carried forward under the engine, via rods and bellcrank, to another spring/damper unit just ahead of the crankcase. The remote reservoirs of both dampers are located on the rider's "dashboard," within easy reach for compression-damping adjustment.

During initial testing in New Zealand, riders using the new fork applied brakes at their usual shut-off points, only to have to re-accelerate into most corners because of the shortened braking distance. Unlike a telescopic fork—which becomes jerky and stiff under braking because of the side-loads on its sliding bushings—pivoted-joint suspensions like Britten's remain supple, and so offer better traction over rough surfaces. Hence the shorter braking distances.

At Daytona, Britten and his crew worked essentially around the clock. Not only was the machine almost completely untested, but there were un-looked-for problems. First, intake-valve clearances were disappearing at the rate of .005 inch per 40 laps. While not a threat to the bike's ability to finish the SuperTwins race, this lash loss was new. Britten thought it might have arisen from his relocation of the fuel injectors to a new position very close to the valves.

Next, water had somehow been lost from the engine during practice, causing a cylinder liner to crack. The crew completely disassembled the engine overnight, brazed the crack, and rebuilt. On top of that, the electronic fuel injection had a lean spot that hurt acceleration. After the crew downloaded the injection system's fuel-map program onto their laptop computer and enriched the weak region, the problem was gone.

The three days of practice and qualifying passed quickly and with little sleep. Hampered by the troubles the team had encountered in practice, Stroud qualified on the third row—a disappointing 12th—some 10 seconds slower than Picotte.

But when the final went to the grid and the flag dropped, everything came right as Stroud ran effortlessly with the leader. The Britten had been transformed from a mass of questions into an integrated, powerful answer. The brazed cylinder liner worked. There was no water loss. Handling was good. There remained one unknown defect: During Thursday's all-nighter, a very tired John Britten had installed the small ignition battery incorrectly, so only part of its power served the load, while the rest leaked slowly to ground.

As the race laps passed, Stroud was clearly continuing to test the machine, evaluating how fast he could pull up to Picotte as they approached the chicane. But just as onlookers began preparing for the seemingly certain dramatic finish, the battery expired. The silent Britten rolled to a stop.

Picotte rode well on a fine machine to win the race without further challenge. Britten, Stroud, and crew were left with only the glory of all they had dared. And the bright prospect of all they seem destined to achieve. Soon. Very, very soon.

# Voxan

# Boxer

*Run up the flag and see who salutes it. Sometimes it's no one.*

Voxan went to last fall's Paris show to demonstrate that its French-designed-and-built machines were reaching production. They were upstaged by an unofficial prototype on their own pavilion—the Voxan Boxer VB1. This machine was created by Boxer Design, a group directed by Thierry Henriette, himself a Voxan dealer, with consultation from British stylist Glynn Kerr. The VB1 is a study of what a Voxan superbike might look like. There are no plans for production.

Henriette's VB1 is "racing-conventional" in appearance, contrasting with the flamboyant playfulness of the production Voxans. Existing FIM regulations and common sense require this. The best available suspension and brake components, applied in proven and reasonable ways, yield a shape like that of other narrow, compact, racy machines. It will be small and smooth, its windscreen will be low, its rear section will be spare and open, and its streamlining will be concentrated forward, concealing the engine.

Within these limits, Boxer Design has tried its hand at some of the optional shapes that attract the eye on other machines. Ducati bunches curving, writhing exhaust tubing to serve two underseat mufflers. The VB1 likewise makes its pipes an attraction. The swingarms of Grand Prix roadracers are graceful shapes that sculptor Constantin Brancusi might have appreciated. The VB1's swingarm is of this kind. Visible also are the rear arches of the machine's hybrid steel-tube and cast-aluminum chassis, rendered here in eye-catching stainless instead of Voxan's painted metal. Aside from its YZF-R1-like "cat's-eye" headlights, the VB1's fairing is Grand Prix–functional—slab-sided and narrow, as aerodynamics requires. Its bellypan continues to the rear tire in modern style, and its cooling-air opening at the front is mildly shark-like. Generous exit holes in the fairing sides release the air that emerges hot from the rear of the radiator. A Showa fork, Öhlins shock, and Brembo brakes are employed.

Expensive materials such as carbon-Kevlar and alternative metals are used to achieve the claimed low weight of 407 pounds. This, Henriette notes, is a $75,000 project. When pressed to price a hypothetical VB1 with reasonable production economy, the creator suggests it might be achieved in 20-per-year quantities, for perhaps $15,000. The matter is under study.

The VB1 is not now a hot challenger for Ducati's 996 and Aprilia's RSV Mille. It is speculation; an elaborate message from one Voxan dealer to his manufacturer. Paris attendance figures show that 400,000 Frenchmen got that message.

Official Voxan spokesmen kept their distance from the VB1, insisting it was not their toe in the water. They must keep their heads down, get production up, and make their shareholders happy before considering future projects.

Can we find the company's ultimate intentions hidden in its engine design? Bore and stroke at 98 x 66mm are the same as those of Ducati's 996 and the new Japanese liter-twins. Double-overhead cams driven by Hy-Vo chains operate four large valves per cylinder. Combustion chambers are compact as a result of the very narrow 21-degree included valve angle. Short-skirted, Formula 1–style pistons are used, with titanium connecting rods. Engine V-angle is a compromise. No balancer shaft is used and engine management is by Marelli. Don't be fooled by the claim of 100 crank horsepower—20 or more down on other sport-twins—this is no cruiser. It is a high-performance engine strangled to meet French law. It can make more power when and if the need arises. The VB1 shows how it might look in this role. Let us hope its day will come.

## Whither Voxan?

France is a nation intensely conscious of its own history and importance— where laws are made to prevent foreign words and usages from creeping into the language. Imagine, therefore, the position of French motorcycle enthusiasts. A pioneer of motoring at the turn of the century, France evolved a strong, multibrand domestic motorcycle industry only to lose it all to economic depression and war. Imports from Japan and elsewhere have carried French riders for years, but there exists a powerful motorcycle vacuum that can only be filled by genuinely French machines. French technology is alive and powerful—the French aircraft industry is highly respected, and French F1 engines define the state of that art. Why no motorcycle industry revival?

The missing element has been the sustained economic prosperity that affords investors a chance to risk capital in new business. French motorcycling revived strongly during the 1970s on imported machines, and many fine French racers won championships in that period. Since then, Europe has emerged once more as a world economic force.

Two and a half years ago, the Voxan motorcycle was announced to the world at the French Grand Prix at Le Mans. At that time, there were suggestions of pneumatic valves in its future, an implied relationship with French F-1 engine designs. Since then, the process of recreating an industry has lagged behind promotional promise. The models soon to enter full production are the Roadster and the Cafe Racer, to be followed by the Scrambler, all powered by a liquid-cooled, 72-degree, 1,000cc V-twin limited under French no-fun laws to 100 bhp. Any idea of export has been carefully suppressed until production catches up.

As of last summer, the factory was still largely empty. Voxan is not the only manufacturer to discover the difficulty of sourcing equipment and parts of high quality. The company stated that its first machines required 1,800 different parts, of which 900 were unique. As some early deliveries of parts did not measure up to required quality standards, there have been returns and adjustments. All this has taken time. Currently, the first work stations are in place and operating, and true production was scheduled to begin by January 21, 2000.

# *Part 2*

# TIMELESS TECHNOLOGY

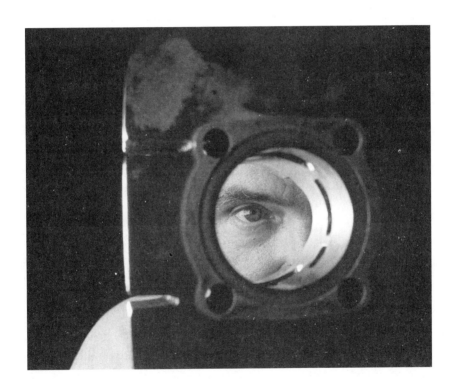

# All About Transmissions

*I had to learn about transmissions in order to make my
500cc Kawasaki H1-R shift properly. My rider, the late Cliff
Carr, and I did 26 meetings in 1971, and that year was an
intense (I nearly said "crash") course in gearbox durability,
problems, and maintenance.*

The ideal motorcycle engine would not need a primary drive, clutch, gearbox, chains, shafts, or any other such complex, failure-prone and power-robbing nonsense. It would couple directly to the rear wheel, run at its speed and supply the necessary torque at all speeds from zero to maximum.

There is no such internal combustion engine. This most imperfect prime mover not only makes zero power at zero engine revolutions, but it must actually be turning at some fair speed to make even enough power to idle, overcoming only its own internal friction. It must turn faster yet to begin to move a vehicle. This consideration requires that there must be a clutch to allow the engine to spin at power-producing speed as torque is gently applied to the drive wheel to accelerate the vehicle.

Besides a clutch, we also need a speed reducer, or transmission, between engine and load because useful engine power always occurs at much higher rpm than wheel speed. At 60 mph, a 4.00 x 18 tire is making some 900 rpm, and many modern engines don't even idle this low.

Early machines used a flat leather belt as both transmission and clutch. Because of their low-horsepower, industrial-type engines, they needed only one drive ratio. A 500cc single might produce only two horsepower, idle down as low as 250 rpm, drive away at 500 rpm, and then waffle along at a peak of some 25 mph at 1,500 rpm. This meant that at minimum rpm, the machine would be moving at only 4 to 8 miles per hour (mph). Slipping the belt-clutch to get from zero speed up to a brisk-walk pace wasn't too much to ask; complications multiplied as the motorcycle evolved from inventor's curiosity into a practical conveyance and the sporting nature of the machine emerged. Our hypothetical ancient 500 quickly doubled its horsepower. Then, to realize its higher potential top speed of over 40 mph, the drive ratio had to be raised. This lifted the minimum speed as well as the maximum, so the rider had to slip the clutch much more to get moving.

The improved, sportier 500 wouldn't pull as well down low without its huge "industrial" flywheel, making the starting situation even worse. Two ratios were needed now—one for making a snappy start and one for hurtling down the macadam at a breakneck forty per. This still wasn't too bad. The problem was solved by installing a second set of pulleys, belts, and idlers. Except a leather belt to transmit four or five horsepower was getting rather wide, and two of them took up a lot of room. Maybe too much for a motorcycle, engineers of that period must have thought. How about Mr. Renold's commendable 1894 invention, the roller chain? There's never any slippage, even in the wet, and it's ever so compact and narrow. Using a chain would require a separate friction clutch and new kinds of gadgets to route power through the desired set of sprockets. Perhaps some shields would be necessary as well, to prevent Edwardian knickers from being caught in the works. A fine arrangement, simply smashing!

And then World War I. Airplanes, tanks, submarines, and trucks all needed lighter, more powerful internal-combustion engines to hasten the death-dealing process. Engineers began to grasp the parameters of engine performance, and these newly refined engines needed three or even four ratios to make best use of their power. Even the relatively compact roller chain was much too bulky to provide the necessary ratios. Designers turned to gears.

Gears are miracles of compact strength. A modern six-speed gearbox designed to transmit 100 horsepower can be held in one hand and weighs less than 10 pounds, but such refinement hasn't come easily. At first, constructors copied bicycle practice, putting planetary gear sets into the rear wheel hub as in an English three-speed bicycle. The steady advance of engine power against nineteenth century metallurgy turned this attractive idea into a gritty stew of broken parts and gear grease. By the time engine torque had been multiplied in reduction to wheel speed, the pressure on these slow-turning gears was just too great. To survive, gears would have to turn faster, and this meant that they would have to be inserted in the driveline ahead of the final drive. The engine would drive the gears through a primary reduction, and the gears would drive the wheel through a secondary reduction. In their new location the gears could live.

These early gearboxes were gate-shifted. From neutral, any of the ratios could be selected by an appropriate movement of the lever. The rider not only had to take one hand off the bars to grasp the shift lever, but also had three or four choices of where to move it. Disastrous for rider concentration, this also surrendered the machine to the charming uncertainties of one-handed steering. The AJS company introduced sequential shifting, which limited shifter movement to simply two choices: upshift or downshift. Finally the shifting function was transferred from hand to foot, and the modern form of transmission was created.

Today we bestride our modern machine, thumb the engine into life, snick the transmission into gear, and whir smoothly away, shift after reliable shift, protected by warranty, the DOT, and three million man-years of human technology.

For most owners, the gearbox is among the deepest of mysteries, but like many things governed by simple principles, the details provide the confusion.

The simplest gear transmission has two states: engaged and neutral. When engaged, it transmits power at a fixed ratio, which is the tooth number ratio of the two meshing gears. One is connected to the engine, the other to the load. When engaged, both gears are fixed to their shafts. In neutral, one gear is made free-spinning on its shaft and there is no drive. Transmissions with more ratios are simple multiples of this. Their apparent complexity comes from the need for a mechanism that will engage one and only one ratio or gear pair at a time while disconnecting all the others.

Motorcycle transmissions use straight-cut spur gearing. This means that the gear teeth are parallel to the shafts, and that the shafts are parallel to each other. Modern motorcycle gearboxes are of the *constant-mesh* type in which every gear pair is always in mesh, but in early times *sliding-gear* transmissions were the rule. Such transmissions engaged each gear pair by actually sliding the teeth sideways, into, and out of mesh. To permit such sliding, the moveable gear was splined to its shaft.

Sliding-gear transmissions had terrible limitations. Gear tooth surfaces must have precise contours for efficiency and long life, but these were damaged by being crashed together while spinning. Gear teeth operate best with very small tooth-to-tooth clearances, just enough for heat expansion and a good oil film. With such small clearances, sliding-gear teeth had to be lined up very precisely before they would slip together. Even sharpening the ends of the teeth to aid engagement didn't help much because the thin edges chipped and broke easily.

It wasn't long before someone sensibly decided to separate the functions of power transmission (accurate gear teeth) and engagement (something else). That something else was engaging dogs. While the teeth occupy the *circumference* of a gear, the ends could be used for this other function. Rugged engaging pegs, called dogs, are cut into the ends of free-spinning gears. To connect such a gear to its shaft when desired, we provide similarly dogged *engaging rings*, sliding on splines and located adjacent. By sliding the engaging ring's dogs into those of the desired free-spinning gear, it too was locked to the shaft, transmitting power to its mesh mate.

In the interest of saving space, this function is commonly handled by other gears in the transmission, rather than by separate engaging rings. The free-spinning gear we wish to lock to its shaft can be located adjacent to another gear which is splined to the shaft. This splined neighbor is slid along the shaft like an engaging ring until its dogs engage those of the desired gear, locking it to the shaft. This doesn't engage two ratios at once because the mesh mate of the splined gear is not also locked to its shaft, so that pair windmills. Gear teeth don't slide out of mesh because the engagement of dogs requires only five or six millimeters of lateral movement.

A curious variant of the constant-mesh idea is the *ball-lock* transmission. This system places its dogs *inside* each gear, and they look much like splines, but these gears are free-spinning. A compact stack of them is carried on the smooth, hollow input shaft. Their mesh mates are all splined solidly to the output shaft. The hollow input shaft is perforated in two or more places under each free-spinning gear, and in each hole rides a hard steel ball, held below the shaft surface by a spring, and projecting slightly into the shaft bore. A short plug is moved through the shaft bore by a thin rod, and when this plug arrives under the desired gear, it forces the steel balls outward so they engage the dogs/splines in the inside diameter of the gear. This locks it to the shaft, for the balls are now half in the shaft, half in the gear.

This is the most compact of transmissions because it can offer as many as six ratios in a space two or three inches in width, but its fragility limits use to lower-powered machines.

There are two major schemes for routing the flow of power through a gear transmission: *direct* and *indirect*. Most motorcycle transmissions today

*Lee Klancher*

are of the indirect type in which power enters on one shaft and leaves from the other. There is one meshing pair for each ratio, and one gear of a given pair is carried on each shaft. One of each pair is free-spinning, the other splined to its shaft. Ratio selection takes place by locking the free-spinning member of the desired pair to the shaft. All other pairs   windmill.

British motorcycles of older design, and most automobiles, use the direct scheme. In lower gears, power enters through a mainshaft, passes through one gear pair to a counter-shaft, then back again through a second gear pair to a free-spinning output gear concentric with the mainshaft. Top gear locks this output gear directly to the mainshaft, and all gear pairs windmill. The direct gearbox eliminates all major gear friction in top gear but doubles it (two meshes transmit power) in lower gears. Direct gearsets were originally designed for applications calling for top gear most of the time.

By suitable design of the shift mechanism, a direct box can give as many as six speeds from four gear pairs, but the choice of ratios is limited compared with an indirect box.

Again, remember this: It is the details of a gearbox that are frightening to behold, but the principle is always the same. There is only one solid path for power through the gearbox in any ratio. Only through the desired gears is the drive solid. All other gears are windmilling.

The face-dog gear engagement method is not without its problems. One of these is driveline backlash, the curse of many Japanese-made machines for which there is a well-known but unfortunately expensive solution. The requirements of fast, no-miss shifting are best served by providing wide spaces between engagement dog teeth. But large gaps make for a loose drive, in which free backlash of perhaps a quarter-turn of the transmission output shaft may be created.

There is a way to get clean shifting without excessive backlash. You double the number of shifting dog teeth, from the three found in most Hondas, Yamahas, etc., to six—and then cut back alternate teeth by a depth of perhaps two millimeters. This provides, effectively, a wide spacing as the longer dogs snag into engagement, followed by tight, no-lash coupling as the shift is completed.

To engage and disengage the dogs, we need to be able to slide the splined gears or engaging rings along their shafts at will, and to hold them in the desired positions. Each sliding element is provided with a grooved collar into which fits a semi-circular shift fork. Such shift forks slide along guide-rails parallel to the transmission shafts. When a shift fork moves, it moves its gear or engaging ring.

The shift forks are in turn controlled by a rotatable shift plate or drum into which are cut wiggly slots. Each shift fork has a peg which fits into one of these slots. As the drum rotates, the forks are made to perform the back and forth movements of engagement and disengagement, selecting one gear after another in sequence. A spring-loaded detent holds the drum in position for each ratio.

The shift drum is moved through an angle corresponding to one full shift's worth of rotation by a claw connected to the shift pedal. Moving the pedal causes the claw to engage pegs or notches in the drum, and then rotate it. A stop is provided to prevent this claw from moving the drum more than a single shift, after which a powerful spring returns both claw and shift pedal to center position, ready for another motion.

When concept, engineering and manufacturing are all correct, you get perfect shifts, but there are some common problems. Fortunately some of the most common are also the easiest to fix. They come from faulty adjustment of the stops controlling the movement of the shift claw. If a full stroke of the shift pedal doesn't pull the drum around far enough for it to reach the detent of the next gear, there will be no shift at all or a false neutral between the original and the desired gear. If a full pedal stroke pulls the drum too far, there will be a false neutral *beyond* the desired gear or a double shift. Because the shift claw and its stops are usually located in the primary case, service does not require complete engine disassembly.

Other problems come from deep within and are harder to trace. One common scenario runs as follows: As you make the shift, and the two sets of dogs approach each other, they hit head-on-head, rather than dropping neatly together. Normally this is fine because the faces of the dogs are smooth and oily, and they slip over each other to drop into engagement anyway. The dogs, however, aren't necessarily smooth. They may be covered with nasty little machining marks, or the dogs may get all banged up from hard shifting. When the dogs hit head-on-head, these little imperfections lock together and prevent the dogs from sliding off each other and into engagement. Consequently, the shift pedal won't go the full stroke, and this condition is symptomatic of this annoying problem. Because the difficulty appears random to the rider, he is tempted to kick and stamp at the shift pedal. The gears don't care. The rider will get even. Take that and that.

Instead of burning your machine and putting the insurance payoff into a sailboat, simply set aside a few hours to take your engine all apart. With a nice sheet of 220 carborundum paper on a flat surface, lap the faces of the dogs until they are smooth and bright. Reassemble for a soothing shifting experience.

Here's another gearbox quirk. Just as you are making the big shift, there is a moment's hesitation and just the suggestion of a noise from the gearbox. Or was there? As time passes, you become sure there was, and is, every time you make that shift. It spoils your rides. That gear is easy to miss, and you can't think of anything else. Finally you must use your foot to hold it in that gear, and when it misses, the crunching and munching sounds make you sorry for your machine. The tension may find complete release with a bang. Your transmission's broken.

Here's the inside story that led to the final demise. As the dog sets move into engagement, they don't penetrate each other to the full depth of the dogs, so the load is carried on the edges of the dogs. A little pounding from sporty shifting works over those edges, rounding them off. Now the dogs crash over each other until they get a bite. They get worse. Finally they are so rounded off and peened over that they just grind ineffectually over each other without driving the machine. The end thrust produced in this attempted engagement burns the shift forks as they try to hold the gear engaged.

This evil process is caused by incorrect shimming. The sliding gear is located on the shaft by the shift fork, but the gear it tries to engage is usually located by circlips and shims. If these shims are the wrong thickness, the gear may be just too far away to ever engage to full depth of the dogs. And that's the beginning of the disaster coming later.

An ideally shimmed transmission, when in neutral, has each of the dog-sets missing its neighbor by the minimum possible clearance. But when the dog-sets engage, they do so to the maximum depth without bottoming.

Shallow engagement doesn't always lead to failure, but all too often it does. Not only are the gear dogs battered and the shift forks bent or overheated, but the retaining circlips may be forced out of their grooves, permitting the gear to wander away. This can result in simultaneous selection of two gears, which is no joke. Simple replacement of the parts without correct reshimming will only postpone recurrence of the problem.

Sometimes the adjustment and finish of the gearbox are not at fault; sometimes the problem is in the design. Certain street machines, shifted hard and fast, will miss shifts because the slotted shifting drum's diameter is too small and the ratcheting portion of the mechanism too flimsy. The shift drum's slots are cams of a sort, and their ramps get steeper as the drum diameter is reduced, which means more pressure is required to make the drum turn. Combine that stiff action with a long-link ratchet mechanism that flexes under pressure, and you have a shift that can't be hurried.

Another design anomaly is the grown-up engine with the adolescent gearbox, very common in the present era of displacement escalation. Last year's model has to be pumped up to win the sales race, but without spending any money. The clever designer crams in bigger pistons and cylinders, but the increased power has to funnel down through last year's transmission. The gears just can't carry the load gracefully, and bad things begin to happen.

The reason for such failures is that gears, good as they are, have limitations. There are limits to how much pressure can be exerted through the teeth. There are limits to how fast the teeth can move through the mesh. Choices made in materials and manufacturing can move these limits up or down, trading cost against life and strength, but the limits are always there and sometimes overstepped.

Gear design and manufacture is among the most sophisticated of the mechanic arts, yet gears are really nothing more than levers. Consider a pair of gears in mesh, with all of their teeth removed except for the pair in the center of the mesh. As the driving shaft rotates, its lever, or tooth, presses on the lever, or tooth, of the driven shaft, making it turn as well. The gear ratio is simply the ratio of the lengths of these two levers. A complete circle of such levers on each hub ensures that the drive is continuous.

Gear teeth cannot be simple pegs attached to a hub, interlocking with similar pegs projecting from another hub. Such an arrangement of levers could not transmit smooth power from one shaft to the other because the gear ratio would change as the levers passed through the mesh. At one moment the tip of one tooth would press on the root of the other, then vice versa. Such variation in leverage would produce a cyclic rpm variation, or "wow" on the driven shaft, producing shock loading under power.

Therefore the teeth are specially shaped to preserve a constant "gear ratio" for the entire time a pair of teeth is in contact. This shape is derived from an involute spiral, which is the curve described by the end of a cord being unwound from a cylinder. When teeth having this contour operate in mesh, a steady, shockless drive is maintained at a constant ratio.

To prevent shock loading from another source, the load is carried by more than a single pair of teeth at a time. In this way, load is transferred smoothly from each tooth pair to the pair following it into the mesh, rather than dropping it with a crash. To accomplish this, the tooth profiles must be very carefully controlled in manufacturing. A profile error of even a thousandth of an inch can produce fatal shock loads in power gearing.

The important variables in gear design are tooth-to-tooth contact stress (determined by shaft torque, gear diameter, and width) and the speed of the mesh (derived from shaft rpm and gear diameter). The smaller the gear diameter, the higher the tooth contact stress in psi. The wider the gear, the lower the stress. By increasing gear diameter to reduce tooth stress, we are at the same time increasing the mesh speed, and may run into troubles with tooth profile accuracy or lubrication.

Tooth-to-tooth pressure has a very high upper limit in steel gears. Truck gears operate routinely at contact shear stress levels of 500,000 psi. As the curved tooth surfaces roll and slide over each other in mesh, the contact between them would theoretically be a line, but the elasticity of steel widens this under load into a rectangle. Such deformation produces large shear stresses in the material below the surface of the tooth.

The other limitation, mesh speed, imposes different compromises. At low mesh speeds, gear tooth profiles can be less accurate and still work reliably under pressure. Designers are always tempted to run gear speeds higher using less gear to transmit more power, but speed shows up the inaccuracy of gear teeth in the form of dynamic loads. Gears sufficiently accurate to carry heavy loads at high mesh speeds are expensive, so there must be compromises. The crank phasing gears of the Kawasaki KR-250 roadracer must be extremely well-made to survive, for the teeth enter the mesh at over 200 feet per second!

To approach these upper limits of pressure and speed, power gearing must be made of exceedingly hard and fatigue-resistant material, and only steel will do the job. The teeth not only have to carry the high stress of contact but must also resist the bending loads produced, and those loads are trying to break off the entire tooth. Steel at full hardness can take the contact stress but would snap like glass under the shock loads of vehicle drive. Conversely, if the entire tooth were heat-treated to a toughness and ductility sufficient to accept the shock and bending load, it would lack the surface hardness required for the contact stress.

Therefore the teeth are case-hardened, leaving the core tough and ductile, yet with a super-hard skin over it. The gear is held at high temperature in a nitrogen- or carbon-rich environment, causing extremely hard compounds to form in the steel surface. The longer this process continues, the deeper the hard zone.

If this case is too thin, contact pressure may flake it right off the tooth like paint. If case depth is too great, there will be too little tough core left to carry the bending load, and the tooth may snap.

Well-designed gears will not fail in the lifetime of the vehicle, but, if run long enough, any gear will fail eventually by surface fatigue. The high shear stresses of tooth contact, repeatedly cycling over millions of revolutions, will eventually propagate tiny cracks, nucleated by impurities or dislocations in the metal. When such a crack intersects the tooth surface, bits of metal may break out, leaving a microscopic pit. When such pits become numerous, some join together to produce results visible to the naked eye, and it's time for replacement. It is to search out such incipient failures that racing mechanics scrutinize the load-bearing face of each tooth for signs of pitting.

The cleanliness of the steel, its composition, and the nature of its heat-treatment all determine its response to fatigue. The better the steel, the longer failure is postponed, but even with today's super-clean vacuum-remelt aerospace alloys, there are the same problems. All materials contain the ingredients of failure.

It is easy to imagine a way of making gears. A cutter made in the shape of a tooth space would cut the spaces one at a time, finally leaving a finished gear. This is inefficient because every different number of teeth would require a special cutter, and the indexing of the gear blank from one tooth to the next is inaccurate and time-consuming.

Therefore most gears are made by a method called *gear generation*, in which the cutting action results not only from the rotation of the cutter, but from that of the blank as well. Cutter and blank revolve together like gears in mesh, as the gear-cutting machine feeds the cutter deeper into the blank. When teeth cut in this way reach the desired depth, the process is finished. A typical type of cutter used in gear generation is called a hob, and it resembles a worm gear with serrated teeth. No indexing is required and a single cutter cuts all tooth numbers in a given pitch range.

Gear steel is cut in a soft, annealed state, and is then case hardened and heat-treated afterwards. Gears at this state of finish can be used immediately in many lower-precision, lower-duty applications. Steels do distort somewhat in heat-treatment, and the cutting action of gear generation can leave tool marks. For the highest orders of precision, the gear teeth must be further refined after hardening. Only abrasives will cut hardened steel well, so for final finishing, the teeth are either lapped or ground with profiled abrasive wheels. This leaves the teeth with the characteristic bright, fine-ground surface finish that distinguishes the best of gears.

Motorcycles use gears in many places outside the transmission. The drive from engine to clutch is often by gear and is a much higher-speed drive than the transmission itself. There is thus a potential for considerable noise generation. Helical gears are often the choice here, for the angling of their teeth places more of them in mesh at a time, smoothing the drive.

Unfortunately, helical gears produce some end thrust, and this is not desired in racing and other high-power applications. For these, straight-cut gears are used, and the noise is enjoyed. Camshaft and accessory drives place lesser loads on gears, but there is still a premium on accuracy. Again, straight cuts prevail.

Shaft-driven machines need one or more right-angle drives, and these take many forms. The temptation is to save weight, using the smallest possible gears to control unsprung mass, and this works the gears very hard. Most shaft-driven machines are expensive touring models and this means that noise is undesirable. The more complex and quiet-running gearing systems involve a large component of sliding in the tooth contacts, and this places special requirements on the lubricants used. These gears require the very best in manufacturing, adjustment, and lubrication.

Without the protection of a lubricant, a steel gear of any type would soon fail under load. Moderate to heavy loads are carried by a complete film of viscous lubricant separating the rubbing surfaces. This is called hydrodynamic lubrication. Heavier loads are able to break down this film, and the metal-to-metal contact that would result without further protection would cause tooth-to-tooth welding and tearing. Early failure would occur. Further protection takes the form of boundary lubrication. Chemical additives (compounds of phosphorus, chlorine, etc.) in the lubricant form compounds on the rubbing surfaces which are strong enough to carry heavy loads, yet are weaker than the steel beneath. When the heaviest loads are applied, it is this solid film which is scoured away by friction, sacrificing itself to protect the underlying steel. As the scored surface leaves the mesh, the additives in the gear lubricant quickly react with the exposed steel to replace the surface layer, ready for the next encounter This process actually produces a chemico-mechanical polishing that refines the gear surfaces during break-in and increases their load-carrying ability. This action is why specially compounded gear oils can give better protection than ordinary motor oils less rich in such additives.

Another lubricant function is to carry away heat. Even a very accurate and efficient gear pair seldom exceeds 98 percent efficiency in power transmission. The lost power is consumed in shearing the lubricant or additive film between the gear teeth as they slide over each other, and this lost power appears as heat. A gear pair transmitting 100 bhp at 98 percent efficiency would have to rid itself continuously of two horsepower in heat. This is 1,500 watts, equivalent in output to two toasters; if not removed, the heat burns up the gears. The lubricant does remove heat, bathing the parts with liquid that picks up the heat and carries it away so it can be transferred to the inner surfaces of the gearbox.

Early gearboxes were lubricated by grease, which was easier to contain than oil. Grease is a mixture of an oil and a stiff carrier, such as a soap. The apparent viscosity of grease is high, but it is the oil, wicking slowly from the carrier that actually carries the load. Obviously, small amounts of oil melting from a mass of grease cannot carry away much heat, and so it happens that grease lubrication is not suitable for modern gearboxes.

The common form of gear lubrication in today's machines is oil bath. The gear case is filled to a level that ensures that every gear inside at least dips into it. This is a great advance over grease because it guarantees every gear a plentiful supply of cooling, lubricating oil.

This can be too much of a good thing at very high revs. A meshing pair of gears can act as an oil pump with a very loose casing. Oil in the mesh must be violently squeezed out as the teeth close the spaces, and this squeezing action generates heat in large quantities. Thanks to a close casing and excessive oil level, the Kawasaki KR-250 roadracer encountered gearbox temperatures of 300° F in development! A lower oil level and special deflectors to keep the oil away from the gears reduced this to a reasonable level. At high speeds, the gears don't dip into the oil like millwheels on a summer day. The inside of the gearbox is more like a confused vortex of air and oil in a Waring blender.

Better than oil bath is lubrication by oil jet to each mesh. Such machines as the Kawasaki Z-1 and Yamaha TZ750 roadracer have pumped oil supplied to a gallery over the top of the gearbox. A drilling above each mesh supplies the right amount of oil, no more. Since the oil level is well below the gears, oil churning losses are minimal.

Gears and the problems of their design and manufacture are interesting in themselves, but the reason we want gears in the first place is to get the best possible match between an internal combustion engine and the power requirements of a road vehicle. This gives the choice of ratios great importance.

We know that first gear must be low enough to permit starting without prolonged clutch slip, and that top gear must be high enough to match maximum speed and power, but what about in between?

The obvious thing, making all ratio steps identical, is unfortunately not the best way. As the engine winds up in one ratio and reaches the top of its powerband, the transmission must be shifted to the next higher ratio. The shift pulls engine rpm down, and the wider that ratio is, the further down the engine will be pulled. Since our beloved engine makes its greatest horsepower at the top of the band, with progressively less available lower down, it's obvious that the wider the ratio step is, the less real horsepower we will have available to accelerate the vehicle in the next gear. The wider the step, the lower the average horsepower yielded across that ratio.

At the same time, remember that the power required to maintain a constant rate of acceleration increases as the square of the speed, and that air resistance increases in power consumption as the cube of the speed. Both facts make it harder to accelerate the faster we go so it's obvious that making all ratio steps equal would hurt acceleration in higher gears prohibitively. To obtain the quickest overall acceleration across the gearbox, the lower ratios are spaced farther apart than are the upper ones. The first/second shift on a big street bike might pull engine rpm down from a shift point of 8,500 to only 6,300 at the bottom of second, but the fourth/fifth shift might only see a drop from 8,500 back to 7,500. It is planned this way simply because the engine makes much more power at 7,500 than at 6,300, and the machine needs the power much more in fifth than it does in second.

Why not just put in enough ratios to keep the engine up near the top of the band all the time? We have already come a long way towards this situation. There is a world of difference between a one-speed belt-drive machine and today's five- and six-speed roadburners. But why not eight, ten, or twelve speeds? Extra ratios mean extra cost, complexity, and bulk. More speeds require more from the rider, and motorcycling is still supposed to have a small component of *fun*. A point can be reached where gains are wiped out by losses. Shifting takes time, time when the engine is doing nothing. Finally, the current thrust of engine development is towards wider rather than narrower powerbands, which work well with five or six transmission speeds.

Different applications call for different ratio spacings, and overall ratio spread is the key here. This is the number obtained by dividing the lowest gear ratio by the highest, and it represents the ratio of maximum speed in top gear to maximum speed in first.

Trials machines must be capable of a walking pace while traversing difficult terrain, yet must still have a roadable top speed of 50 or more miles per hour. Trials engines have an extremely wide useful powerband, and so their gearboxes are widely spaced, with overall spreads of 3.5 or more.

Small street bikes have less flexible engines, yet must still have low first gears to drag a heavy rider and passenger away from an uphill stoplight. Their overall spreads range downwards from 3.25.

Larger street bikes have larger, higher-torque engines which can pull taller first gear ratios gracefully. The need for sporting performance crowds their ratios closer together, giving total spreads of 2.5 or less.

The extreme end of the spectrum is the roadracing machine, with a narrow powerband and little tolerance for being pulled way down the rpm scale at each shift. Some have total spreads as little as 1.9, but the common figure is 2.25. This means that the familiar Yamaha TZ750D, when geared for its maximum of 180 mph in sixth gear, can run as fast as 80 mph at the top of first!

There is no reason why we must put up forever with rider-shifted, fixed ratios. Automobiles in their millions are driven by torque converters which smoothly vary the ratio between engine and load over a range of 2.1 or more. Snowmobiles and the unique Rokon motorcycle enjoy stepless drive from their variable belt transmissions. There are a few motorcycles using fluid torque converters, following the pioneering Rabbit Superflow scooter of the last decade. The inherent efficiency of fluid drives cannot match that of straight-gear drive, however. So until motorcycle engines offer large amounts of surplus power, the automatic transmission will likely be limited to heavy touring and utility applications. The variable belt drive suffers the same limitations, but its simplicity, lack of expense, and lightness are attractive features.

One unique variant is the Husqvarna automatic, which couples the engine through centrifugal clutches to a multi-speed planetary gearset.

Shifting takes place without any decoupling of engine and load, and power is at all times transmitted by efficient, low-loss gears. There is none of the torque converter's viscous loss. Despite its complexity, this gearbox seems a success and will probably appear in other forms in the near future.

There are other forms of stepless drive fairly bursting from the files of the patent office, but most of them are heavy and strictly limited in their torque capacity. Nevertheless, who can say? Honda machines equipped with a curious hydraulic drive were photographed by industrial spies a few years back, creating a sensation at the time. Though they were never introduced, the work no doubt goes on in many places. Humans are persistent. There's a lot more to come.

*May 1979*

# The Ignition Process

*A friend who was making detectors for high-energy physics set forth the core of this story for me—the idea of an avalanche of ionization in a gas, brought about by an intense applied electric field. A spark.*

Every power stroke in a spark ignition engine is initiated by the timed electric spark used to set the fuel-air mixture alight. If it does not ignite, there is a misfire, a break in the steady flow of power. The energy in that charge will never be released and the energy used to induct and compress it will be wasted. Power and efficiency drop; fuel consumption and emissions rise.

A big 500 single lazing along a country road may need only 20 good sparks per second, while a multi-cylinder, high rpm racing engine could require nearly 1,000. Every one of these sparks must produce ignition. The lifetime of a motorcycle may require a total of half a billion such sparks. To deliver consistent performance over such a long span requires not only adequate design initially, but excellent durability and resistance to deterioration in service.

There are mixtures that are ridiculously simple to ignite, requiring only the weakest of sparks across the tiniest of gaps. Propane engines, with their accurate and perfectly mingled fuel-air charges are examples of this. On the other side are the new lean-burn clean air engines whose mixtures are made deliberately marginal in flammability. To fire them may require very large plug gaps, powerful ignitions capable of sparking them, or even systems which deliver not a single spark but an entire train of them at each firing.

The point here is that there is no *best ignition*; there are only adequate ignitions and inadequate ones. The most advanced ignition, with the highest energy and voltage output will not improve on the performance of an ordinary system that is already adequate. The reason for the existence of so many systems is not necessarily progress but the great variety of ignition requirements of the types of engines in production today.

Consider what happens as the piston rises towards top center on a power stroke. The plug's electrodes are poised in the dark, their gap filled with the swirling, turbulent fuel-air mixture as the piston forces it to higher and higher density. Now the ignition process begins.

A voltage difference appears across the plug electrodes, the leading edge of a pulse arriving from the ignition system. The plug's center wire is rapidly becoming negative with respect to ground. No current can flow because the gases in the plug gap act as an insulator, or dielectric, preventing electrons, which are the charge carriers in electric current, from moving from negative to positive electrode. The voltage difference establishes an electric field in the gap whose strength grows rapidly, exerting a force on any electric charge in its range. Every molecule of fuel and air is normally electrically neutral, with the positive charges on its nucleus exactly balanced by an equal number of negative charges in the form of shells of electrons orbiting them.

The voltage pulse arriving at the plug gap from the ignition system soon raises the electric field strength there—high enough to tear off some of the outer electrons from molecules in the gap. This is called ionization. These free electrons are quickly accelerated by the electric field to very high velocities and they collide with other molecules in their way, ionizing them, in turn releasing yet more electrons until an avalanche of high-energy electrons is streaming towards the positive plug electrode. Such ionization

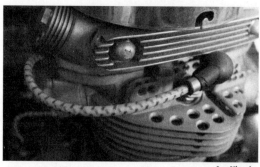

of the plug gap changes it from an insulator to a conductor; the moving charged electrons are in fact an electric current. Now the gap is said to have broken down. Voltage has accumulated until it ionizes the gap,

*Lee Klancher* generally several thousand

volts. This accelerating voltage is now able to force a heavy current surge across the gap, a thin channel of fast-moving electrons whose energy is now enough to break molecules apart into their constituent pieces, ionizing everything many times over. This particle bombardment also has the effect of raising the temperature of the material in the spark channel to some 60,000° K. For an instant, the inertia of the particles so heated keeps them together, and their internal pressure rises to hundreds of times that of the atmosphere. Finally this internal pressure begins to accelerate the material radially outwards, cooling the spark channel and reducing the density of charge carriers there. As the temperature continues to fall, many of the broken molecules are reassembled, but not necessarily into their original forms. Some of the fragments of broken fuel molecules will combine with oxygen from the air charge, releasing heat from chemical reaction. Such reactions constitute burning. If enough such reactions are initiated, their increasing heat will take over from the cooling spark channel the job of breaking down and recombining fuel and air. If the heat yield of this chemical reaction is greater than the heat lost to cooler surrounding gases, to the metal plug electrodes, and to the nearby cylinder head, a nucleus of self-sustaining flame has been created. It can now spread throughout the combustion chamber in the familiar way. If the heat yield is too low, there will be no continuing flame and a misfire will result.

An oscilloscope trace of the voltage across the plug gap will show the abrupt rise prior to ionization, then a rapid fall as the electron conduction across the gap takes place.

The initial spike of high voltage is dropping as the current peaks, but there is a short period when both are very high. Since power in watts is the product of voltage and current, this is the time of maximal energy release in the discharge, perhaps as high as a hundred kilowatts instantaneously. This initial current surge is supplied by the electrical capacitance of the wiring leading to the plug which in a sense is "stuffed with electrons" by the high voltage built up before breakdown of the gap.

This local source of current is quickly exhausted by such a heavy discharge across the gap, and the gap voltage now falls to a value just high enough to maintain ionization, some thousand volts or so. This later lower current, lower voltage part of the discharge is called the inductive phase because in a conventional ignition system (inductive coil and battery), the current that continues to flow is supplied by the coil's inductance. Current continues to flow at this lower voltage until what is stored in the ignition system for that spark is exhausted and voltage drops too low to maintain gap ionization. Current flow stops.

The capacitive phase, or spark head, occupies very little time, while the inductive part continues many times longer. The very high energy of the spark head makes it most likely that ignition will take place at this time or not at all, but there are exceptions to this as to everything else in this business. When the first Spanish Femsa CDI system was developed for the old Yamaha TD2 racer, it would not reach as high a peak rpm as the old, unreliable points magneto. Further investigation showed that the high-voltage CDI discharge was too brief to ensure ignition under the poor mixture/mixing conditions in that engine. When the output coil was changed to extend the inductive phase of the discharge, the high-rpm performance returned. Obviously then, the way in which an ignition delivers its energy is as important as the total amount.

A typical coil-and-battery inductive system might have a rise time (the time from 10 percent of maximum output voltage to 90 percent of maximum) of 100 microseconds, which is 3.6 crank degrees at 6,000 rpm. Its arc duration (period of conduction across the gap) might be of the order of 1,500 microseconds, or over 50 crank degrees. Its voltage output might reach 25,000 volts, open circuited. When connected to a plug, of course, any system can rise no higher in voltage than the breakdown voltage of the gap, which acts as a load.

A magneto system would differ from this in having a shorter rise time of 40-50 microseconds, a somewhat shorter arc duration, and a similar output voltage.

A capacitor discharge system of modern design would have an extremely short rise time of 2–4 microseconds, a short arc duration of 100 microseconds, but a much higher open-circuit output voltage capability of 35,000 volts.

Two systems may in fact have identical total spark energies but behave quite differently. The inductive system distributes its energy over a long time period, with relatively little "up front," in the spark head. The CDI system, however, puts most of its energy up front, and has little left over to maintain a long arc duration. Each energy distribution has its uses. An engine with poor mixing of fuel and air may not run properly on a short arc duration ignition, because the spark may arrive when the plug gap is occupied by mixture too lean or too rich to burn. On the other hand, only the true CDI system would be able to fire and keep clear modern surface gap plugs.

Ignition is often marginal, for stock systems provide little more than the plug's voltage requirement under difficult conditions of operation, such as starting and acceleration. Manufacturers must compromise often in providing components. Large, high-current ignition coils are expensive and their operation burns points faster than weaker items. High arc current to the plugs causes faster deterioration there, too.

Successful ignition depends on the heat yield from the volume of charge heated by the spark. There are many factors controlling this.

Since there is only one chemically correct fuel-air ratio for each fuel type, only that ratio will yield maximum heat in burning. This is why ignition is more difficult when the mixture to be fired is richer or leaner than the correct value.

It is not enough to supply just the correct proportions of fuel and air. They must also be intimately mixed so that the sample near the spark plug is flammable.

The temperature of the air charge and of the spark plug and its surroundings is important, for cool material can bleed heat away from the beginning flame nucleus, quenching it. Massive plug electrodes can be guilty here. A further effect is that of pressure. The gas in the plug gap acts as an insulator, and increasing the gas pressure makes it even harder to break down the gap. Engines with very high compression are harder to fire for this reason. In some cases of marginal ignition it is easier to get an engine to run with lots of spark advance than at a more attractive, late timing. This is because the earlier the spark is timed, the lower the combustion chamber pressure it opposes in trying to break down the gap, and the more sure will be the spark.

Excessively rapid motion of the charge past the plug electrodes can actually blow out the spark, removing the ions faster than they can be created. The same can happen with the incipient flame nucleus; it can be cooled or dispersed by such turbulence and thus extinguished.

The presence of inert material in the fuel-air mixture naturally makes combustion less likely, for these molecules act as "spacers," between the reactive substances. There is always nitrogen in the charge, for this gas makes up 78 percent of the air. Another source of inert material is exhaust gas residuals from the previous cycle, or deliberately introduced, as in exhaust gas recirculation (EGR).

There are three principal ways of dealing with these difficulties, and all of them involve means of increasing the sample of mixture that is exposed to the spark.

A large plug gap is the most obvious means, and modern automobiles call out gaps ranging from .035 in. up to .080 in. instead of the former .018 in.–.024 in. The bigger gap ensures that there is a larger sample through which the spark must pass, and there is an improved chance that this sample will be flammable. The larger gap has a higher voltage requirement.

Another approach is to increase the duration of the spark, depending upon charge motion to circulate the desired larger sample of mixture through the gap during the arc. This type of ignition, usually in the form of multiple spark discharges, has had good success in solving the problems of lean-burn engines with marginal mixtures, and with heavy EGR ratios.

A third useful method is placement of the plug gap away from the stagnant boundary layer near the combustion chamber wall and out in the stream of moving charge. Such projected tip plugs have improved performance in many automotive and motorcycle applications. Because of space constraints, they cannot be used in very compact chambers where there is danger of contact with piston or valves.

A corollary of this idea is the use of very fine electrodes, which produce less masking of the gap region, allowing freer circulation of charge to the gap.

The spark plug itself is nothing more than an easily removable high-voltage spark gap that threads into the wall of the engine's combustion chamber. The steel outer shell is sealed to the aluminum oxide ceramic insulator which passes through its center, and within that is the rivet, connected on the outside to the spark plug wire and on the inner end to the center electrode or center wire. This wire is normally designed to be the hottest running part of the plug. There are two reasons for this. First, the insulator surrounding it must run hot enough to spontaneously burn off any conductive carbon deposits that may form on it. Secondly, the center wire is usually made of the negative electrode because it is easier to pull electrons out of a hot surface than from a cool one, reducing the voltage requirement in running.

The high temperature is the source of problems because the center wire is more quickly eroded by electrical and chemical attack when it is hot, leading to growth of the gap and a higher voltage requirement. If the center wire temperature or that of its insulator rises high enough, it will act as a source of premature ignition in the cylinder, setting off the charge before the spark does. Such preignition leads to overheating, detonation, and possibly destructive results.

As is usual in engineering, the plug designer is caught among contradictory requirements and must compromise. If the insulator nose temperature drops too low, as during idle running, carbon may be deposited on it, acting as a shunt path for plug voltage, draining it away fast enough to reduce spark energy or prevent sparking completely. This is fouling. This cold-fouling region begins at some 700° F.

When the temperature of the center wire or insulator nose reaches up towards or above 1,700° F there is danger that it will cause preignition. Again, the higher the center wire temperature, the more rapid is gap growth. This makes short, thick electrodes look attractive, but we have already seen that these have drawbacks for other reasons.

To counter cold fouling, the insulator can be made long and thin, making the heat path from the hot tip to the cooler shell of the plug longer. Such hot-running plugs are good for low-power applications but can get too hot at high duty.

Colder plugs have shorter insulator noses which are often fatter as well, joining the shell quite near the chamber end.

In especially severe conditions of service (sustained open throttle, heavy supercharge, and/or special fuels), special measures have to be taken to control center wire and insulator temperature. The center wire may be made from high-heat-conductivity material such as copper or silver, to take the heat away more quickly, or the heat path from wire to insulator may be improved by use of a thermal cement.

As the insulator is made shorter to resist severe service, a point may be reached beyond which it is the ground electrode, not the center wire, which is dangerously close to preignition temperature. It can then be made shorter and thicker. The limiting case in a conventional airgap plug is the push-wire type, in which a stubby wire is pressed through a hole in the plug shell so just its tip projects towards the center wire. Such retracted-gap plugs were formerly obligatory for racing engines, in which placement of valves and piston dome precluded use of anything else, and marginal conditions of carburetion and ignition timing required the very greatest in preignition resistance. With the advent of improved center wire materials and improvements in engine systems, such plugs are rarely used today.

For the very maximum in preignition protection there is the surface gap plug, which discharges not across an airgap but along the surface of the insulator, which entirely fills the space between shell and center wire. Such plugs require high-energy, fast rise-time ignitions to fire them and keep them clean.

After preignition rating, the major concern of manufacturers is gap growth in service. The chemical and electrical attack eats at the electrodes, rounding them off and increasing the gap. The rounding alone can increase plug voltage requirement by 25 percent, for the original sharp edges concentrate the electric field, making breakdown of the gap easier. The side wire or ground electrode is made to present a flat surface to the center wire, requiring removal of more material for a given increase in gap space than a round wire. The side wire is made from a nickel or nickel chromium alloy, resistance welded to the plug shell.

To preserve a reasonable voltage requirement, finer wire can be used, which never has a tip radius larger than half its diameter. To prevent rapid erosion of such fine wire, it is made from chemically resistant metals such as platinum or iridium. Various schemes have been tried to maintain sharp edges on the sidewire as well.

Much effort in plug engineering goes into locating the operating points of the plug well away from the fouling region on the low end and the preignition range at the upper end. A given plug will have a definite relationship between its insulator nose and center wire temperature on the one hand, and the severity of operating conditions in the combustion chamber on the other. We can draw a temperature versus load curve in this way. A steep curve means limited latitude in heat range, with less room between the undesirable extremes. A small change in engine load will cause a relatively large change in plug temperature.

A less-steep curve puts the extremes farther apart. A plug of this kind is said to have wide latitude. A recent development which makes a considerable contribution to such latitude is the use of projected gap design. Although such a design looks as if it would run hotter than a conventional plug because the insulator and center wire project so far into the chamber, this very feature makes it run cooler than expected at high load because of the cooling effect of fresh charge blowing over the exposed parts.

Spark plug preignition rating is an SAE procedure carried out in a precise way on a special test engine, using instrumented versions of the plugs being tested. The plugs are modified during assembly to include a fine-wire, high-temperature thermocouple in the insulator tip that permits measurement of its temperature continuously as the engine runs.

The preignition rating engine is a ruggedly constructed 17.6-cubic-inch single cylinder test unit made by Labeco, connected to an electric dynamometer which applies the load. The severity of the heat generated in the combustion chamber can be varied all the way from idling to very high supercharge. The actual variable measured in preignition rating is the indicated mean effective pressure (IMEP) at which the plug becomes hot enough to cause preignition. IMEP is the pressure which, were it to act constantly over the entire piston stroke, would result in the same pressure-volume work as does the real, complex varying pressure in the running engine. It is therefore an average combustion pressure. Brake mean effective pressure (BMEP) is simply the IMEP with losses from friction and pumping subtracted. The higher the IMEP, the more severe the thermal environment in the combustion chamber. The colder the plug, the higher the IMEP rating.

In the test, the engine's oil and cooling water temperatures are brought to specified values and the rpm is brought up to the test point. Now the inlet pressure is increased (the throttle is opened or the supercharger boost is turned up) by small amounts, the dynamometer keeping the rpm constant by applying more and more load. The spark plug's tip temperature is noted for each power level and IMEP. At some IMEP the steady, measured increase in plug temperature turns into a sudden rise, signaling the onset of preignition. This is the plug's IMEP rating, and it allows plugs of various designs to be compared by a fixed standard.

Other types of testing are carried on routinely as well. Computer-controlled dynamometers cycle engines endlessly through various loads in gap-growth tests. Engines run hour after hour at tick-over speeds in fouling resistance tests.

Actual road tests are carried out as well, with portable equipment being carried on running vehicles to measure and record plug temperature during various regimes of operation. In this way unusual situations of plug fouling or overheating can be discovered before new models are released, and plug engineers can use the tools at their disposal to eliminate such problems.

Spark plug fouling can arise either from carbon deposition or from lead deposits. The familiar carbon fouling results either from poor engine condition (excessively rich mixture, poor oil control, etc.) or from incorrect selection of plug heat range or type.

Lead fouling is more complicated. In normal moderate power running, the lead anti-knock compounds used in gasoline are deposited on the plug insulator in a chemical form that is electrically nonconductive. When the throttle is opened, however, the increased heat changes these nonconductive forms into conductive ones, and spark voltage may be shunted away to ground down the insulator nose. The classic case is the large outboard motor used for trolling. For hours the engine drones at low power, but finally the anglers tire of the mosquito bites and head for home at full throttle. The lead compounds become conductive or a whisker is formed across the gap, and the plug is shorted.

To counter this phenomenon as well as that of carbon fouling, makers have had recourse to very high energy, fast-rise-time CDI systems firing surface gap plugs. The sheer energy of the discharge running along the surface of the insulator evaporates the deposits, seeking them out because they are the lowest resistance parts of the gap. Outboard engine manufacturers have been the leaders in this field and remain so.

Simply screwing surface gap plugs into an engine whose ignition is not designed for them will only result in fouled plugs or no ignition at all, for without the voltage to jump the gap and keep it clean, there can be no result.

Other engines may require the rapid rise time of a CDI ignition without the extreme spark energy needed for surface plugs. Certain types of two-stroke engines will do very well with such ignitions and conventional plugs, for the fast rise time alone will keep them out of the fouling region which their messy mixtures offer them.

Such complexities are some of the reasons why the ignitions used on Superbike racers are so mundane compared with those of the 250 and 750 Yamaha two-stroke racers. The Superbike can do very well with its slow rise time, moderate energy coil and battery system, perhaps even fired by reliable old points, simply because its charge is so easy to light. There is little point in bolting up a patent arc welder of unknown reliability when the existing system is adequate.

But then try running a two-stroke racer on one of the older systems. Back in the days of points magnetos it was often necessary to use hotter plugs for

*Lee Klancher*

starting and warming up, then switch to colder heat range for racing. There was the real possibility that you could go into a turn as a twin and emerge as a single. Fouled plug. Out of the race. No fun. With the modern CDI systems, we use the same plug heat range all day, and if the engines are carbureted right, they will idle right down off the tachometer face.

My informants at Champion Spark Plug insisted repeatedly upon this point: there are no rules in the ignition business, only methods. You cannot say what ignition will be required by a given engine until you investigate it. For each particular variant of ignition there may be an application, but you cannot read the entire future off the manufacturer's advertising.

No system confers an automatic advantage. Taxicab engines idle for hours at the curb, waiting for fares. Then they roar off up the expressway. Their tuning may be indifferent, their gas the cheapest that will burn. Compression is down, oil control is permissive. This may be the ideal place for one of those multiple-spark discharge systems; if the first spark runs into an oil blob, maybe the second or the third will do the job. Maybe.

Lean-burn engines can have trouble with ignition unless large gaps are used to expose more mixture volume to the discharge. This may require more voltage and more energy. May. Years ago we had the choice between a Yamaha racing magneto and the German-made Kröber CDI system. We didn't know it at the time, but the Kröber system had much less energy than did the stock magneto. It was a good thing we didn't know it, because the German system would start our engines and run wonderfully all the same, with hardly a trace of the fouling we had had with the mag. Still, its spark energy was less than one-fifth that of an average modern ignition. Why? Perhaps because its limited energy was all up front, with a fast rise time. Perhaps. Whatever the numbers were, the thing worked.

In the face of some of the torrid claims made for certain ignitions today you might think it a miracle that engines ever ran at all in the bad old days. Classic single-cylinder racers such as the Norton Manx and G50 Matchless had combustion chamber conditions just as severe or more so as any encountered in the most powerful four-stroke racing engines made today, yet they ran happily, never missing a beat, with huge, cumbersome magnetos supplying very moderate voltage with dreary rise time to the plug. The plugs themselves were set with gaps that were tiny by today's standards. It all worked fine because it was designed to.

A good commentary on the progress made recently in carburetion and ignition is the continuing trend towards hotter and hotter spark plug heat range for a given application. An ignition with haphazard spread in timing has to be set so the most advanced possible spark is not too advanced, and to cover contingencies it might be a good idea to use a cold plug as well. The dreadful carburetion we all thought was perfectly OK not so long ago sent alternating blizzards of wet, rich mixture and barely inflammable lean mixture to the chambers; again, the plugs had to be cold enough to deal with the worst case, and that could be pretty bad.

In 1960, the MZ 125 single roadracer developed some 25 bhp, hardly a notable figure today. Back then the plug fitted was the very coldest plug in Champion's air-gap range, the N52-R. In 1970, the recommended plug for Kawasaki's 500 H1R roadracer was the Champion N54-R, a bit warmer than that MZ choice, but still a very cold, retracted-gap design that today would find application mainly in supercharged fuel dragsters. Yet we used these cold sparklers religiously, fervent in our belief that they were the proof that racing is tough and mean. The engines had horrid little coil ignitions with flapping points driven off the flexing crank end, no doubt delivering sparks all over the degree wheel with great impartiality.

Yamaha's TZ-750A of 1974 was a faster machine by far, yet it used a Champion wire-gap plug a full three heat ranges hotter. Now, five years later, the F-model of this same 750 is running regularly with plugs a range or two hotter again, and developing yet more power. This is possible because engines of today are running in a much better controlled and narrower range of operating variables. Mixture and ignition are much closer to the good numbers most of the time. When they begin to act up, tuners still have recourse to colder plugs as mental insurance against any possibility of preignition.

Don't imagine that preignition is some strange and theoretical laboratory phenomenon. It is very real and I have seen the results often enough. It used to be quite common for a harried novice racer to forget to replace his warm-up plugs with cold racing numbers before practice. This mistake usually was paid for in the first lap with a seized engine, the direct result of plug preignition, detonation, and overheating.

In general, however, racing is an easy environment for plugs. The tuning of racing engines is much better than that of street-driven vehicles because the tuner is always correcting it. Racing engines don't run thousands of miles on a set of plugs so gap growth is nonexistent. The load is always high, requiring little plug latitude. On a fast track like Daytona, a 750 machine could run near-identical laps with three different heat ranges of plug because each of them would have its firing tip in the nonfouling, non-preigniting range.

The reason for choosing the hottest plug that will run is that when the engine is at part or closed throttle, the hotter plug will stay more nearly free of deposits that could hinder immediate acceleration afterwards. This is why wire-gap plugs often reduce lap times on tracks like Loudon with many slow corners.

Though it seems a bit odd at first, in general the larger the engine, the hotter the plug recommended for it. This is because full power of such engines is too much for any highway condition, and if it is ever used (a dark night, a straight road . . .) it will be for a very few seconds at most. This means the big motor spends more of its life at part throttle, near the fouling range, than does a little engine that has to work hard just to keep up with traffic.

Engineers monitoring the operation of engines under test have long noted the wide variations in peak combustion pressure from cycle to cycle, under constant throttle. If such cycle-to-cycle variations could be eliminated and performance brought uniformly up to the level of the best cycles there would be a substantial improvement in power and economy. Where do these variations come from? Why don't they go away?

In some degree they are related to mixture in homogeneity. In even the best of cases there is no measurable pressure rise in the cylinder for some time after the passage of the spark. This is called the delay period, and it arises from the fact that there is considerable time from the generation of self-sustaining flame until the beginning of rapid inflammation of the chamber. Combustion rate increases geometrically, so at first the rate can be very low for some time. If the spark passes through a region of very lean or very rich mixture, the initial rate of energy release will be low and the delay period long. Peak pressure will be delayed and reduced.

Even when elaborate means are adopted to eliminate mixture strength variations (such as complete evaporation of the fuel into a vapor by passing the mixture through a steam-heated drum on its way to the engine) there are still cycle-to-cycle variations. This redirects suspicion onto exhaust gas residuals, which, in mixing with even a perfectly prepared fuel-air mix, will do so imperfectly.

When research situations are created to eliminate exhaust residuals there are still variations. This inclines researchers to believe that air motion itself causes some variation. There is no way to eliminate turbulent air motion from the combustion chamber, so there will always be air movement at the plug gap. Turbulent air consists of small parcels of molecules in more or less coherent motion. If the spark occurs at the boundary between two small parcels, the shear zone between them may have the effect of spreading the flame faster than if the spark had occurred inside such a cell, in which the flame might be imprisoned for some time.

Elimination of cycle-to-cycle variations is an attractive idea, but it appears that advances in ignition and plugs will only reduce the effects, never eliminate them.

What about the future? Motorcyclists have anxiously watched the proliferation of Federal standards for auto exhaust emissions, wondering when their turn would come. The constant stream of weird and often counter-productive technologies pressed into service as quick-fixes for emissions made us all wonder if our vehicles could even survive such official attention. Most of the clean-air equipment and modifications have made ignition more difficult through use of very lean mixtures, inappropriate ignition timing, or complex precombustion and turbulence schemes. Long-burn ignitions and multiple discharge systems firing projected tip plugs seemed to be the trend, with conditions getting ever more stringent.

Now it appears there is hope. The coming of computer-controlled fuel mixture and ignition timing may extend the life of the spark ignition engine in recognizable form into the foreseeable future. The new system has much in common with the racing situation, but instead of a tuner scrutinizing the spark plugs and then correcting the mixture and the timing, there is an oxygen sensor in the exhaust which continuously monitors the engine's fuel-air ratio. Any deviation from the chemically correct ratio of some 14.5:1 is signaled to a small computer which then adjusts the delivery rate of the fuel injection system. The ignition timing is simultaneously adjusted to suit several other variables, being reset as often as every firing event. The minimal exhaust pollutants from this clean-carbureting system will then be conducted to a three-way catalyst pack which oxidizes unburned hydrocarbons and carbon monoxide and reduces oxides of nitrogen.

Ignition of such accurately metered fuel-air mixtures is a simple task compared with the troubles of the earlier schemes.

The real beauty of the oxygen sensor system with three-way catalyst is that we may be able to retain the valuable, proven technology that has given us strong, reliable, understandable piston engines for so many years. We may not have to struggle with Buck Rogers lithium hydride/freon/element 109 engines of mind-breaking complexity and expense. We may just have the possibility of soldiering on much as before, but with clean air and good fuel economy. And good ignition.

# Chassis and Suspension, Part 1

*I was first involved in motorcycle racing in the 1960s, so we were all mesmerized by horsepower. The one inkling I had of this other world was when I replaced the 125-pound-per-inch stock chromed springs on my Yamaha TD1-B with softer Girling 70-pounders. With my rear tire more often on the track rather than hopping above it, I had grip. We're still looking for more.*

O ur first and finest chassis and suspension is the human body, articulated in bone and moved by muscle, controlled by that most versatile of computers, the brain. No other system can monitor the surface ahead, adjust power, direction, and damping, and chew gum at the same time.

For the much simpler vehicles we ride and drive, we must be satisfied for now with passive suspension, unable to act of its own will and simply reacting to the road. Even these basic systems of springs, dampers, and moveable parts needed years of invention and development to reach their present excellence.

The inventive process differs from what myth would have us believe. Nothing is invented in a vacuum. All inventions come about because people work on a problem whose only solution is a new idea. When one of these people finds an answer, we remember his name, call him a genius, and know nothing of all his colleagues and all their work. It's silly to suppose there would have been no steam engine if James Watt had never thought of it. In his time there was a need for mechanical power and there was therefore a general ferment of thought, after which, sooner or later, the new engine would have come about.

The first wheeled vehicles had no suspension but the "give" in their joints. Because nothing is ever improved until there is a need, these conveyances remained unchanged for many centuries—early tuners never found a way to double the speed of a horse or an ox.

When speed did finally arrive, it came first on rails and was only for the well-to-do. Transport for everyman had to await the coming of the bicycle. The first of these were impractical curiosities—too heavy in their wooden-wagon construction to make useful speed. The world, however, headed into an explosion of technology at the end of the nineteenth century, causing entire clusters of new materials and technologies to appear, and these made a practical bicycle inevitable. The tension-spoke wheel, the ball bearing, the roller chain, the pneumatic tire, and the production of light, stiff steel tubing were combined by 1885 into Starley's famous "Rover Safety Bicycle." The possibilities of rapid individual travel created a bicycle boom, in the wake of which entire industries sprang up to supply better tubing, tires, bearings, and chain. Quick business success stimulated rapid development.

The internal combustion engine appeared as well. Though there had been steam-powered, bicycle-like contraptions before, the union of the IC engine and the bicycle created the motorcycle.

The first motorcycles were bicycles with clip-on engines, driving either the front or rear wheel by belts of twisted rawhide or flat leather. Even a 1-horse-power engine has 10 times the continuous power of a man, so these hybrid machines hit bumps much harder than did bicycles. Bicycling societies lobbied hard for better roads, but travel remained rough. Forks bent or broke and frames cracked. A bicycle absorbs shock by flexing, but the new mechanical power was too much. Early alloys fatigued and broke constantly.

Matters sorted themselves out and by 1903 most motorcycles started by pedaling like a moped, had their engines in the current location, and drove their rear wheels direct from a pulley on the engine crankshaft. It's tempting to laugh at these putt-putts now, but you must try to imagine the incredible feeling of freedom they gave to their riders: to travel faster than any horse, and without the crushing expense of carriage house, carriage, horses, and all the stuff that went with them. This was a dramatic time and motorists would undergo almost any hardship to enjoy their machines. Change was rapid and constant.

Why belt drive? It was almost universal as a drive for factory machinery. It needed no lubrication, was largely immune from fatigue, and was naturally shock-absorbing. As the early motorcyclist pedaled furiously off, fiddling desperately with his air lever, his big single was apt to start with a terrible bang. A solid chain drive to the rear wheel would result only in broken spokes or a broken chain.

Belts require constant tension to transmit power, so any form of rear suspension was all but out of the question. The evolution of the chassis depended on the evolution of drive systems. The classic diamond bicycle frame was ideal for belt drive because it placed a solidly braced triangle of metal between engine and rear wheel.

A bicycle's front fork consists of two gracefully curved blades which join the front axle to the steering stem. The joint between blades and stem often broke, injuring many riders. The first advance in forks made especially for motorcycles was, therefore, an extra pair of steel braces from axle ends to the top of the steering stem. This multiple-load-path structure was safer because the failure of any one member did not spell the rider's downfall. These extra braces took the flexibility out of the front end, making riding very hard on the rider's hands. Some form of front suspension was then a must.

In five years, hundreds of schemes were tried by as many makers, including all the ideas we now think of as modern. Fork blades that hinged perilously in the middle, and forks with long or short leading or trailing links appeared. Leaf springs, compression springs, tension springs, and even air springs operated them. Telescopic forks were made which "telescoped" in every conceivable place. Since suspension dampers were still 15 years away, more than an inch or so of suspension travel resulted only in comical bouncing. Short-travel designs were the ticket. The leaf spring, whose inter-leaf friction provides its own limited damping, won out over the coil spring. Anything with sliding motion (such as a telescopic fork must have) was impossible to seal against billowing road dust with only felt or leather washers. Forks that operated by pivoting outlasted those with sliding motion. The dynamic American pioneer, Indian, adopted short trailing links which pivoted from the lower ends of the fork blades. With no more than this, there would have been only the tightness of the axle to keep the links parallel and the wheel centered in the fork. To correct this, Indian added a tuning-fork-shaped yoke which connected the two axle ends to the limber end of a short leaf spring above, projecting from the top of the steering head. In order for the wheel to twist or tilt, it would have to bend or twist this spring sideways. The design succeeded, even if all it did was clip off the peak forces from bump impacts.

In England another concept matured. Designers were attracted by the stiffness and safety of those four independent load paths in a reinforced bicycle fork. They reasoned that the wheel together with such a fork made a light, stiff unit. Why not attach this to the steering crowns by four short parallelogram links and a pair of springs so that wheel and fork could rise and fall as one? This was the girder fork, the most successful front suspension concept for the next 30–40 years.

Ideas for rear suspension were also irrepressible. Indian adopted chain drive soon after 1900, probably because of the advanced state of the U.S. chain industry, and this gave them a freedom the belt-drive builders did not have. A chain required no tension to function: The rear wheel could move up and down without interfering with power flow; Indian pursued advanced experiments while others persisted with rigid frames and belt drive.

The Norton that won the 1907 Isle of Man TT had a Druid girder fork, a rigid diamond frame, and a single-speed flat-belt drive. Meanwhile the TAC machine tried out shaft drive and suspension at the rear. Four parallel leaf springs projecting from the rear of the machine acted in pairs like two parallelogram swingarms. Any shaft-drive lift forces were thus reacted to the frame. This idea went nowhere. The flexibility of all those springs in all directions made the machine unstable. Indian, on its road machines, went straight to a fully modern swingarm design supported by the ever-present leaf springs, yet for its powerful racing machines it retained the stiffness and handling certainty of the rigid diamond frame. After all, they could spring the rider by putting coils under his seat.

Tires were narrow, hard, and poor, so cornering was always subject to the "dreaded side-slip," especially on the luxury in-line four-cylinder machines with very long chassis. Because stable and short chassis were easier to arrange with compact singles and V-twins, these types prevailed.

Thinking about these first machines, remember that they were not much heavier than bicycles. The addition of anything extra, be it suspension, variable gearing, or whatever, prompted suspicion. Those engines were barely up to the work of pulling a very light and simple machine; anything new had to be worth the weight.

In France a unique development was unfolding—track racing on smooth velodromes. Engines as big as two liters were fitted into grotesquely swollen bicycle frames with a multitude of extra braces to hold the vibrating mass of metal together. Giant flat belts over 2 inches wide, running on drive pulleys nearly as big as the wheels themselves, transmitted the "monstrous" power of these 20-bhp machines. Progress along this line of development was clearly nearing a dead end.

Less power but better handling was the direction taken in England, where useful speed over convoluted country lanes required constant deceleration, cornering, and acceleration. Adding variable-pulley schemes permitted altering the drive ratio while under way, but this did nothing to hasten the coming of rear suspension. Belt drive still looked very comforting to the conservative element in design.

So stifling was this conservatism that the TT organizers deliberately outlawed pedaling gear for their 1911 event, hoping to hasten the coming of real clutches and variable-ratio drives. The advanced Indian, equipped with a friction clutch, two-speed transmission, and primary and secondary chain drive, dominated this event 1-2-3.

From this time until the First World War, English machines were increasingly equipped with rear-hub-mounted planetary gears, driven now by special segmented leather V-belts that could double as clutches.

Innovation continued to gleam out of the murk of conservatism, but it was frequently punished by poor handling or durability. Time and again designers were forced back to the trusty diamond bicycle frame. Scott experimented with linear-motion forks in 1908. In 1912 NSU built a rear suspension suggestive of the monoshock later used by Yamaha. In 1920 ASL used air pressure in modern-looking, rolling-seal housings to spring its machine. In the face of inadequate materials and punishing highways, the innovations died out almost as fast as they were born. This left engineers with the incorrect notion that their ideas were at fault rather than their application. Failure's aftertaste prevented many sound concepts from being tried again.

Most machines then used the girder fork, but it had drawbacks. Forces applied at the tire multiplied many times by the time they reached the four little links attaching the girder to the steering crowns. The stiffness of the fork depended on the stiffness of these links and on the clearances in each of their eight pivot bearings. A small clearance at the pivots became a large backlash at the wheel. Lateral stiffness was low because of the light-gauge tubing used, braced as it was in the fore-and-aft direction only. Increasing fork travel meant making the links longer, and subsequently more flexible.

Another fork gained popularity as well. This was a development of the Indian trailing-link fork, but turned around and made more rigid. In this so-called Castle pattern, or H-D fork, two rigid blades projected downward from the steering crowns to the level of the front axle. A pair of very short leading links connected the blades and axle, providing minimal travel. Protection from tilting and twisting was accomplished with a yoke rising from the axle ends upward, parallel with the fork blades. The upper end of this yoke was tubular and rode up and down in a guide attached to the upper steering crown. In a variant, the upper end of the yoke pivoted from a second set of links attached to the upper crown. This Castle fork acquired the reputation of "hair-line steering," probably because of the lateral rigidity of the heavy vertical blades and because the pivot links were right at wheel level where any bearing looseness had minor effect.

Although many machines had engines as big as 1,000cc, power was low because of low compression (set by poor gasoline), low rpm (limited by bearing materials and oiling systems), and inefficient drive systems. Such engines were unable to distort frames under acceleration. Feeble brakes were also the rule, based either on industrial models or bicycle practice. Without powerful forces to bend these motorcycles under power, braking, or cornering, builders had little incentive to advance chassis design.

World War I arrived and the world changed. A post-war business slump eliminated many motorcycle brands and delayed the progress of others, but soon the application of wartime engine know-how made obvious the weaknesses of bicycle frames and suspension.

More power needs more brakes. In 1922, Norton gave up its bicycle-type stirrup rim brakes in favor of the automotive-type internal expanding shoe. Higher speeds and more brakes put more force through front suspensions. Riders needed either stiffer springs or more travel to cope with this; since suspension was already very stiff, travel won out. To stop the disturbing bouncing that resulted, Norton and others added automotive friction dampers to their front forks the following year. With signs of progress at the front, was there a matching advance at the rear? Not immediately. If anything, a little more power was still a good reason to keep the back end rigid. No one wanted additional wobbles. More hinges meant more trouble.

In America, long, straight roads encouraged increases in power rather than advances in handling. There, engines grew bigger. Design on the two sides of the Atlantic diverged.

BMW began production of its long-lived flat-twin in 1923 and conservatively equipped it with the Indian trailing-link fork. In 1925 the fast and powerful British Brough SS100 sports bike was equipped with the Castle fork. Its big JAP V-twin engine had the power to pull the extra weight and its speed required accurate steering.

In 1928 came the invention that would permit riders at last to use their brakes hard and continuously: the positive-stop, foot-operated gear change. Before this, the rider had to take one hand off the controls to downshift. Now chassis and suspension could be on duty all the time.

AJS tried to combine the steering accuracy of the Castle fork with the lightness of the girder by fabricating the Castle blades in girder fashion from several small tubes. After two years of trying, they found that the stiffness really does increase with the fourth power of the tube diameter. Unwilling to settle for the weight of a stiff, big-tube Castle fork, they reverted to girder. Norton dropped the old Druid fork for the newer Webb girder in 1929. The next year, rising power and the new footshift demanded that Norton revise its brakes again. As engineer Phil Vincent drew plans for his machines, which were to employ the engine as a frame member and use a monoshock-like triangulated swingarm, Matchless was trying out a similar rear suspension on its expensive Silver Hawk model. The triangulated swingarm looked good to designers of heavy, powerful machines after the failure of lighter rear suspension schemes on earlier motorcycles.

In 1933 Moto Guzzi began to experiment with longer-travel leading link forks in hopes of finding a safe way to more wheel grip. Norton enlarged the brakes on its racers yet again. On the continent, BMW engineers ignored suspension in favor of supercharged power, nearing the 100-bhp mark from their 750 speed-record machine equipped with Indian's turn-of-the-century fork and rigid rear end.

Conservatism like this received a hard smack in 1935 when Moto Guzzi, evidently having discovered something in their experiments, won the 250 TT with a motorcycle having swingarm rear suspension. This was the first time *any* TT had been won by a "springer." A year later the progressive English maker Velocette fitted its works racers with modern swingarms controlled by hydraulic dampers. Prevailing thought believed that the extra weight of a triangulated swingarm would be too much on a race bike.

The Italian and German makers were benefiting from pre-war nationalism now—their governments directly encouraged them to seek racing prestige. Their supercharged engines were now making so much power that British makers, with less money, had to scratch hard for suitable replies. Better acceleration out of corners now clearly depended more on wheel grip than on pure power; at the 1936 Swiss Grand Prix, Norton's team bikes appeared with rear suspension by plunger. Each end of the rear axle was bolted to a short, vertical, round plunger that rode up and down in two guide bushings attached to the rear frame. This gave a straight-line wheel motion that was very hard on chains; there was a large variation in chain-line center-distance as the wheel rose and fell. Why, in the face of the other makers' success with swingarms, did Norton adopt the plunger system? First, there was no doubt Velocette's scheme was less than ideal, and the Norton men knew it. Velo's oleopneumatic suspension units were a "first try." Previous history had shown designers that the classic diamond frame always offered a haven from frame problems. Velo's design, a pivoted swingarm, had to feed wheel loads through the spindly arm itself into a dangerously novel, truncated chassis. Plungers, on the other hand, allowed the designer to keep his beloved diamond frame and to mount his new gadgetry at its rear—obviously a low-risk proposition. Never mind that the slightest clearance in the plunger bushings produced wobble-generating tilting of the rear wheel. Never mind that the best angle for the plungers and chain was the worst angle for action over bumps. Many makers hastened to adopt the new plunger design, including eventually BMW, NSU, and Benelli.

Norton also accepted the need for increased stiffness at the front. They abandoned the light but flexible girder fork for a telescopic fork, albeit with only two inches of travel and without hydraulic damping. Two inches sounds tiny today, but it was equal to the best of the girders. One step at a time. After a season with this new frame and suspension, Norton engineers had to add extra reinforcing stays leading back to the plungers; their system wasn't as good as they'd hoped.

In Germany, DKW tried a hybrid approach. Attracted by the more compliant action of a swingarm and by its benevolence toward chains, they adopted it; yet also attracted by the legendary stiffness of the diamond frame, they fitted their new swingarm between the rear triangles of such a design, locating the supporting suspension units at the apexes. Apparently, their belief was that the real cause of motorcycle instability was not so much tilting of the rear wheel out of plane as it was distortion of the entire frame. If so, the diamond shape should eliminate it. They were wrong and their machine handled no better for it.

By 1937, BMW's supercharged horsepower was so competitive in Grand Prix racing that it compelled the company to revamp the 500's dreadful handling by adopting plunger rear suspension and an oil-damped telescopic front fork. Why were telescopics suddenly respectable again, after so many years on the "rejected" list? New aircraft designs in the middle-1930s were incorporating retractable wheels for the first time, and tele-scopic suspension was the most compact form conceivable. The aviation industry wasted no time developing suitable seals and hydraulic dampers, and motorcycles were indirect beneficiaries of this work.

Despite the efforts of Norton, Velocette, and the other English makers, the battle of continental horsepower versus British chassis and suspension ingenuity was slowly beginning to favor the big numbers. Norton advanced its brakes again, adopting large conical hubs, but BMW won the 500 title in 1938, their leaping supercharged racer demanding the utmost bravery from its riders. The only British company with a powerful supercharged design, AJS showed that power and weight were truly far too much for existing suspension by breaking a girder fork link while leading the 1938 Ulster Grand Prix. The Italian Gilera Rondine, with its smooth water-cooled, supercharged four-cylinder engine, showed what combined power and improved handling could do by taking the title in 1939. This machine had a twin-loop chassis, girder fork, and a rear swingarm.

World War II left motorcycles largely unchanged because they offered little scope as weapons of mass destruction. When the hostilities ceased, the world needed transportation. The revived Italian industry's new offerings were all equipped with up-to-the-minute rear suspension. By 1948, Velocette models could be had with production versions of the oleo-pneumatic fork and suspension units used on the pre-war racers, made by the aircraft landing-gear firm, Dowty. In the U.S., too, replacement forks of telescopic pattern were offered to fit big V-twins by another landing-gear maker. By 1951–53 Velocette was offering conventional spring-supported teleforks and swingarm suspension on all models. AMC machines (the combination of Matchless and AJS) sported the "Teledraulic" fork and their own hydraulic rear dampers. Even Triumph grudgingly acknowledged the validity of the trend by offering (as an option only, mind you) the "sprung hub," a form of plunger rear suspension in which all the mechanism was stuffed inside the rear hub.

Supercharging was banned from racing at this point, so the pre-war British designs were again successful. When Gilera resumed racing, its beautiful engine was housed in a succession of improbable and unstable frames with rear suspension via torsion bars, levers, springs, or bell cranks. It was to be the same story all over again. The first post-war title was won by AJS's new racing twin, the "Porcupine," fitted with teles and swingarm. With no budget for engine development Norton replied the following year with an all-new chassis and suspension, later called the "Featherbed." The Featherbed was a synthesis of all that was best in the large variety of concepts reviewed in racing over the previous 10 years.

Like the pre-war Rondine, the Norton had a twin-loop chassis but was specifically reinforced to withstand heavy braking and lateral loads at the steering head. Its swingarm attached across the full width of the frame and not, as in previous designs from other makers, by only a narrow lug behind the gearbox. Front suspension was by hydraulic-damped teles, at the back by coil-over hydraulic dampers. The engine was a further refinement of what had reliably gone before. Gilera horsepower took the title that year, but when the Featherbed was perfected, its corner speeds, braking, and accelerating were without precedent. Common sense has its merits. Norton took the 500 title in 1951.

BMW also returned to racing with the overhead-cam flat-twin but abandoned the telefork in favor of a long leading-link design, the Earles. A leading link offers minimum unsprung weight and has very low stiction. It also let its designer try any of the many kinds of tubular shock absorbers then coming into production. These were an outgrowth of wartime needs for rationalized design in mass production. Tubular shocks can be made largely of sheet metal, while the previous lever types employed expensive castings and forgings.

In 1950 a newcomer appeared in racing—MV. They had hired the designer of the original Gilera Rondine, Piero Remor, to conceive a new four-cylinder racer. In a flash of intuition, Remor decided that longer suspension travel combined with softer springing and damping might cure many of the handling ills preventing the powerful fours from using their high horsepower. We know today that he was right, but it took much better dampers and far stiffer chassis than he had to make it all work.

With all the chain center-distance problems of other designs, wouldn't shaft drive offer a neat way out? No doubt he discovered that a simple combination of shaft drive and soft suspension produced shaft-drive lift, a phenomenon familiar to present-day BMW owners. This results from the drive pinion's trying to walk up the rear wheel's ring gear, creating a reaction torque on the drive-shaft housing, lifting the swing-arm pivot. Remor wouldn't have this; he decided to react the torque of pinion-walk directly to the frame rather than allow it to lift the machine by twisting the swingarm. To do this he needed two parallel swingarms, much like those of the old TAC machine, and two universal joints, one at the gearbox and one at the rear drive pinion. In operation, it was the same idea as a full-floating brake linkage. Of course an extra swingarm and a big gearset jumping up and down with the wheel were no asset to handling either. With then-current Italian ideas about weight distribution (set that engine way back there) chassis geometry (plenty of it), and damper design, this first MV was a handful.

Gilera, those masters of four-cylinder design, began a long winning streak in 1952 but always against strong British opposition. MV continued to fight against itself, replacing their truly massive torsion-bar sprung girder fork with a tele, then dropping the shaft drive for chain and a single arm. MV's adviser in much of this was Les Graham, the rider who had given AJS the title back in 1949. Graham thought the Earles fork offered advantages lacking in a tele, and in 1953 his 500 MV was so equipped. The heavy mass of such a fork lies mostly behind the steering pivot, so hitting bumps while heeled over produces a strong, out-of-phase steering torque on the front end by a sort of pendulum effect. The MV was

*Lee Klancher*

still a handful with the Earles—so much so that Graham was killed on it at the 1953 TT. In that same year, BSA began a project that had obscure but lasting significance. Designer Bert Hopwood and his advisers laid out a 250 Grand Prix roadracer which, like the Featherbed of three years before, included all the best of current thinking. Its strongly braced twin-loop frame was certainly the ancestor of both the very successful Trident/Rob North racing chassis of 1970 and the derivative but very influential Yamaha TZ750 frame. The swingarm was of true monoshock pattern, the steering head wonderfully braced. Hopwood may be forgiven the leading link fork; there is such a thing as fashion, and for a time all English special-builders embraced this concept. The little BSA, however, had the finance cut from under it by "people upstairs" and was never raced.

Nineteen fifty-three was also the year in which Norton's star rider, Geoff Duke, went to Gilera, convinced that British industry could not compete horsepower-for-horsepower with the Italians. At his suggestion the Gilera was lowered, its brakes enlarged, bigger tires mounted. Eventually a Featherbed-style frame appeared as well. He made Gilera engineer Taruffi so aware of chassis flex that even the upper and lower steering crowns were welded together to reduce fork twist. (This is a greater problem than you might think—even on the most modern machines.) Gileras were to win many more world championships.

Faced with the onslaught of Italian power, Norton designers responded in the only way they could afford—with more chassis innovations. They tested 16-inch wheels. They built an ultra-low chassis which made the rider kneel rather than sit. They built a special low-center-of-gravity model of their very reliable single with its cylinder horizontal, like those of the winning Guzzi 350s, and suspended it from a beam frame stiffer than anything active today. They even began work on a four-cylinder water-cooled engine. Money is never a problem until you have none. Norton reached that point in 1954 and their works team left the Grand Prix circuit forever (along with those of AJS/Matchless and NSU). Falling automobile prices forced the motorcycle into a small corner of the transportation market.

Yet so timeless was the design of those British singles that private riders continued to put them into the top three in the world championships until the late 1960s.

The mad scramble was largely over. In a panic to discover ways to go faster, engineers had re-sifted all of the pre-war ideas to come up with reasonable answers. A fixed pattern had emerged. With careful machining and attention to sealing, they could build a fairly rigid telescopic fork which would handle all the forces of modern braking, cornering, and power. Its natural weaknesses were a tendency to bind up under load (why do we praise teleforks and condemn plunger, when they are really the same idea?), and lateral stiffness that depended on internal fit and the rigidity of the axle's attachment to the sliders. Oil dampers built into the legs gave decent wheel control except over short, high-frequency bumps. At the back, swingarms were flimsy but there were not yet tires that made this a big problem. The major issue decided, handling became a more refined matter of correct weight distribution, spring and damper rates, and steering geometry. Budget had compelled the British to study handling instead of power, and they had become the oracles in this specialized field. The Italian companies tapped these resources by hiring away the best British riders.

John Surtees began his brilliant riding career on a girder-forked Vincent 500, but by 1956 he was ready to go to MV to make the chassis choices their engineers were unable to make for themselves. He cut the suspension travel of the 350 and 500 in half and forbade MV technicians ever to make any changes to the machines without his express consent. In Europe, academic degrees were exalted and the engineer's world was thus law. Riders tested merely to confirm the excellence of the maestro's decisions. Surtee's, even more so than Duke before him, introduced a much more effective development system in which the rider was the most important decision maker. Based on his knowledge, he proposed the changes and then tested them himself, one step at a time. He knew from his English riding experience what was possible, and he certainly knew what he wanted. Surtee's MVs quickly evolved into a new standard of excellence. The great Mike Hailwood later continued Surtee's winning streak on these machines and said at the time that they handled better than either the Norton or AJS singles. Quite a leap forward. High horsepower could, at least within limits, be tamed.

Moto Guzzi personnel never quite accepted the new orthodoxy of teleforks in the 1950s, preferring instead their own short leading-link design. Their most successful design, the 350 horizontal single, was so very light that the limited lateral stiffness of this fork design was adequate. Guzzi's only attempt at a super-power machine, the water-cooled V-8, had as many handling problems as any other of its time. In any case, the Italian motorcycle industry was next to suffer the decline that had hit England. The major teams quit by mutual agreement at the end of 1957, leaving only MV, whose income derived from helicopters, to inherit the position so long held by Gilera. Without opposition, MV had no need of any suspension development. It was the old story of the ox-cart: adequate is good enough. The machines remained largely as Surtees had left them until finally challenged by Honda almost 10 years later.

English machinery did not win a world title after 1952, but the British design philosophy lived on in decent road machines which handled well even though powered by mundane engines. The Italians weren't in the large motorcycle business, Germany's BMW was specialized for a limited and sedate clientele, and America's motorcycles were as inflated and unwieldy as its automobiles. Britain's motorcycles were therefore the finest in the world. Aspects of their technology, carried off to Italy in the heads of British riders, would live on in relative dormancy there until the Japanese challenged anew.

The handling combination of the 1950s—teleforks, swing-arm rear suspension, and correct geometry—was to prove adequate for street motorcycles for the next 25 years.

The swingarm and telescopic fork were failures in 1905, but they saved the day 30 years later. Monoshock suspension was tested by BSA in 1955, but it didn't find a home until Yamaha desperately needed it in 1974.

When a new technology opens up, as did that of the bicycle in 1885 or of the motorcycle in 1900, a tremendous outpouring of ideas is the first result. When these ideas are tested by experience, not all of them are found practical for the needs, technology, and materials of the time. Most often we remember these failures as bad ideas, not bad applications. When new conditions arise in which those old ideas may provide a solution, only the most open-minded designers have the discernment to recognize the future buried in the past. The irony is that when these same ideas do reappear many years later, they are usually hailed as breakthroughs.

*April 1983*

# Chassis and Suspension, Part 2

*Chassis and handling can't become a subject until there's something important to talk about. In this case it was failure—the failure to make bigger-engined motorcycles as fast as their horsepower implied they should be. New ideas were needed and as so often, they came from motocross—long travel, with dampers more sophisticated than the previous 25 years of crude door-closers.*

*The motorcycle set-up problem is never solved—just elevated to a higher level of performance.*

History shows that motorcycle engineers resort to suspension development only when a deficit of money or ideas blocks the way to more power. After all, engine work is measurable. What is handling? No gauges measure it; only riders can. The very concept of handling comes from riders, not from engineers. In the minds of traditional engineers, handling is an imprecise study and thus an improper one. If it can't be measured, it doesn't exist. A barrier therefore arises between riders and engineers, who in effect speak different languages and have different goals.

At various times and in various places, this barrier has broken down. It happened at Norton in its classic years, it happened at MV with Surtees, and at Harley-Davidson with Calvin Rayborn. As a general rule, however, the wall stays up.

In any case, a new suspension orthodoxy had come into being by the time the Italian makers withdrew from racing in 1957. Front suspension was by telescopic fork, set at the "British numbers"—27-degree rake and just under 4 inches trail. A swingarm and a pair of spring/damper units controlled the rear wheel, while the chassis in between looked much like a Norton Featherbed. Wheel travel was in the range of 2 to 4 inches; long wheel travel was as yet unworkable, as MV had discovered in 1950. Consistent shock absorbers could not be had. Because short travel suspensions had to be very firm to avoid bottoming, stability was still a matter of hugging Mother Earth where possible, and simply slowing down where not.

Honda began Grand Prix racing in Europe in 1959 and predictably made the same errors everyone else had made before. By hiring the best riders and imbibing their experience, as the Italians had done, Honda slowly evolved chassis that were usable showcases for their triumphant engine technology. Success did not come, however, until the company had put its transverse-four 250 engine through two complete redesigns and several chassis. When the little Honda 250 began to win races, it produced such low lap times that it obviously could succeed in the 350 class as well. The MV dominating that class was a scaled-down 500—overweight and oversized for its power. As soon as Honda fielded an enlarged 250, they captured the 350 title as well. Only the 500 class remained to MV.

Two years later, in 1965, MV engineers fought back with a compact new 350 triple—five inches narrower than the old four, much lighter, and housed in an up-to-date chassis.

What did up-to-date mean? Racing tires change more often than chassis. The old MVs had been designed in 1956–58 to run on fifties' tires, but 1964–65 saw a revolution in rubber compounding, with synthetic butadiene-styrene rubber replacing natural rubber for tread materials. Whenever tire grip improves dramatically, riders brake and accelerate harder, and they ride bumpy sections faster. The weight distribution and suspension that had been just fine on bikes with 1958 tires were nonsense with the new rubber. Riders formerly losing the back end under heavy throttle were instead picking up the front wheel out of corners and then running off the course. Engineers rebalanced the new MV's chassis to exploit this increased traction. Lighter and lower, it responded faster to the rider's control forces, and that meant less distance wasted in laying the machine over and picking it up again—distance that could be used either as more straightaway or as a larger corner radius. MV nearly took the 350 title away from Honda with the new design, and began to apply its concepts to a new 500. Honda had announced its entry into the 500 class for 1966.

Yamaha and Suzuki were learning their lessons in Grand Prix racing too. Yamaha arrived in Europe with its T1 frame—a near-copy of the

G50 Matchless that MV had already copied in 1956. This simple design of backbone and twin downtubes had a completely unbraced swingarm welded up out of three pieces of pipe. It was too weak even for the 48 horsepower of the early engines. After a careful look at the opposition, Yamaha came up with the T2, based sensibly on Norton Featherbed lines. With it and a reliable air-cooled two-stroke twin, Yamaha took the 250 title from Honda in 1964 and 1965. Honda responded with its 250-6, and Yamaha retorted with a complex and bulky V-4. When fitted into the T2 frame in the traditional fashion—back against the rear tire—this engine made the resulting machine very difficult to ride. Because lack of steering response under acceleration was blamed on forks rather than on weight distribution, Yamaha tried adjustable steering heads and even Italian-made Ceriani fork legs, to little result. The later Honda sixes just kept slipping away from them out of corners. Honda had built the six to be narrow—just about 14 inches—so it could be set low in the chassis. Under continued rider complaint it was set well forward and the chassis acquired additional bracing and a heavily built swingarm. It had become a motorcycle in the English style, meant to be ridden out of corners under early throttle, gaining speed and distance before the straight.

Suzuki began in the small classes, mastering two-stroke technology. Once the company had a successful 125 twin, it was doubled into a 250-4. Two 125 cranks were idler-geared together, one ahead of the other, into a square-four configuration, the carburetors sticking out at the sides. Behind the cranks sat the two gearbox shafts. The engine was huge—five shafts in length. The motorcycle Suzuki built to carry this power station was ultra-conventional for the time. It had the weak three-piece swingarm, the tiny frame tubes, and the primitive fork that had been just fine in smaller versions on the 125. The engine made power, but the bike was a monster. Under throttle, the engine pulled the chassis into shapes never imagined by the designers, and the machine tried to go several ways at once. When the staff understood that the engine was too bulky and long, they completely redesigned it to be more compact. The shorter engine was a fine idea but there were no ideas for the chassis. Suzuki withdrew the 250.

Looking over these struggles with hindsight, we see a pattern emerge. Whenever horsepower rose high enough to make chassis trouble, designers might do just about anything. When that anything was a stiffer chassis with "British numbers," the handling improved. When it was not, nothing desirable resulted.

Honda's new 1966 500 racer was disappointing. Instead of breaking new ground, like the 250-6, it was just a great big old transverse-four, as high, bulky, and heavy as the old MV. Honda, so busy racing cars, was perhaps tempted to rely purely on engine technology to win in the 500 class. A derivative motorcycle resulted.

MV replied at first with a 420 version of the already proven 350 triple, and later enlarged it to 489. Though 10 percent down on Honda's 80–85 bhp, it had enormous advantages in handiness, lightness, and weight distribution. MV beat Honda in the rider's championship in both 1966 and 1967 despite all Honda's engine know-how.

The Honda was almost unridable. When the machine emerged from a corner under power, it did so swerving. There are two possible causes. First, the weak chassis was pulled out of shape by a very powerful engine, perhaps into geometries that actually steered the rear wheel to generate the swerves. Second, this was now the era of the Dunlop Triangular tire, which had a narrow traction strip for acceleration in its center, flanked by broad, nearly flat cornering areas. To use this tire, the machine had to be either straight up or at full lean. In between, the contact patch migrated from the center of the tire to the broad cornering flat, changing the tire's thrust direction by as much as two degrees as the bike approached full lean. As the rider accelerated out of a turn, the rear tire would break away as soon as it came upright enough to lift off its flat, grippy cornering area. Then the tire would slide back down onto the flat again, and the cycle would repeat. Indeed, Dunlop was preparing special new tires for the Honda's next season when the big four was withdrawn. Like their counterparts at Yamaha, Honda engineers tried "everything"—stiffened the frame, added extra pinch bolts and gussets, built forks with eccentric trail adjusters at the bottom. Nothing worked. Hailwood had a special chassis privately built, and Honda took it away. Whatever disease the 500 had, the medicine that had cured the 250-6 had no effect. Had Honda crossed some horsepower barrier?

When humans are thwarted by a certain class of problems, often they haven't seen the problem or aren't thinking about it. When Rex McCandless drew the Featherbed frame for Norton, he had indeed identified the problem. Nortons with single-plane chassis and plunger suspension wobbled when ridden hard, and McCandless concluded that the chassis was acting as a spring, storing up energy as oscillations started by bump impacts. This called for both a more rigid frame to resist the oscillations, and more compliant suspension to prevent impacts from reaching it in the first place. McCandless provided both and made them work. He replaced the single-plane chassis with a big box—a twin-loop design partly inspired by the 1939 Gilera. He braced the steering head to resist deflection from all directions and attached a trailing-fork rear suspension across the full width of the box. Result: Nortons went faster over rough pavement.

Others copied this design's particular features without understanding the thinking or the methods behind them. Many of the copies didn't work.

When Triumph people battled the Harley Flatheads in the U.S. racing of the 50s and 60s with their little 500 twin, they discovered that a motorcycle could handle just as well as a Manx without looking like one. Triumph's steering-head angle dropped in the process from a conservative and heavy 31 degrees down to the 27–28 degrees of a racing machine. If there was power to pull a lot of metal, and that metal was in the frame, then a simple chassis could be just as stiff as any twin-loop design.

Harley became justly famous for the handling of its roadracers, yet their swingarms were not attached across the broad width of a twin-loop frame, but rather to a narrow little forged-steel lug bolted to the back of the gearbox. So effective was the cooperation between H-D development staff and rider Calvin Rayborn that when one of these "obsolete" machines went to the English Match Races, Rayborn used it to run away entirely from the cream of British riders and machinery. Handling is not a matter of where you live or of what orthodoxy you believe. There are no pat formulas.

There *can't* be any pat formulas because the most important parts of the equation—power and traction—won't sit still long enough. How much is available? Well, when do you mean? And where? At Hockenheim last month? Next spring? Tires change fast. The 60-horsepower engine of a 1950 Italian 500 racer was set back against the rear wheel to prevent wheelspin under acceleration because the tires of the time had only that much grip. The 500 Suzuki that won the 1982 500 title had its 145-horse-power engine so close to the *front* wheel that its radiator had to be notched for clearance. Tire traction has improved to the point that unless the front wheel carries maximum weight, it will be picked up under acceleration and the machine won't steer out of turns.

People's ideas about engines change too. In the era of singles, Moto Guzzi laid down its engines to get the low center of mass that permits extremely fast direction changing, an important and effective design goal. Since compact singles can no longer give competitive power, designers have simply accepted the huge bulk of multi-cylinder engines as normal, discarding low center of gravity as a design goal.*

While the Japanese advanced the powerplant arts in Grand Prix racing of the 1960s, British National racing evolved some modest gains of its own. Colin Seeley bought the rights to once again build Matchless G50 racing singles and was putting them into a striking new chassis. For the idea of the Featherbed box frame, he substituted a pair of direct members straight from the steering head to the swingarm pivot. These prevented side to side wagging of the swingarm, something that was possible with the Featherbed.

U.S. racing expanded in scope when in 1970 the AMA raised the capacity limit for OHV engines to 750cc, with two-strokes at 500cc. Triumph's design for this new formula was a developed version of its three-cylinder 750 engine, in a novel chassis designed by Rob North. Like the Featherbed, it was of twin-loop design; but also like the Seeley, its two top tubes did not lie horizontally under the fuel tank. They went almost straight from steering head to swingarm pivot. Rather than being added on, the steering-head bracing was integrated into the main frame. To allow the fork crowns to accommodate the width of disc brakes in 1971, Triumph fabricated them in welded steel sheets, much like those of the last Gileras. These Triumph/BSA racers were successful as long as their modest power would permit, but rising two-stroke capabilities threatened them when they were barely a year old. The threat came with the reliable Yamaha 350 production racer's light weight and with Kawasaki's horsepower.

Kel Carruthers and Don Vesco collaborated in 1971 to build and race a modified Yamaha 350 entirely competitive with machines twice its size. To add weight to the front wheel they straightened the front downtubes of the T2 chassis and moved the engine forward three inches, spacing it at the back with plates. To slow the breakaway of the Dunlop Triangular tires, they extended the swingarm. With 55–60 horsepower, this 280-pound roadracer was *fast*.

Kawasaki's H1R 500 production racer had a three-cylinder engine 21 inches wide (remember the Honda six at only 14 inches), riding tall in a frame that had been designed in 1968 for a 125 square-four. Originally

---

*The year after I wrote this nonsense about low center of gravity, Honda built its NSR500 racer with the fuel carried under the engine and the exhaust pipes routed over the top. This bike's low center of gravity made it *slower* in rolling over than a conventional bike.

What makes a bike fast to roll over is to place its major masses as close as possible to its center of mass, which is roughly 20 inches above the pavement.

one of many Featherbed look-alikes, it had been enlarged in 1969 for a 250, then again in 1970 for the 500. Its rearward engine location was correct for a 125, and its steering head was braced, but only to withstand 250-sized tire loads. Intense vibration demanded the engine be mounted in rubber, so the frame derived no stiffening from the crankcases. Though its chassis was no stronger than the Yamaha's, the Kawasaki was much heavier and more powerful. Such limitations held it to a single win in 1971.

When the AMA simplified its rules further, giving all corners a straight 750cc for 1972, a crisis in handling arose: Both Kawasaki and Suzuki immediately began developing three-cylinder 750 racers with 100 horsepower, and Yamaha began to think in terms of a four-cylinder, reed-valve 750 street bike with racing possibilities. None of these companies had any previous experience with 100-horsepower racers, and none had solved the handling problems of its most powerful previous racers.

Suzuki had a very smooth test track, but even there its TR750 racer prototypes were unstable. Following the accepted techniques for adding stability used on choppers and at Bonneville for years, Suzuki raked out the front end and extended the wheelbase. Consequently, these first Suzuki 750 racers had heavy steering and a wheelbase more appropriate for a full-dress touring bike than a Grand Prix contender.

In 1972 Kawasaki's only secure test facility was an instrumented drag strip that ran through the factory complex—hardly the place for handling trials. The chassis chosen for the first 750 H2R was yet another rehash of the early 125 design. Time had not improved it, but Kawasaki showed surprising tolerance for its importer's efforts at constructing better chassis in the U.S. Such liberality contained the seeds of future enlightenment.

When the big Suzuki reached the hands of expert riders, they were amazed. Here was a 100-horsepower engine in a street-derived chassis extended and slowed down "in the interests of safety." How would they race such an overpowered, flexible and dangerous lumberwagon? Although the Kawasaki was less powerful than the Suzuki, riding it was no vacation either.

How did this happen? Although Suzuki had years of Grand Prix experience, it was mainly *engine* experience. The only time they had run into real handling trouble they had backed away. Kawasaki had almost no experience at all. Factory engineers were not motorcycle people the way Norton's men had been. Only abstract engineering principles guided them, and within those principles they were acting reasonably. They were unaware how hard racers ride and were as yet unable to understand how valuable input from experienced riders would be.

Yes, on the straights the new two-stroke 750s blew past everything—in the corners it was another story. They wobbled, they twitched, they swerved. In these gyrations they ground off their tires, stretched out their chains, crashed themselves to pieces. Race after race went to smaller or less powerful motorcycles.

While U.S. Kawasaki got down to welding up its own experimental chassis, Suzuki management wanted no subversive outside advice. They wanted to win races direct from the home office. More power! By the end of 1972 Suzuki had 112 horsepower and a powerband so steep no one could use it. Officially, Kawasaki disregarded the delay caused by extra fuel stops (early 750s got 10 mpg) in the belief that more and more power would easily make up the difference. They would learn otherwise.

*Brian J. Nelson*

In the meantime Yamaha was winning race after race with its little 350, by now completely reliable and nimble as only small machines can be.

Kawasaki would accept suggestions, but only from its fastest rider, Yvon DuHamel. When Paul Smart came to Kawasaki in 1972, laden with Triumph development experience, he was told to mind his own business about handling until his lap times were as quick as Yvon's. This silly idea supposed that a man must be World Champion before he can understand how a chassis works. By ignoring its development rider and concentrating on the fastest man, Kawasaki wasted a lot of effort.

In 1973 official Suzuki team orders at the twisty, 10-turn Loudon circuit were *not to race at all*; just ride around and "show the flag." Had the company given in and accepted its handling problems as insolvable?

Many engineers at the time did believe these handling troubles were inherent at the 100-horsepower level. In 1974 Yamaha introduced its full-sized racer, the TZ750A, which had a gentler powerband than piston port bikes and was based on components proven in the 350. Although Agostini won Daytona on it, the A-model was far from immune to handling problems. It frightened many of its private owners and at Talladega shook the team riders' feet right off the pegs (a manufacturing error was found in the fork). Containing 100 horsepower was a delicate task that permitted no mistakes. Kel Carruthers, by now the Yamaha team manager, remarked that anyone who wanted to go fast on a 750 would have to put as much time into the chassis as into the engine. The slightest trouble with the shocks, the least looseness of a pivot or twist in chassis could set these machines into terrifying wobbles. Over bumps they shook their heads viciously. Such stability as they had was not inherent; it was forced upon them by hard preparation work.

In that same year Suzuki cautiously sought outside opinion and gave development funding to rider Gary Nixon and engineer Erv Kanemoto. Kanemoto designed a motorcycle with a short, stiff chassis, forks set at a much-reduced rake and trail, and a usable powerband and gearbox. When they got to Loudon—the race Suzuki had conceded a year before—Nixon won easily. Officially, Suzuki turned up its nose at this; in secret, engineers studied how it had been done. Apparently 100 horsepower *could* be contained in a racing chassis.

Two-strokes had come to motocross long before they arrived in heavy-weight roadracing. Their advantage was power without weight, but with their short wheel travel and stiff springs, these light motocross bikes were difficult to ride. The slightest bump set them rocking like rodeo broncs. An obvious solution was softer spring rates, but motocross suspension must absorb hard landings without fracturing vertebrae. Lots of wheel travel was the answer. Then, although the spring was soft, it had to compress a long way to bottom, and on the way the dampers could stop the motion smoothly. This stimulated work on better dampers and led to gas-pressurized construction.

Roadracers also suffer from pitch problems, complicated by high wheel rpm. Each spinning wheel is a gyro, resisting twisting around axes other than its own bearings. When a roadracer leans over in a corner and hits a bump, first the front end rises, then the back. This pitching upsets those gyros—the wheels—and sets them to nutating, a fancy word for wobbling. This is disturbing enough to the rider, but if the frame is flexible, it can act as a spring, storing or even appearing to amplify the wobbling of the wheels. If there is enough natural damping (the fancy term for friction) this wobble energy will be absorbed and the wobble will die out. If not, the wobble may increase without limit until the bike throws the rider.

If the pitching produced by bumps could be reduced or at least slowed down, the wobbling would be controlled. Perhaps longer wheel travel would reduce pitching in roadracers as it had in motocross bikes. Yamaha bought its concept from a Belgian patent-holder named Lucien Tilkens;

when developed, it consisted of a triangulated swingarm like that of the old Vincent, acting against a single, large horizontal spring/damper unit. Because normal dampers wouldn't work horizontally, Yamaha had to adopt the new gas-pressurized damper technology as well.

Yamaha gained revolutionary advantages with this suspension. First, the triangulation greatly strengthened the weakest part of the motorcycle— the swingarm. Second, the extended wheel travel did indeed prevent pitch-induced wobbling. Third, the need for a pressurized shock absorber proved the huge advantages of this design by providing consistent damping.

Yamaha applied the Monoshock concept to its production-derived 350 twin in European Grand Prix racing, and Agostini used the machine to take the 350 title away from MV. That same year it was applied to the 500, the Grand Prix–racing little brother of the TZ750A, and a year later Ago used that to win the 500 European title as well. In 1976 Yamaha offered the new suspension on its 250 and 350 production racers and added it to the 750 works machines to produce the revolutionary OW-31, a bike so successful it later drove all other makes out of the class.

Monoshock suspension worked well enough to take the handling of the super-power machines out of the "hazardous duty" class. Private owners of OW-31 replicas felt that their racing careers had been rescued.

MV, with its 350 and 500 Grand Prix triples now outdated, developed new four-cylinder designs. With a new MV-4, Phil Read brought MV its last 500 title in 1974. The power of disc brakes had made them universal after 1972, but they worked really well only on two-strokes, which have little engine braking. When the MV four-strokes were braked hard enough to stop with the Yamahas, they had so little weight on their back wheels that engine braking made them skid and hop. While Yamaha riders exploited the new stability of Monoshock over rough pavement, MV was forced to try to keep up by increasing rake and trail. Their steering became heavy and the machines were slower through chicanes. Their large engines placed more weight high in the chassis than did the simpler two-strokes. Finally the roles had been reversed; the Oriental company showed the Europeans the path to good handling. MV failed to learn the lesson of long travel, instead continuing with conventional and outmoded solutions. When two-stroke domination of the 500 class arrived in 1975, it came from superior handling, not power. MV had always had a top-speed advantage over Yamaha, but uncontrolled power had become almost useless. Machines were just too light and powerful. The new wisdom seemed to be this: Keep the machine still by letting the wheels do all the moving.

In 1974 Suzuki responded to Yamaha's challenge in 500 European racing with the RG500 square-four two-stroke. This compact engine, with two cranks stacked on top of its gearbox, showed that Suzuki engineers had carefully considered the lessons of the failed 250 of 1963. Unfortunately they still had much to learn about suspension. The first RGs wobbled and lifted their front wheels out of turns so badly that Paul Smart, one of the first works RG riders, had a special chassis built for himself. The company promptly seized it. No help wanted.

In time, Suzuki modified this policy and began to work hard on suspension. The engineers moved their engine ahead and stiffened their chassis. For 1976 they experimented with air pressure in the fork. Although a soft spring rate prevents pitch-induced wobbling, such light springs bottomed easily under hard braking. The usual answer had been progressive springs—those whose rates rise as they compress. Indeed, Yamaha had provided progressive spring action on its Monoshock suspension through gas compression. Suzuki then applied a similar idea to keep its front ends from bottoming. Suzuki's wheel travel was increased to 125mm at the front and 135mm at the rear—a tremendous increase over the earlier chassis. In 1976 Barry Sheene won the 500 title for Suzuki.

What had happened? Yamaha's initial head start in long-travel suspension had provided a crushing advantage in 750 racing. Why not in 500? Committed to piston-port engines, Yamaha, to keep competitive with Suzuki's rising horsepower, had to sharpen the powerband until acceleration suffered.

Suzuki's powerful disc-valve acceleration allowed the motorcycle to remain heavy enough to be stable and not skittish over rough surfaces—just the way Sheene liked it.

Yamaha, to help its peaky engine accelerate with the Suzuki, had to resort to extremes of light weight—even the removal of material from the chassis. To a point, long-travel suspension encouraged this; by keeping the wheels from bottoming, it reduced the need for chassis stiffness. Yamaha continued the process so far that the chassis began to wobble again. The coming of Kenny Roberts gave Yamaha a momentary advantage that allowed them to believe they were on the right track, but after Kenny had won Yamaha three 500 championships, Suzuki's advantages finally overcame Kenny's talent. Perhaps unwittingly, his effect on Yamaha development had been like DuHamel's at Kawasaki: he was so good his ability masked the machine's fundamental troubles.

With the long-travel revolution came slick tires and their increased traction. As a result, braking forces increased and forks had to be made stiffer and stronger. The larger forces now possible under braking and acceleration made it easier than ever to pick up either the front or the back end. For better braking, a rearward engine position was better; the reverse was true for better acceleration. Unless the engine was mounted on rails to move back and forth as required, no engine position could satisfy the conflicting requirements. Other routes were to (a) make the chassis longer, (b) use aerodynamic devices to push the front end down, or (c) lower the center of mass of the entire machine. The first was out because a long machine steers too slowly. Suzuki tried and rejected the second. This left the third, and Suzuki engineers therefore set about completely redesigning the engine, which shows how completely their outlook had changed in just a short time. The 1978 engine had its cylinders stepped on two levels, moved forward and down. Finally, engine design was being dictated by chassis considerations and not the other way around.

In 1979 Suzuki added an antidive device to cushion the machine's forward pitch during hard braking. To cope with the large braking forces, Suzuki increased fork-tube diameter, though the forks remained conceptually what they had been in 1937.

By now Yamaha had removed so much weight from its 500 frame that it wobbled on the straights as well as in the corners. Trying desperately to cut weight, Yamaha's designers used carbon-fiber-reinforced plastic fork tubes, titanium fasteners, and finally an aluminum chassis. Aluminum had arrived in motocross in 1976 in the form of swingarms. With problems of alloy, weld technique, and heat treatment better understood, Yamaha was ready to make entire chassis. These early frames cracked constantly but improved. Aluminum weighs one-third as much as steel but has only one-third of steel's rigidity. Where is the advantage? In bulk. For equal weight, a piece of aluminum tubing is three times as thick as steel, and the thicker aluminum part gives an advantage in stiffness. By 1981 all Grand Prix racing factories were testing alloy chassis. Kawasaki and Morbidelli experimented with monocoque aluminum chassis, but deficiencies in other areas masked any advantages they may have had.

To cope with varying track conditions, suspension builders gave dampers external adjustments, and trackside tuning became possible.

With tires improving weekly, chassis forces also rose constantly. An urgent need for yet more suspension travel arose—springs heavy enough to carry the maximum loads were too stiff otherwise. The harder the spring, the more pitch motion it imparts to the chassis over bumps, creating *more* wobble. What was needed was a suspension soft initially, rising in rate as it compressed. More travel would either destroy essential ground clearance or make the machine too tall.

Yamaha's gas-progressive Monoshock, Suzuki's air fork and air shocks, and multi-rate springs all suffered from the same drawback: The damper and its spring were matched to each other at only one point in the suspension's movement. Below that, there was too much damper for the spring's soft initial rate; above it the stiffening spring was too much for the damper. A machine with such suspension would be overdamped when upright and underdamped when loaded down in a corner.

Why not build progressive dampers? This had been tried in motocross, but such dampers were hard to construct, and impossible to adjust.

The final answer was rising-rate suspension, an idea already in use in auto racing and patented for motorcycle applications. In the Kawasaki system which appeared on the KR250 roadracer in 1978, a large single spring/damper unit was linked to the swingarm by pushrods and a lever that varied the ratio between wheel movement and spring/damper compression as the wheel rose. Now a rising rate of both spring and damping could be provided across the whole range—soft rates initially increasing in firmness towards the top of the travel, a suspension properly sprung and damped for both upright and cornering conditions. Yamaha's Monoshock, with its fixed 2:1 ratio between wheel and damper movement, was soon obsolete.

Suzuki adopted rising-rate suspension on its RG500 in 1980 and went on to win several Grand Prixs that year. The RG500 took two world titles in 1981 and 1982. Suzuki had come a long way from its impasse with the 1963 250 square-four.

Ultimately Yamaha replied with a dazzling array of new engines and its own varieties of rising-rate suspension.

Honda, out of Grand Prix racing since 1967, re-entered in 1979 with the curious NR500 four-stroke. Though the machine was unsuccessful, many of the ideas Honda applied to it have greatly influenced motorcycle engineering. The first influence was small wheels; the NR was planned to run on 16-inchers front and rear. Second, a one-way clutch in the gearbox eliminated the wheelhop under braking that had so plagued MV in their final year. Third, Honda concentrated completely on the development of highly superior suspension components.

Heavier tires and brake discs have come with the growth of traction. These have increased the rotating inertia of the front wheel, requiring more steering effort from the rider, particularly at high speeds. When racers first tried the smaller 16-inch front wheel, they likened it to power steering.

Tires have come to overshadow all other components of the motorcycle. Modern rubber chemists have produced tire compounds of enormous grip—at the expense of life. Currently no tire grippy enough for use on a modern Grand Prix racer will tolerate maximum-effort racing through an entire Grand Prix race. Riders must use judgment and restraint to exploit the tires they choose. They must know when to race hard, when to protect and coddle the tires, when to simply hold position. Any rider who tries to race right off the start grid will find his rear tire overheating and losing grip after only a few laps. Slowing down won't help, for by then the chemistry of the rubber is irreversibly changed and the tire useless. The rider, sliding around helplessly, can only watch as his competitors pass him.

This development has enormously complicated motorcycle design because now power, speed, and even handling mean nothing unless accompanied by extreme kindness to rubber. Any motorcycle design that causes excessive wheeelspin, hop, or sliding is therefore bad.

To supplement its slow-developing four-stroke NR, Honda in 1982 fielded a small and simple two-stroke Grand Prix 500, the NS2. While Yamaha and Suzuki neared the 150-horsepower mark, Honda could summon only 125. Vibration-induced cracking prevented the Honda from being built any lighter than the opposition's 275 pounds, yet in its first season this apparently underpowered and overweight little machine won three Grand Prixs. How is this? The answer, as we have observed, no longer lies in power-to-weight ratio. Remember kindness to tires? Honda riders could race harder and longer than their Yamaha and Suzuki rivals, and could take corners faster. These corner speeds gave the Hondas their high speed-trap figures, in some cases higher than more powerful machines.

Though handling technology has progressed greatly in the last 10 years, major unsolved problems still confront motorcycle chassis design. The current orthodoxy of big-tube telescopic fork at the front, rising-rate single-shock swingarm at the back seems not to resolve current conflicts.

Steering remains troublesome, more so with increasing power. Motorcycles must be short to have quick steering response, but a short machine picks up its front wheel out of turns even when the engine and rider both move forward to the practical limit. When the wheel picks up, the rider loses directional control.

As an interim solution, riders are setting up suspension to let them break the back wheel loose out of the slowest corners—if the front end won't turn, let the back end do it. This works so long as tire-heating is limited in the process—but it's clearly not a real solution to steering problems.

Tire makers have tried to spread wear and radiate heat over larger and larger acreages of rubber by building super-wide tires, but these have produced strange wobbles not unlike those of the old 1966 Honda 500. Can a tire ever be developed with a flat tread that remains centered and flat on the ground as the machine leans over? This would certainly be one possible solution to certain traction problems.

Because it affects chassis design, the engine can be considered a chassis component. Can more compact engine configuration be developed that will permit a really low center of gravity and a true solution to the steering dilemma?*

Motorcycles remain in many ways just motorized bicycles. As Continental tire engineer Manfred Kuntz has said, "The design of the bicycle was finished in its original conception." Is this to remain true for motorcycles?

Many recent suspension and chassis innovations have been promptly incorporated into street motorcycles—often within less than a year of their introduction into racing. These include big-tube, Teflon-bushed forks, rising-rate adjustable rear suspensions, gas-pressurized dampers, aluminum frames, 16-inch front wheels, and one-way clutches in the driveline.

Already, 550 street motorcycles are every bit as fast around a tight race circuit as were the all-out racers of just a few years ago. This kind of progress arises mainly from suspension and tire improvements, which mean greater safety and control for all riders at highway speeds. Can the rate continue? Will further suspension and chassis advances be so fundamental that the results won't be recognized as motorcycles at all?

---

*Woe is me! Here I am, contributing to the long-disproven low-center-of-gravity myth.

# Chassis and Suspension, Part 3

*Only now are we seeing concepts like active ride height implemented. It will probably be banned as soon as officialdom realizes that ride-height control motors might exist for reasons beyond compensating for fuel burn-off. Don't just moon over these ideas as I have done—act on them! Never, never tell yourself, "If my idea were so hot, someone would be using it by now."*

The 1984 model motorcycles are for us the pinnacle of development. Did the be-goggled rider of 1905 feel any differently about his belt-driven machine? Sophistication is relative, and people always feel a false sense of finality about the present. When we look back on this time in 10 years, no doubt we'll find it hard to imagine how we admired these machines so much.

Technological change moves in cycles. Development is the refinement of accepted ideas, but its by-product is the accumulation of problems and bad compromises which in time strangle progress. People struggle with the old ideas until a new thought breaks the deadlock and opens up fresh areas to development. Then the cycle repeats.

What will the future bring? The true shape of the future is concealed in the shape of the present predicament—problems and compromises in the ways we build machines today; we are just standing in the wrong place to see it clearly. By examining today's major suspension and chassis problems, however, we might glimpse tomorrow's solutions and the shapes of tomorrow's motorcycles.

## Compromises of Wheelbase, Steering Response, Acceleration, and Braking

Here is pure conflict and little progress. We need the engine forward in the frame to keep the front wheel down under power, and we must have it all the way back to permit maximum brake use. We'd like the engine high in the chassis for cornering clearance, and we want it low to limit weight transfer under braking and acceleration. For quick steering, we need the shortest possible chassis, but then the bike lifts the front or rear wheel too easily, so we actually want a long chassis. This sounds like a political speech—we want a chassis high, yet low; long and in a sense short; with its weight forward and at the same time well to the rear. What are we to do? Put the engine on a little combination trolley/elevator?

Modern high-power motorcycles are limited by the amount of acceleration it takes to lift the front wheel off the ground. Gas it any harder and over backwards you go. Sure, leaning forward or even climbing up the gas tank will help to keep the front end down—but at some level of available throttle, the bike flips and that's all the squirt you can possibly use.

Watch expert qualifying from Daytona's turn two, where riders brake very hard. You'll see their rear tires just floating along the ground, threatening to lift up and over in an instant. The tire could stop the bike harder, but the chassis is limiting the braking that can safely be used.

So let's build the chassis longer to get that improved braking and acceleration. Kawasaki did just that with its KR500 racer. But at the next chicane, the other fellows on the short-chassis bikes flick through while the KR is still drawing a bead on the first apex.

Well, then, let's lower the center of mass so we can have *both* a short wheelbase *and* lots of desirable wheelie resistance. Not easily done in this day of complex, bulky powerplants, but it's just what Suzuki did four times since 1975, completely redesigning its entire engine in more compact form. Small gains cost big money. Engineers must search for slightly better compromises among all these conflicting requirements, and any gain in one area is likely to cause a dead loss in all others.

## Poor Emergency Steer Response

Cars can turn as fast as the driver moves the controls, but motorcycles must wait until they have rolled over into the cornering attitude before turning can even begin. In an emergency this extra delay means danger. More complications: In a car, we steer away from a threat and are saved. On a bike, this actually makes the machine fall over *toward* the threat and is probably the origin of many injuries. People usually learn to drive a car before they learn to ride a motorcycle and so are reflex-set to steer away from threats. Correctly, the motorcyclist must first countersteer toward the threat, which rolls his machine over so it can then turn away from the danger.

Although manufacturers can easily build more responsive street machines and racers, they have preferred to compromise. If many motor-cyclists' initial reflex is to steer away from threats, wouldn't quicker steering just get them into trouble more quickly? Nevertheless, more and more machines are now available with 16-inch front wheels; these offer less resistance than larger wheels to the rider's steering torque, and so steer faster. Additionally, sports machines with racerly 54-inch wheelbases are on showroom floors. As stiffer chassis appear, steeper and quicker steering geometry may follow.

All this is fine—if you have the correct reflexes when that car swerves across the centerline. If you do, all that quick-steering technology will help you. If not....

Ultimately, means exist to resolve the conflict between car and bike accident-avoidance reflexes, but for now it is a tough nut.

## The Suspension Nexus

A motorcycle is an assembly of mechanical oscillators. Give it a knock and each of them vibrates for a time at its own natural frequency. If our machine is designed well, this vibration will quickly be absorbed, or damped, and die out before it can cause any harm. The machine can rock back and forth on its suspension like a boat—pitch oscillation. A front wheel can wobble on its steering pivot like the casters on a beat-up supermarket cart. The rear of the machine can weave from side-to-side in similar fashion. The wheels can jump up and down, reflected alternately from the suspension springs above and the springy tire below—because they are either out-of-round or out-of-balance. The chassis can twist back and forth like a torsion bar. The front wheel and fork can spring backward and forward on the flex of the tubes and steering head.

Normally these controlled oscillations give no trouble, although a sharp bump will excite them for an instant until the appropriate systems damp them out. The front- and rear-suspension dampers take out pitch. Tire hysteresis (internal damping) or a steering damper sponge up wobble. Tire properties absorb weave. Wheel vibration, though always there, is kept low by balancing or tire quality control; the vibration goes into the tires or suspension dampers. The best designs make the chassis so stiff its natural vibration frequency is too high to allow twisting. The same is true of front-end bending.

Bad instabilities result when any of these oscillations builds up uncontrollably. Among other things, ineffective dampers, a broken frame, broken engine bolts, or a weak chassis can cause problems. Real trouble starts when two oscillations come into step with each other. In such a case, each one helps build up the other, swamping out the normal damping mechanisms to produce extravagant chassis motion which can buck the rider off. This coupling requires pathways by which energy transmits from one oscillator to another. The familiar big-bike 35-to-40-mph wobble results from the front tire's vibration (show me a perfect tire) coming into step with the steering wobble frequency; they are coupled by the fork and the tire's contour. The old H1/H2 Kawasaki triples developed wonderful and terrifying coupled "Dutch roll" oscillations—the chassis pitched, rolled, and weaved all at once.

Older motorcycles had many pathways to transport oscillations. Because a motorcycle has only two wheels, we can't stop it from rolling from side-to-side (except at stoplights, where we put one foot down for this purpose), but the right dampers can now effectively control chassis pitch. Very stiff chassis (finally coming into street use) also prevent storage and transport of vibratory energy in the roll, or twisting, direction. This blocks another pathway of energy transport.

Bumps don't bother a competent machine running straight up. They act directly under the machine's central plane, lifting first the front wheel then the rear to produce pure pitch motion. The suspension dampers absorb this promptly. Now hit those bumps while heeled over in a corner. They no longer act right under the machine's center of mass but off to one side where the tires meet the road. Instead of simply lifting the machine, they both lift and twist it. The spinning wheels fight this with counter-torques that twist the chassis and joggle the steering. If the motorcycle's damping mechanisms fail to deal with this extra energy, the surplus becomes available to drive one or more of our oscillators into wilder and wilder motion, and may cause loss of control.

Bump energy is proportional to the weight of the wheel hitting the bumps (the unsprung weight) multiplied by the square of the upward velocity given to that wheel by the bump. This velocity depends both on the size of the bump and the speed at which we hit. If a machine is marginally stable through a given corner at a given speed, it's easy to understand why only a small increase makes trouble.

If our suspension were perfect, with zero-mass wheels controlled by zero-rate springs and dampers, the motorcycle would track bumps perfectly. Having no weight, the wheel also would have no upward kinetic energy to be absorbed by the suspension. The zero-rate springs and dampers would transmit nothing to the chassis, so it would feel nothing. Like a majestic ocean liner in a light chop, plowing on unaffected. Pretty nice. How can I order?

In real life, wheels have to weigh quite a bit. When a bump kicks this weight upward, it carries energy into the suspension; absorbing that calls for substantial springs and dampers. These in turn transmit quite a bit of force to the chassis, causing it to roll and pitch in corners.

We try to approach perfection, but it's hard. Wheel weight is down to a practical minimum and further decreases will be tough. So we attack from the other direction—by reducing spring and damper rates. Reducing wheel mass would reduce the energy put into our system by a given bump and speed; making the suspension softer transmits the smallest amount of that energy to the chassis in the form of oscillations.

This was precisely the reasoning used by Ing. Remor, the Italian designer who gave the first MV 500 racer its six inches of suspension travel back in 1950. It should have worked. The soft springs and dampers should have isolated that big MV from road bumps, allowing it to hustle through rough sections at record speed. It didn't work because an important element was missing.

Example? Take a car from the American Overstuffed Era—say, a 1950 Lincoln—and another from the old sports-car tradition—a 1948 MG-TC. Head out to a road with long, wavy undulations in it. Run that big Lincoln through there, and what happens? The car begins well enough, but soon the low-frequency energy coming into its suspension from those waves has the car pitching extravagantly in step, bottoming front and rear in big, scary leaps and plunges. Now try the old MG for an incredible difference. That little car runs up and down those waves like a little mouse, no rocking and heaving. This car carries nothing with a low enough oscillation frequency to come into step with this road of ocean swells. The Lincoln has lots of suspension travel and not enough damping to prevent it from using all of it to get right out of control. Energy enters the Lincoln's pitch mode faster than the dampers take it out, and the surplus appears as uncontrolled motion.

Now try a different road—a dirt road with a vicious washboard surface. The heavy Lincoln runs across this smoothly, its tires bobbing up and down over the bumps, its soft springs and shocks leaving the chassis unaffected.

Now the MG. We are immediately out of control as the stiffly sprung wheels hammer the bumps, half the time in the air. The Lincoln, with little damping and soft springs, can track the fast bumps; the MG, with strong springs and damping, cannot. Yet the Lincoln is useless at high speed on a wavy road because it develops uncontrolled motions of its own.

Our current big street bikes with their suspensions set on soft are like the Lincoln. They have poor high-speed stability because their suspensions are designed for comfort, with soft springs and dampers. Firm up those settings and you increase high-speed stability, the porpoising (low-frequency motion) and wallowing now absorbed by the dampers or prevented altogether by the springs.

The obvious question is can we have the best of both worlds? Can we build a suspension combining the ability to track high-speed bumps with good resistance to wallowing? Can we have both comfort and sports handling? The answer, until recently, has been no. Suspension dampers, always a black art, have traditionally had simple damping curves that resisted motion in rough proportion to wheel velocity. If you had enough damping to control porpoising, you had too much at high speeds. This is why Remor's MV, with its six inches of wheel travel, did not work. On the track, it wallowed like our test Lincoln and no rider could control it. When John Surtees cut its travel in half and firmed up its suspension, he in effect made an MG of it, and it worked as well as any other machine of its time.

How has long-travel, soft suspension ever been made to work? Engineers eventually created dampers that worked predictably (no easy matter). Once that was done, they could easily provide extra resistance just in the range of velocities associated with pitch, leaving the damping low elsewhere to achieve good response to high-frequency wheel movements.

Why did long travel work so well? First, it generally increased the suspension's ability to absorb energy. A long-travel suspension can suck up more bump energy without swamping out its damping and setting up oscillations. Second, long travel allows the use of very soft springing that converts sharp impacts into longer, softer, less-disturbing pushes on the chassis. For riders the gain was enormous. No longer was there any need to be a genius or a hero to speed through rough sections. At any speed, machines were more secure.

To get more and more of this good effect, designers increased suspension travel quickly until at about 6 inches (road) or 12 inches (dirt) the process stopped. The barrier to further travel was ride height. Put in more travel and you must make the machine taller. Beyond a moderate increase, new problems erased any gains. Compromise number one. Still, people wanted to go faster.

Designers found other ways to reduce spring and damper rates, even with travel limited to 6 inches. Just soften up the first part of the suspension travel, where most running is done, and firm up the last part to prevent bottoming. This was done with linkage, and we call it rising-rate suspension. At this point, development took over from new thought, and the last three years have been a process of finding optimum damping curves, the best rising-rate curves, and proper ways to apply them—the classic case of development within a body of accepted ideas. For the moment, the suspension revolution is over. Still, people want to run harder and harder over rough surfaces.

Look at some of the recent accomplishments. In the previous era, spring rates measured at the rear axle of a roadracing machine were of the order of 200–250 pounds per inch. With the coming of the Yamaha TZ750D, the common rate was down around 150 pounds per inch. With the much improved dampers and rising-rate suspension of the recent era, axle rates have fallen lower yet. A similar process is visible on the street, complicated by the need to provide for a passenger's weight.

Though new softness does permit higher speeds over rough surfaces, it has brought special problems as well. The older stiff suspensions were hard enough to easily carry the extra loads imposed by braking. The new ones need special help in the form of add-on devices like direct-jacking or hydraulic dive-limiters that add weight and complication. Compromise number two.

Here comes number three: Watch the suspension of a motorcycle as it angles over into a turn; it compresses visibly because the suspension must carry part of the centrifugal load of cornering. At racing speeds, this load can be 40 percent of the machine's weight, enough to compress a soft modern suspension more than an inch. To prevent this from giving us cornering clearance problems, we'll just make the bike an inch taller to begin with and . . . *Hey, wait a minute*! That's going to cut further into our ability to brake and accelerate without lifting a wheel! That's not progress! You said it. It's compromise, and we are stuck with it for now.

Inevitably we'll add other gizmos to our chassis; this time, an automatic ride-height adjuster. Simple calculations show an effective system could cut two seconds from a Daytona lap. Someone will build it soon.*

Fine. We develop this new system and bolt it on. Do we have the best of it now, finally? Good acceleration and braking, coupled with plenty of

*MotoGP teams were working on this in 2008, but it has now been prohibited.

cornering clearance and the freedom to use soft suspension without penalty. Sounds pretty good. But how will we control it? If, like antidive, we tie the ride-height adjuster to the brakes and throttle simply, what happens if the rider jiggles the throttle or pumps the brakes? Will the suspension jump up and down like an excited child? Will it interfere with the rider's cornering by failing at the exquisitely wrong moment? The solutions may be worse than the compromises. Maybe that's why we haven't seen the hardware yet. Give up. Live with it. But soon the variation in machine weight caused by fuel use may have a similar effect. And another compensating system will look pretty attractive. Does it ever end?

Go back to the beginning of the argument—where we decided to go after lower spring and damper rates because they were easier to achieve than lower wheel weight—and let's consider unsprung weight for a while.

Car buffs talk about an "unsprung weight ratio" as though it were sacred. What is it? This is the ratio between the weight of the parts that move at bump speed (wheel, tire, brakes, moving suspension parts) and the weight carried by those parts. Obviously, bumps would knock about a light machine on heavy wheels more violently than a heavy machine on light wheels. Bump energy is proportional to wheel weight, and for a given energy input, the smaller we make the machine, the more it will be disturbed. This is why the Cadillacs of 30 years ago were believed to handle better than the Fords. Both had wheels of similar weight, but the Caddies weighed much more. In those days people said that extra weight "made the car stick to the road."

The unsprung weight ratio also has a definite physical meaning. When a bump falls away beneath a wheel, how fast can the suspension accelerate that wheel to follow the bump's contour? To find acceleration, we divide the driving force by the mass to be accelerated. In this case, the driving force is the load above, the sprung mass, transmitted through the spring, and the mass to be accelerated is the unsprung weight. If a 50-pound front wheel is carrying a 300-pound share of vehicle weight, that wheel can accelerate downward at $300 \div 50 = 6$ times the force of gravity, or 6G. (The actual figure can be smaller because the vehicle may be pushed up by the spring even as the wheel is pushed down, and because the suspension damper slows wheel movement.) Unsprung weight ratio is therefore a direct measure of how fast the wheels can accelerate in tracking the road.

Compare that with the tracking ability of wheels on a rigid-frame machine. How fast can they accelerate downward? Exactly 1 G, because all such machines can do is fall back onto the road after bumps throw them up. This is why the old rigids stepped out in turns; their wheels spent a lot of time up in the air where the traction is poor.

It appears, then, that a full-dress tourer with luggage suite and chubby passenger, running on tiny, caster-sized wheels would give us the ultimate suspension. It would too, except that wheels have work to do in addition to tracking bumps. We can't all be happy with a half-ton bike, either. At the moment, racing machines actually have worse unsprung weight ratios than street bikes because they are so light. Figures of 5–7:1 don't look very good against good car numbers. Compromise again.

Although motorcycle wheel weight is hard to reduce, it does go steadily downward. Steel rims gave way to aluminum, wire wheels yielded to cast, and now Honda has replaced thick, heavy cast metal in rim and spoke areas with lighter, stronger stuff. Their Grand Prix roadracers use carbon-fiber-reinforced plastic (CFRP) in these areas. From the present-day 8-to-12-pound cast magnesium racing wheel, we may in time arrive at a 5- or 6-pound plastic wheel. Costs permitting, such a wheel will appear on the street.

Present brakes are made of iron or steel; alternate materials are either troublesome or expensive. Why not just run smaller or thinner discs? A fixed relationship exists between vehicle weight and speed on the one hand, and brake thermal mass on the other. This thermal mass (weight of discs multiplied by the material's heat-storage capacity) is necessary to store the energy of a single maximum-speed stop for long enough that the heat can be dissipated down the next straightway. If we don't provide enough thermal mass to store this heat at a reasonable temperature for the material we are using, the discs get too hot and warp or crack. Taking heat out of the discs as fast as it's put in during braking is not a viable alternative; it would require internal water passages, a powerful pump, and radiators more than twice the capacity of those provided for the engine.

Present iron-disc technology being what it is, we must burden a fast machine's front wheel with 20 pounds of brake discs, carriers, bolts, calipers, and lines—a lot to have whacking up and down with every little bump, loading up our suspension system with all its energy.

Then let's not use iron. Certain aircraft (Concorde, for one) use very light carbon brakes which store energy at super-high temperature—hot enough to melt conventional rotors into glowing puddles on the ground. Carbon's disadvantage? It produces very little friction at room temperature. Only as the discs heat up do they begin to work. This is fine for Concorde, which stops only once per journey. A motorcycle may need maximum braking at any instant. When ways are found (as they will be) to get instant friction from carbon-based brakes, discs might weigh less than one-third as much as iron parts. Our 20-pound front-wheel brake system would weigh 13 pounds. With carbon in the disc carriers and calipers as well, perhaps brake weight will one day be cut in half.

Want light brakes right now? Lay out a tidy little stack of thousand-dollar bills and vendors will rush to supply all the discs you want out of light, high-heat–storage-capacity beryllium metal. The big C5A transport aircraft uses such brakes, and race cars have proven them successful on the road as well.

How about lighter tires? Talk about compromises. The tire question is extremely involved, but a short comparison with the car world will show the potential. First, understand that cars (racing cars, that is) *do not* derive their superior cornering power from fancy suspension and low unsprung weight, though they have both. Consider a class of racing car with no suspension at all and no ground-effects devices: Superkart. These machines, powered by six-speed 250cc bike engines, lap most racetracks faster than the fastest motorcycles without regard to displacement. How do you like that? If you really want to go fast, junk everything off your bike but the engine, make yourself a rudimentary frame out of old pipe, and set it on four of these cute little slicks here; it will corner so fast your vision will blur. This is a fact: Rubber on the ground is the key to cornering power.

Consequently, even if we do somehow resolve the problems of high unsprung weight and chassis instability over rough surfaces, our miracle suspension will still depend on the feeble traction of narrow, hard tires of a kind last seen in car racing in the 1950s. Why? To remain stable and to avoid destruction from overheating, motorcycle tires must be inflated to approximately 30 psi,* and this places an absolute upper limit on how much footprint they can spread out on the ground. Traction, since it depends to a great degree on the area of this footprint, is limited as well.

Cars get their traction by using big tires, inflated very little. This spreads out a lot of rubber on the ground—rubber which can be made soft enough to key into the pavement for incredible grip. Unlike a bike tire, car tires are mainly curved in only one direction—around the tread. This limits the amount of bending and therefore heating that occurs in flattening out on the road. Bike tires are curved from side-to-side as well, which generates more heat and puts complex strains into the tire carcass, making it hard to get uniform pressure on the ground.

---

*This has now fallen as low as 12 to 15 psi in MotoGP tires.

All this forces motorcycle tire designers to concentrate on getting more and more traction from the same old contact area, and that's difficult to do. Making tires smaller only exaggerates preexisting problems. Some new thinking is needed.

Reduced to essentials, a tire is just an endless flexible band of rubber tread provided with means to get driving, braking, and cornering thrusts from it. Currently, we connect this flexible band to a metal wheel by means of fabric sidewalls and call it a tire. The flexible band moves in a circular path except where it lies flat on the road. When this tread contact patch hits a bump, not only that bit of the flexible band but the whole tire and its metal wheel with drive system attached must rise to pass over the bump. Looked at in this way, a tire seems a ponderous and inconvenient way to do what should be a much simpler job. Any ideas?

Back to the problem list:

## Excessive Structure Weight

Consider 1,000-pound race cars with 50-pound chassis. Ratio? 20:1. The best racing motorcycle chassis designs, on the other hand, struggle through the problems of aluminum welding and special heat treatment even to reach a ratio of 10:1. Why the difference? Car chassis usually don't have to deal with the extreme vibration of simple engines running at high rpm. Therefore such chassis can be stressed just for the suspension loads expected, without extra reinforcement against vibratory fatigue failure. Bike chassis must be heavy in order not to crack up, or if the engine is rubber mounted, its function as a frame brace is lost and must be made up for by extra metal. Cars, with twice the number of wheels, feed stresses into their chassis at many points, none of them highly concentrated. Bike suspension loads concentrate at the steering head, swingarm pivot and rear shock mount; frames need plenty of metal there to take it.

This is part of the reason monocoque chassis haven't worked—and by the time we add engine hangers, rad mounts, fuel tanks, and what-not to our lovely, strong monocoque beam, we have come right back up to the weight of the tube frame. No gain.

Many engines (some made for racing) now have balancer shafts or are constructed in Vee form to minimize vibration levels. This will bring progress in chassis weight.

Everyone knows tubes are strongest in pure tension or pure compression. Put bending loads into a tube and you are using it inefficiently; you must use more metal to do the job than if you devised a way to carry the loads in pure tension or compression. Hence the space-frame—a structure of straight tubes devoid of bending loads.

Look at front ends. Under peak braking, a front tire may generate a 600-pound force at ground level, but it doesn't enter the chassis until its leverage has been multiplied by traveling up those long, bendy fork tubes to the steering head, some 30 or more inches above. When it arrives, it has grown to 1,500 foot-pounds of torque or more, and must be received by two small bearings only 6 inches apart. Thousands of pounds of force are trying to yank the top bearing out of the frame and crumple the lower one onto it. You can see why Grand Prix chassis presently use double triangular yokes to brace their steering heads. Furthermore, the flexibility of fork tubes and steering heads can produce vibration unless the parts are extremely stiff. More weight.

Can space-frame structure save weight? Though such frames look like Tinkertoy creations, they do work. Nevertheless, expect the realities of motorcycle design and of the marketplace to keep curved tubes on the job despite their obvious shortcomings. Only when the going gets so rough in the search for weight reductions that people don't care how a frame looks will designers be forced to adopt more rational structures. Indeed, the double-triangle steering-head bracing may be regarded as creeping space-frame-ism.

For the moment, Honda seems to have the best of it in racing and street chassis, continuing with traditional but well-detailed structures that work because of the development in them. With Honda's experience with CFRP in wheels, can a CFRP Honda racing chassis be far behind? All the Grand Prix contenders have had terrible troubles with cracking of aluminum chassis, and plastic materials resist fatigue much better than metals.

This sounds great, but isn't manufacturing traditional chassis out of non-traditional materials rather like building some new Greek temples out of steel I-beams instead of stone? Do we want new Greek temples? Or is there a better way to build motorcycle chassis?

Our present machines are too short to accelerate and brake as we'd like, and too long to turn as fast as we want. Too low for ground clearance, too high to prevent wheelies. Spring rates are low enough to need help from gadgets, but not low enough to realize the potential of tire grip. Our tires give only half the grip known to be possible. Each compromise is a blockade to progress.

Back in 1939, as aircraft approached 500 mph, it was clear that no conceivable amount of refinement would produce a supersonic machine.

Piston engines lacked the power, and even had that power been available, propellers were wasting half of it as they approached the speed of sound. While the piston-and-propeller men struggled to squeeze another half a percent from accepted ideas, a completely new engine and drive took shape: the gas turbine, driving by direct thrust. Thirty years later, aircraft were flying at 2,500 mph with the new technology.

Motorcycles are tangled in the grip of compromises today. To get a balance of abilities in one machine, each ability must be limited to make all work together. Fortunately new materials and concepts are at hand with which to create new technologies. When ways are found to break the present compromises, motorcycles will become far more capable than they are today.

*May 1984*

# Chassis and Suspension, Part 4

*More mooning and dreaming, I fear. Where's John Britten when we really need him? Innovation has to go carefully because race teams know that anything that works and isn't immediately shared with everyone will probably be banned. Racing appears to be a meritocracy, but is also a bureaucracy.*

The better we understand suspension, the more its compromises hurt. Even after this decade of rapid progress, suspension still cannot do exactly what we want it to do.

Let's follow a wheel through a bump/rebound cycle: First, connecting wheel and chassis is a spring, put there to hold up the machine. As the bump accelerates the wheel upward, it sends a substantial kick to the chassis through this spring. We can soften the spring to reduce the kick, but only until the machine bottoms on rough roads. What's more, the shock's compression damping transmits even more kick, adding up to a lot of chassis disturbance—possibly enough to provoke a wobble if the bump is large. Eliminate the compression damping and the machine is more likely to bottom, having only the spring to stop the wheel from flying up off a big bump and into the air where the tire finds no traction. We must have *some* compression damping to get the wheel stopped.

Once its rise has been stopped, the wheel is pushed back down toward the road by the spring. Then rebound damping, which is far more powerful than compression damping, *slows* the movement. Why is rebound damping more powerful than compression? We need a certain total amount of damping to prevent the machine from continuing to bounce and rock after the bump has passed, and that damping disturbs the machine least when most of it is concentrated on the rebound stroke. As you can see, the qualities we need at one moment work against us a moment later. We are left with choosing the least of evils, and we call this good suspension. It's an exaggeration to say we can squeeze nothing more from current concepts—anything can be improved. The point is that we can now figure out exactly how much improvement remains to be had—and not much is left.

Engineering is conservative, especially when tied to manufacturing costs, market prejudice, and tradition, and safe progress usually means bit-by-bit improvement of current concepts. Exceptions are appearing, however. Before his recent death, the great race car designer Colin Chapman predicted the demise of the conventional passive suspension systems. Instead of trying to improve existing hardware, he thought engineers ought to look at what exactly they want the suspension to do, and then try to create systems that would do those things.

Here, roughly, is how suspension looks from such a viewpoint: Here comes the bump against the wheel. We want to limit the disturbance to the chassis in this impact phase of the bump, so we dial in a spring with zero rate—just enough to hold up the vehicle. We also want zero compression damping as the bump accelerates the wheel upward. As a result, the chassis stays level and undisturbed. As the wheel nears the top of the bump it is no longer accelerating upward; it is coasting, and unless we stop it, it will fly up off the road and the tire will lose traction. To prevent this, we now "switch on" heavy compression damping. This action provokes a reaction on the chassis which can't be avoided. In any case, it is less than the initial impact would have been with a conventional suspension. As the bump falls away under the wheel, we want to force the wheel downward to follow it, so we now "turn on" the spring, but without any rebound damping to slow the movement. After the bump has passed, there is some chassis motion from the impulse of stopping the wheel and maybe some tendency of the flexible tire to bounce on the road. We switch in just enough damping now to take out this unwanted residual motion.

Because the parameters of this kind of suspension are switched on and off to suit conditions, it is called an active system. Progressive engineers are working with them in several countries.

Toyota engineers, wanting to combine the soft ride of a limousine with the firm responsiveness of a sports sedan, developed quick-acting damper valves which could be cycled electrically from soft to hard in one-tenth of a second. As with previous adjustable suspensions, the driver can select soft, normal, or sports ride characteristics, but this is not the fascinating part of Toyota's concept. Imagine moving along the rutted streets of a big city, the soft suspension isolating you well from the pounding. Suddenly, a garbage truck lurches out of an alley. You twist the wheel, expecting sickening body roll and a long delay before the car responds. Instead, a rate sensor on the steering column informs a computer that a hard turn is beginning. The computer orders all damper settings to hard to prevent body roll, and the car responds smartly in a flat, quick turn to evade the attacking truck. The system responds similarly to sudden braking and acceleration.

Ford's experiments include using a computer to continuously adjust the ride height and chassis attitude of a car to maintain optimum aerodynamics at all speeds. On rough roads, where more wheel travel is needed, the system raises the car to provide more wheel travel.

These ideas seemed tantalizing but outrageous 20 years ago when discussed at MIT and other universities. The control computers would have been large, expensive and unreliable, made up of hundreds of transistors soldered to numerous circuit boards. Now, however, 400,000 switching elements can be etched onto a single silicon chip one-tenth of an inch square. Computers that would have been military secrets 20 years ago today provide home entertainment for gifted twelve-year-olds.

Now for the shocker: Lotus, the company created by Colin Chapman, proposes to eliminate springs and shock absorbers entirely. Instead, hydraulic rams powered by an engine-driven pump will force the wheels up and down. When a wheel hits a bump, the ram will lift the wheel, stop it, then force it to follow the far side of the bump back down, all while keeping nearly uniform pressure on the tire's footprint. Here is how it works. Each corner of the car carries an accelerometer. As a bump begins to lift one corner, its accelerometer signals the initial disturbance to a central computer, which in turn orders the hydraulic system to move that wheel in such a way as to limit the vertical acceleration of the chassis to some small value. The computer's operating instructions must be sophisticated to deal with special circumstances like bumps taller than the suspension travel, but those are details of software. Although the hardware sounds exotic, it is based on high-speed aircraft hydraulic control system technology that has been highly developed for a long time. What makes this suspension system possible now is the sudden availability of cheap, small and powerful computers.

Early testing by Lotus indicates the active system can boost race car cornering speeds by 10 percent—a huge jump. Lotus also asserts that the occupants of a sports sedan hitting a brick in the road at 100 mph will be almost unaware of it.

Think of the implications. All the traditional flummery with spring and damper rates, ride-height roll stiffness, roll center height, and so on disappears, replaced with coded instructions in a programmable read-only memory. The active system even greatly reduces the problems of unsprung weight because it eliminates the compromises associated with handling it. Unsprung weight, however, does remain important in an active system; when the hydraulics push or pull on a wheel they react equally hard on the chassis, and this varies directly with the wheel mass. Lighter parts will still be desirable.

The drawbacks? First, it will take time to exploit correctly the new freedoms offered by the concept, while passive systems are already well understood. Also the active system uses engine power and requires extra hardware—pumps, hoses, and hydraulic cylinders. Passive systems use power too. We know this because their dampers get very hot in use, and that energy ultimately has to come from the crankshaft. Lotus believes its suspension's power consumption will be about 3 percent of engine peak power, while critics say it might go as high as 10 percent.

Will this be a crippling disadvantage? Many recent developments have sacrificed top speed to increase corner speed and have worked well. Wings, super-wide tires, and flatter powerbands all lowered lap times at the expense of top speed. If we could create a bike that could run around Daytona at an unvarying 115 mph, never slowing for corners, never accelerating for the straights, it would win the race hands-down; 115 mph is the *average* speed of the lap record. A conventional machine must accelerate to 180 mph and slow to 80 mph to do this—an exciting but inefficient process. It takes only one-quarter the power to run 115 mph as it does to achieve 180. Active suspension offers to raise average speed at the expense of top speed, and that's pure gain.

The big objection to any new level of complexity is complexity itself. More parts, we are told, cause more failures. This may be true of simple machines, but consider this: First, little in the Lotus system has not already been well proven in jet aircraft control systems. Second, the most complex part of the system is the computer with its thousands of elements. Duplication will make this as reliable as we want. Instead of one control computer, why not provide three, four, or five computers? Remember, these things are tiny. Having five computers means only four extra little black rectangles on our circuit board. They will operate by logic voting; if any one computer disagrees with the majority, it will switch out of action automatically and record an error signal. The remaining computers carry on with the work. Another way to enhance reliability is to send a test program through the system periodically—interrupting the work for a tiny fraction of a second. If the system gives the wrong output from the test program, it is switched out of the circuit as defective.

Do you resent the idea of a computer-controlled motorcycle? No matter—you will ride one eventually; it is becoming cheaper to use computer logic to control machinery than to develop complex mechanical systems. Do you like those ghastly air-pollution carburetors—the ones that make your engine die five times before it can be driven away? It's either that kind of inadequate passive control or it's the computer. I'll take the computer, thank you. Every engine will soon carry a powerful computer, constantly adjusting the ignition timing and fuel mixture for best performance. Once the computer has to be there for one good reason, engineers will find plenty of other work for it. Suspension is a fine place to start.

Finally, if the conventional wisdom were true—if more parts really do always mean more failures—then a human being should die within minutes of birth. Isn't every one of us a tangle of interconnected automatic systems made of trillions of cells? We survive.

Now consider what active suspension could do for motorcycles. All our big worries—brake dive, chain or shaft jacking, ride height, spring and damping rates—become just matters for sub-programs to handle. Bothered by wheelies under acceleration? Just instruct the computer to squat the bike, limiting weight transfer. Now the machine squirts away like a dragster because, for the moment, it has been re-configured into a dragster. Need extra ground clearance for cornering? A few more coded instructions, plus a roll sensor, and it's possible. Does suspension pitch oscillation encourage weave? Forbid it. Perhaps you want to try a horizontal chassis attitude during braking? Just ask the computer.

Naturally we must wait to see if active suspension can be built, and then if anyone can afford it. Perhaps in a while. Perhaps never. If it is possible, we may be tempted to move on—to extend the computer's domain to include steering stability. The steering of some sports machines is only marginally stable. A loose head bearing, the wrong tires, or worn fork internals can cause a violent wobble. Yet we must put up with this possibility to get responsive steering. Otherwise, every machine would have those old Bonneville numbers—30 degrees of rake and four and a half inches of trail—specifications that make a machine so stable even the rider has trouble deflecting it from a straight line. This is the compromise inherent in all vehicle handling: You choose between stability and response, because you can't have both. A *really* twitchy roadrace bike with a 23-degree steering head and a light, flexible aluminum frame may be so unstable that its rider returns from every practice with blistered hands and his hair matted in sweat. His own reactions must supply the stability his machine lacks. Make that steering head a little steeper or shave a bit more weight out of that frame and it will be too much for him to control.

Aircraft design has passed through the same stages. Hands-off stability is fine for private light planes, but in combat quick response is vital. Soon aircraft designers had built machines that caused their pilots' hands to blister and their foreheads to sweat. Many good men died exploring the outer limits of controllability, but they put up with it because if the thing doesn't turn fast enough, you get bullets coming into the cockpit. In a machine that is hands-off stable, you can throw all your weight on the controls and your airplane plows straight ahead for quite a while before responding.

When military jets appeared, the problems worsened. Many of the designers' innovations were impossible to use because of in-flight oscillations that could break airplanes to chaff in less than a second. No one was fast enough to sense the onset of these deadly phenomena, so stability augmentation systems were developed to deal with them. With a fast computer system sensing the instabilities and compensating for them, the pilot could concentrate on flying. Most important, when stability no longer depended on slow human reaction time, designers could obtain previously forbidden levels of responsiveness.

Sport and racing motorcycles are stuck on the horns of this stability/response dilemma. If a feasible technical solution can solve it, isn't it silly to continue playing with marginal chassis configurations? Let the rider point the machine where he wants to go and let something faster than he is compensate for the instability. This means hydraulic-actuated power steering, with the computer superimposing its small compensating movements on the background of the rider's actions.

The aircraft industry has moved beyond this as you might expect. The next step is called fly-by-wire. The pilot's stick is no longer mechanically connected to the control surfaces. Instead it electronically sends the pilot's instructions to a flight-control computer, which then looks up in its reference library the best way to carry them out. This greatly reduces the pilot's work load. In a conventional modern jet fighter, such as the big F-4, the pilot controls several crucial variables at once to execute a tight turn. To prevent high-speed stall he must watch his angle of attack and airspeed; to keep the engine working he must also keep an eye on turbine inlet temperature. Behind him the opponent lines up to shoot at him. Too much work for one mortal man. With fly-by-wire, the flight-control computer keeps its many eyes on all the vital functions while the pilot gets on with the flying and fighting. In addition, the responsiveness of such a system can be varied to any desired degree. During alignment with the tanker aircraft in aerial refueling, the controls are slowed down for precision positioning. For combat, they are turned up to maximum responsiveness.

Now consider our poor motorcyclist. He's fiddling with his throttle to keep the engine in the powerband, possibly shifting gear as well, dragging his body all over the machine to make up for its chassis compromises, and trying to keep the front end from shaking right off the frame—all while holding his line in the corner and planning how to deal with his competitors. Again—too much work. Will he ever get help?

How about another squint into a rosy future? We know that the delay inherent in rolling over to the cornering attitude gives a motorcycle poor accident-avoidance characteristics. What if we could countersteer *both wheels* out from under the machine simultaneously? Couldn't we then flick it over and begin turning in half the time? This hypothetical motorcycle might be impossible to control manually, but a computer system could conceivably manage it.

It's too far-fetched? Mazda is currently developing a car that steers *all four wheels* to enhance handling. This system is, naturally, directed by the on-board computer. Engineers are sick of devices that won't do what they're told, and now they can do something about it. No new brainless Tinkertoy linkage is going to give perfect suspension; what we really need is not a dreadful compromise but a system that continuously reconfigures itself to be always ideal.

Changes in control technology would certainly alter the function of the motorcycle but not necessarily its form. Indications are, however, that soon even the form will change. Normal motorcycles have a primitive form of steering in which the entire front suspension and its structure pivots with the wheel as it steers. This excess weight stores large amounts of oscillatory energy and thus subjects the front end to wobbling, which the flexibility of the long fork assembly aids and abets. It closely parallels the "steering" of a farm wagon, whose entire front axle beam must swing ponderously around in order to steer. On a car, by contrast, only the wheels pivot, leaving the suspension arms and structure attached to the chassis. The motorcycle equivalent to this is called hub-center steering, in which the steering pivot moves from its normal position high above the engine down to the center of the wheel hub. There are two general types. In one a conventional swingarm projects forward to enclose the front wheel from both sides; the other uses two suspension arms, both on the same side of the front wheel. In the first type, a vertical kingpin or steering pivot is fixed at the center of a bar that joins the front ends of the forward projecting swingarm. On the kingpin pivots a sleeve hub, on the outside of which are large-diameter wheel bearings which carry the front wheel.

The second design has two single-beam swingarms, both on the same side of the front wheel, one above the other. The front ends of these are joined by an upright, attached by spherical joints. The two arms, joined by the upright, can rise and fall together to produce suspension movement, while the spherical joints also permit the upright to pivot for steering. The stub axle carrying the front wheel projects from the upright, while the wheel itself must be deeply dished to allow this upright-and-pivot arrangement to reside at its center. In effect, this is simply one-half of a car's front end, the parallel arms turned at 90 degrees, projecting forward instead of to the side.

The pioneering French ELF E endurance racer (see *Cycle*, March 1984), the outstanding recent hub-steering design, is of the second type. And Bimota, the justly famous Italian chassis salon, has recently shown a hub-steerer of its own. The idea is gaining acceptance because it solves some troublesome problems. What are the advantages? First, the low pivoted mass enhances stability. Second, front wheel support can be very stiff and strong because the long, bendy fish-pole fork tubes and sliders that encourage wobbling are gone. The hub-steerer eliminates the stiction of a sliding joint; it shortens as much as possible the load path from rear axle to front axle—right straight through the engine; and it eliminates the heavy and flexible steeple of tubing usually built above the engine to support the conventional steering head, so reducing the height of the machine. Applying any type of single-shock, rising-rate suspension is easy, and the frame becomes lighter because most of it is gone.

Other related but different front-end concepts vie for our attention. The Hossack-built special and the French Sonauto experimental Grand

Prix chassis incorporate one type. These use forward-projecting arms that are mounted high on the chassis; the upright that joins them is a long girder extending downward to attach to the front axle ends. Such a system offers some but not all the advantages of the true hub-steerer.

If hub-steering is so hot, why haven't we seen more of it? Because early projects had the same component problems as contemporary conventional chassis; only lately are the advantages becoming clear. What's more, by contemporary standards, hub-steerers are ugly. To some people the ELF E looks like some mutant insect about to seize its prey with extended pedipalps. If the idea solves our problems, though, we will have to get used to it just as we got used to the "wrong" look of cast wheels and 16-inch tires.

The ELF machine also asks this question: "Why should the heavy fuel be carried above the engine, making the machine unresponsive and liable to extremes of weight transfer? Doesn't the fuel belong under the engine?" The traditional answer is that fuel pumps (necessary to lift fuel to the carburetors) are unreliable. If that's true, then we ought to abandon forced lubrication, fuel injection, and water cooling—they depend on pumps too. There must be a better reason. Is gasoline more dangerous on the bottom than on the top? No, the bottom is at least partly protected by the wheels; nothing at all protects the top. Most likely, the real reasons for having the gas on the top are tradition and the fear that someone will laugh and point when he sees something different. Wear ear plugs and keep your eyes on the road and it won't bother you.

While calling tradition into question, let's look again at rider position. Why should the rider sit on his machine as if it were a kitchen chair? The taller he is in the saddle, the harder it is to roll the machine over for a turn. Height increases wind drag and rider fatigue. The sit-up position prevents efficient weather protection. It's dignified, though—we must say that for it. The other traditional alternative—the roadrace crouch—certainly is not, and it is cramped. The rider's arms carry much of his weight, while his knees are driven up into his chin. Reduced height and air drag seem to be the only advantages (at least of a non-emotional nature).

Aside from really radical alternatives such as lying prone, only kneeling seems worth consideration. Norton thought so and built such a machine. Although it was tested in practice for the 1953 TT, the famous Featherbed frame was in use at the same time, and the kneeler was bypassed. In any case, Norton's racing R&D days were over; they pulled out of Grand Prix racing a few months later. No other riding position places the rider's weight as low as kneeling, with so much room beneath for machinery, and no other is more comfortable. On the other hand, it would be hard to carry other than a very light and intimate passenger, or to dismount gracefully.

More certain than these revolutionary possibilities are changes in materials. New materials don't always bring progress, however, because conservative designers tend simply to substitute the new for the old, with no design change at all. When stone was the major building material, 10 stories was the maximum; above that, walls crumbled under their own weight. When iron and steel appeared, architects made the first metal-framed buildings look just like stone. Public taste will do that. Only 40 or 50 years later were architects finally ready to build 100-story buildings.

We have relied on steel for motorcycle frames for 100 years, so it's not surprising that the first aluminum frames look just like bright, shiny steel frames. Is this really the best way to use the light metal? Even though airplanes and race cars are no longer welded out of pipe, the monocoque idea has made slow progress on two wheels, for a few reasons. Public taste says pressed-sheet-metal frames are cheap and ugly, when in fact they are cheap and strong. They don't, however, like vibration. Motorcycle engines vibrate and vibration will set the thin panels of a monocoque into resonances which will fatigue and crack them, aluminum being far worse in this respect than steel. When Eric Offenstadt brought his aluminum monocoque Kawasaki to Daytona in 1972, it broke in almost every practice. Kawasaki tried a beam frame for its KR500, but with the handling ideas they applied, nothing would have looked very good. Motorcycle accessories are designed to attach all over a tube frame, which has places for everything. A beam frame requires lots of heavy hangers and brackets to do the same job, and these cancel weight savings. We could conceive of a powerplant module on which all the accessories were attached and which could then be simply fitted to the chassis. It hasn't happened so far, and the monocoque remains a curiosity.

The best approach is still to make a multi-tube frame that is a little bit stiffer than last year's, and leave the revolutionary stuff to those whose yearning for change is greater than their will to win. This is what Honda has done with its 500 Grand Prix roadracer, and Honda has the World Championship to prove it was the right approach. Yamaha is trying to break new ground with a twin-beam frame. It has good engine access and is stiffer than multi-tube.

You have read about the factory Grand Prix bikes' carbon-fiber reinforced plastic CFRP wheels, swingarms, and fork tubes. Is this a revolution in the making? When popular magazines predict plastic engines will take over the world in about five minutes, what are we to think? A gradual revolution seems a little more likely. It will take time to (a) find the best ways to design parts around the unique CFRP properties and (b) bring the cost of materials and manufacturing within reach of mass production. Remember that in replacing steel with aluminum, the manufacturers are replacing one metal with another. Both can be bent, welded, drilled, tapped, and bolted—none of which can be done with CFRP.

The tensile strength of CFRP is the enormous strength of the carbon fibers themselves, while the compressive strength (which is important in bolted connections) is only that of the epoxy matrix—very low. Any attempt to clamp CFRP with bolts crushes the part, so metal inserts must be molded in to permit bolted connections. If a CFRP part breaks, it cannot be welded or glued—once the carbon fibers are broken, all the strength is gone.

It is tempting to expect to make carbon parts as easily as we lay up fiberglass in making boats or fairings. Alas, the CFRP parts must be cured under heat and pressure to ensure that the finished item will have the designed fraction of fibers and be free from voids.

The huge strength and fatigue resistance of the stuff are extremely desirable for racing chassis. The English Armstrong 250 has been shown with a carbon frame claimed to weigh five and a half pounds. Until it can be mass produced, however, and until the price of the fibers drops substantially from the present $40 per pound, such frames remain R&D exercises.

The real hope is for better metals. Look at the progress in aluminum fabrication. A decade ago, a factory MX team had to inventory 10 aluminum swingarms to be sure of making it with two bikes through a single national program. Now the metals, the welding, and the heat-treatment are good enough that the arms can be sold without being a warranty headache. Entire aluminum frames will arrive soon on these shores.

Less visible but just as important are the high-strength, low alloy (HSLA) steels originally developed for the auto makers' weight-savings programs. These steels combine much of the strength of traditional aircraft alloys at a much lower price. Of course, fabulous steels have been available for many years, but they have been priced out of reach for production use.

Whatever the changes that do come to the architecture, materials, and components of the motorcycle, it will take time for a sensible new form to gel out of the thick soup of possibilities. What is the best shape for a CFRP wheel? What engine layout best fits with hub-steering? Can the public accept integral streamlining?

This new form will have to be a complete concept—not just a mass of little improvements. It is hard to prove the advantages of wings by attaching them to a toad; they really do work best on a bird. To leap from the toad to the bird is generally too radical a step for conservative business corporations. They have invested too much money in producing better toads.

The novel concepts, therefore, come from nutty individuals, many of whom seem to like change for its own sake. Because of this they can make mistakes that make even their good ideas appear laughable; consequently, these ideas must wait until traditional thinking is completely bankrupt. Then they are widely adopted and labeled "progress."

# TDC: Rods

*A well-designed connecting rod is a steel or titanium image of the stresses it must carry. A kind of art.*

Two centuries ago the first steam engines had no rotating shafts, but were coupled to loads like pumps that could use the back-and-forth motion of a piston directly. Later, the ages-old crank-and-connecting-rod linkage converted the piston's reciprocating motion into rotation. The early engines were very slow, so the only forces on their conrods were from gas pressure on the piston. As engines ran faster, heavy inertia loads from the piston's and rod's quick starting and stopping were added to the gas forces. Along with both of these were bending loads from the rapid side-to-side swing of the crankpin end of the rod.

The earliest conrods were just thin metal bars with round collars at each end, these collars bored and fit with bushings to act as crankpin or wristpin bearings—the Wright Brothers' first airplane engine in 1903 had just such rods. As engines ran faster, the bending loads broke these rods just above the crankpin, so subsequently this area was reinforced. The wristpin bearing only oscillates a few degrees back and forth, but the crankpin rotates and therefore needs a larger bearing. Gradually rods have assumed their familiar modern shape, with a gracefully tapering shank joining a large crankpin bearing to a smaller wristpin bearing.

Because several kinds of stress fluctuate in rods as they run, it's hard to know what the maximum stress is and where it occurs. Metals under repeated stress fatigue and break where the stress is most concentrated. Such concentrations exist wherever a part changes shape or section; rods have graceful, almost organic shapes to avoid these shape changes.

Steel is a marvelous rod-building material—it has the fortunate property of an *endurance limit*. If no portion of a part exceeds this endurance limit of stress at any time, the part will have an essentially unlimited fatigue life. (Forever, in engineering context, means for between a hundred million and a billion stress cycles. In a motorcycle engine, turning 5,000 rpm at 60 mph, a rod will receive 500 million stress cycles in 100,000 miles.) If the part *is* designed to permit stress levels above the endurance limit, it will have a shorter lifetime.

The designer must find out what the stress levels actually are in his proposed design, and must try to eliminate stress concentrations that push stress higher than it need be. If the part is a simple shape, such as a pushrod, this is a matter of dividing the expected load by the cross-sectional area. But a conrod's shape is not at all simple, and for many years, the designer's experience was the key to good rods—the more mistakes he had made and understood, the better his designs. Later, designers used special plastic materials which polarize light under stress. By making a rod from this plastic, designers could predict and observe the actual stress pattern. Sometimes a prototype rod was painted with special brittle lacquer which would flake away from areas of maximum surface stress. Today, computers provide a new method: finite element analysis. This process mathematically models any complex shape as an assembly of many tiny, simpler elements whose behavior under stress can be calculated individually. When these piecemeal calculations are finished, the computer presents a complete picture of stress in the part as it performs its intended motions. The designer can make changes and run the program again. Nothing breaks, no parts need be made, and the design is refined considerably before any actual prototype parts are made.

*Lee Klancher*

Rods for mass-production motorbikes need not use super-strength steel—they don't need it and the buyers don't need the cost. Instead, manufacturers use low-cost materials with endurance limits adequate for almost infinite life under average use. Only when expecting very high loads, as in racing, is it reasonable to use better stuff. Run the peak rpm of that mass-produced engine up by 20 percent and the rod stress almost doubles. Is the material going to last forever now? Maybe not. This is why the specialty shops do a nice little business in custom-made high-quality racing rods.

Aluminum alloys don't display the endurance-limit behavior steel does. No matter how low the stress, an aluminum rod is always accumulating fatigue damage. Such rods are useful in short-distance racing but cannot endure the stress-life steel can. Titanium is a useful rod material because it is 40 percent lighter than steel and, in the right alloys, nearly as strong, so its reduced inertia cuts bearing loads, clearly an asset in super-rpm applications where bearing life is marginal.

If the rods have a hard time, think of the rod cap bolts. When the piston rises on the exhaust stroke almost no gas pressure slows it, so the rod and cap bolts must jerk the fast-moving piston to a halt at TDC, reaching decelerations of thousands of Gs in a high-rpm engine. Unless the bolts are of the finest materials and finish, correctly installed and torqued, they will fail. Always pay close attention to manufacturer's instructions on rod bolts. A two-dollar bolt often wrecks a four-thousand-dollar engine in a hundredth of a second!

Most conrods are forged—a process which deforms the metal grain structure to align with the shape of the part, increasing fatigue life. A forged surface is rough and may contain impacted scale or forging laps—an area of metal folded in against itself. The roughness, scale, and overlapping all create potential crack sites. Years ago, aircraft rods were first forged, then machined all over to remove the forged surface, and finally polished. This benefits fatigue life *provided* the metal removal rate is not high enough to locally overheat and crack the surface, and provided the polishing is carried out along the length of the part, not perpendicular to the stress. Currently we attack the actual cause of surface crack propagation—the tensile, or stretching, part of the stress cycle, which pulls open and lengthens micro cracks—by using shot-peening to put the whole surface of the part into compression. Directing an air-driven blast of hard steel shot at the part covers it with an infinity of tiny, compressed dents. This process must be carefully controlled if it is to work properly, and should not be confused with the cleaning process of bead-blasting.

It's great fun to hear your engine wind up and feel the thrust of acceleration, but remember your busy connecting rods down there in the dark crankcase, whirling, yanking, and bending. Treat them well and they'll last "forever." Treat them badly and pay the consequences soon.

# TDC:
# Pistons

*How many builders have brought strong engines to Bonneville, only to hole one piston after another? If the duty cycle heats the pistons enough to make them weak, they pop. Bonneville's long full-throttle operation demands thicker piston crowns than does 10-second drag racing.*

Ask any kid in high-school auto shop what makes an engine go and he'll probably point to the pistons, as well he should. But how much does he know about those big slugs jumping up and down in the cylinders? Most of the pistons we see end up as ashtrays on some parts counter, or as bead-blasted paperweights on the shop-teacher's desk. Why are they made in the manner they are?

The first internal-combustion engine pistons were made of iron—a durable metal offering an excellent bearing surface, and well understood at the turn of the century. Unfortunately it conducts heat poorly, so as engine power rose, pistons ran hotter and hotter. But why worry? Aren't these things heat engines? Yes, and while the heat lost to the piston is heat we could otherwise use for power, superheated pistons lose strength and break up from operating stress, or expand and seize. Hot parts in the combustion chamber encourage detonation—the sudden shock-explosion of part of the fuel-air charge after the spark has ignited it. Not only is detonation mechanically damaging (like hammers inside your engine) but it also greatly increases heat transfer from burning charge to engine parts.

Normally, a layer of air a few molecules thick adheres to all the parts with a surprisingly insulating effect. When detonation blows this layer away, parts suddenly overheat. A very hot piston encourages detonation, and a very early spark timing or low engine speed provides time in which detonation may occur; this is why piston temperature is crucial to power—too hot and you will be stopped by detonation at even very low-performance compression ratios.

Pistons cool themselves by conducting heat away from the hot crown surface to the cooler cylinder walls mainly through the piston rings. Some heat is transferred through the poor but large contact between piston skirt and cylinder walls. What heat is given up to air swirling around the piston is almost negligent.

The more poorly a piston conducts heat, the hotter it must run to force its heat from the hot to the cooler parts. Larger-diameter pistons gather more heat, and a longer heat path from hot to cool parts means a hotter-running part. The more surface features in a piston's crown—a high-compression dome, deep valve cut-outs, or an old-style two-stroke deflector—means more area to gather heat.

Because of this, cooler-running aluminum pistons superseded the old iron buckets. Aluminum transfers heat three to four times better than iron, and these aluminum pistons were the key to increased gasoline engine performance. As engine power rose, so did the heat load the pistons had to carry. Likewise, engineers found new ways to make pistons run cool. The easiest way to move heat from crown to walls is to make the piston dome thicker and provide a large heat path. There are limits to the usefulness of this (weight, for instance), and heavily supercharged engines—particularly those with large-diameter pistons—use oil or even water piped or squirted up into the pistons to remove the heat directly. Some current turbocharged automotive engines use oil jets of this type. Since motorcycle pistons are usually so small, the hot and cool parts are sufficiently close together for natural temperature control.

Two-stroke pistons have a double problem—they collect combustion heat every time they come to top center, not every other time as in four-strokes. Back in 1912, a 500cc Scott two-stroke ran away with the Isle of Man TT, and people worried this engine type would soon dominate everything. They needn't have worried. As two-stroke power continued to rise, it ran straight into *the* barrier: piston overheating. Real two-stroke development would have to wait until the Japanese solved the problems of super-low-expansion hypereutectic aluminum alloys.

Four-stroke engine builders have their choice of either forged or cast pistons. Forgings must be simple shapes so the dies can pull straight away from the finished blank, limiting the designer's choices. Cast pistons can have almost any shape, but suffer the problems of all cast metal—gas bubbles and other inclusions that reduce fatigue strength. Forging alloys have tremendous fatigue strength if not overheated, but retain their hardness less well than the best cast materials when very hot. Forged pistons are therefore used where mechanical strength is of primary importance—in super-high-rpm designs. Normal cast pistons are cheaper and work well at lower stress levels, while the hottest two-stroke applications use special heat-resistant cast pistons.

*Lee Klancher*

Providing the undersides of piston domes with reinforcing ribs and/or cooling fins would seem to lead to a lighter, stronger, cooler-running part. Experience says otherwise. For a part subjected to thousands of Gs of acceleration, plus high-speed friction, and severe thermal stress, it turns out a smoothly contoured shape gives the best results. Fins and ribs mean sudden changes in cross-sectional area, and considering the large temperature differences from the hottest to the coolest parts of a piston, that means heavy stress concentrations and the likelihood of cracking. Pistons aren't cooled by air, so fins under the dome are without value.

Move the rings closer to the crown and a cooler-running piston results, but the rings get hotter—such a design shortens the heat path from dome to ring pack. If the rings get too hot, the oil on them will gum and glue them to the piston, making them useless. Racing engines, serviced often enough to prevent sticking, use such high-ringed pistons. These pistons run a useful bit cooler and can tolerate higher compression ratios without detonation. In long-service engines the rings are put lower down to prevent the need for periodical servicing to free them.

In general, the smaller the piston clearance, the cooler the piston will run because of the closer thermal contact between the piston skirt and the cylinder wall. As the piston heats up and expands, it makes closer contact with the wall, gets rid of its heat, and cools off again—provided that the surfaces are sufficiently broken-in to operate with only the thinnest oil film.

A well-designed, close-fitted piston is not only a cooler-running part, but also a more accurately guided carrier for the all-important piston rings, keeping them from tilting in the cylinder bore and leaking pressure. Close clearances also avoid the terrible hammering of loose pistons as they warm up, something that can damage more than just the pistons themselves. Quite a bit of technology to be tied up in that ashtray, don't you think?

*March 1984*

# Tires: The Basic Vocabulary, Part 1

*When I first started messing about with bikes I tried hard to ignore what I considered mere "organic material"—riders and tires. I didn't know much! So I had to find sources and learn. The tire industry is secretive, but there are always ways.*

While common sense tells us tires are useful because they are round, the most interesting parts of a tire are not. The part of the tread lying flat on the road and the distorted carcass of the tire transmitting traction forces to the wheel rim are far more fascinating than a tire's roundness.

Any round *wheel* can roll and carry a load, but a *tire's* special mission is traction, giving a vehicle the ability to accelerate, brake, and turn corners. Reduced to essentials, a tire is a band of traction-generating tread, part of which lies flat on the road while the rest is on its way up and over to be laid flat on the road again. A flexible inflated fabric bag—the carcass—connects this band to the wheel rim. Compare this with a tank track system, which uses sprockets, bogies, slides, and idlers to control the motions of its tread loop. The tank track analogy is important because a track system accomplishes many things which would delight a tire engineer. First, it places a maximum amount of its tread on the road at one time, giving maximum traction. Second, its tread band is very stiff in every direction except as needed to bend in passing over its rollers, preventing the tread band from distorting under traction forces and losing its grip. Finally, the tank's track is under excellent control as it moves, guided as it is by all those gadgets.

Although a tire looks simpler, it is much more complex in its action because it must combine in one part all the jobs of tread, rollers, bogies, and the lot as it flexes, twists, and bends.

Tire design has struggled with the same basic problems from the beginning. If we could resurrect a tire engineer from the turn of the century and bring him together with his present-day counterpart, the two would understand each other's work instantly. Traction, wear, stability, structural integrity, and heat effects are as perplexing today as they were at the beginning. Tire problems haven't been truly solved—just pushed to higher limits.

Several major parts make up a tire: the *tread* rubber, which generates traction by continuously receiving the imprint of the road; the laminated fabric *casing* or *carcass*, which flexibly supports that tread; the *beads*, circular hoops of wire wrapped into the edges of the carcass, which prevent the tire from popping off the wheel rim; and finally the *air pressure* inside that casing, which tensions the fabric to define the tire's shape and gives the tire its exceptional springiness.

The center of the tire's tread is its *crown*, its edges are its *shoulders*, and between each shoulder and its bead are the *sidewalls*, which transmit traction forces from tread to rim. That part of the tread in contact with the road is the *footprint*, or *contact patch*.

The carcass is made from one or more layers of *tire cord fabric*.* Instead of an ordinary cloth's interwoven fibers, tire cord fabric has essentially all its fibers parallel, held in alignment by a very few cross-fibers. Embedded into a thin layer of rubber, the fabric is then cut on the diagonal into lengths sufficient to wrap once around the tire carcass. As a tire is built, these lengths of cord fabric are laminated over each other with their diagonal fiber directions alternating. This gives the desirable property of conventional fabric—the ability to resist stress from any direction—but without the undesirable property of allowing crossed fibers to saw at each other as the tire flexes. Encased in their own layers of rubber, tire cord fibers never touch each other.

In a tire plant the builder laminates the tire in the form of a flat band—with none of a finished tire's familiar doughnut shape. Taking the successive lengths of cord fabric from an overhead machine called a servicer, he applies them to a building drum turning slowly in front of him. The fabric plies stick to the drum and to each other because the as yet unvulcanized rubber in them has what is called *tack*. The builder starts each ply in its proper place, keeping it centered and avoiding wrinkles.

*This sentence describes the manufacture of *bias* tires, which have now been almost entirely replaced by *radial* construction, the manufacturing of which is different in many ways.

Next he locates two rubber-coated bead wire hoops over the flat band of plies, and folds each edge of the ply band inward over its bead, sticking them back down to themselves and trapping the beads in the fabric structure.

Finally, the servicer feeds the builder a strip of shaped tread rubber extrusion—thicker in the crown and tapering to its shoulders. He applies this over the ply band, centering it carefully, and finally overlaps its tapered ends into a strong scarf joint. The drum now spins rapidly under rollers which press out trapped air and squeeze the plies and tread into one sticky black ring.

This *green tire* is still a flat band whose diameter is that of the bead hoops, 18 inches in the case of most motorcycle tires. The rubber is doughy, plastic, and uncured, the tire held together only by its own tack.

On command the drum collapses, allowing the green tire to be removed, ready for *vulcanization*, or *curing*.

The cure process does two things. It deforms the flat-band shape of the green tire into the shape of a finished tire, and it chemically transforms the weak green rubber into a tough, elastic substance. The cure press opens like a clamshell, divided around the tread crown. In its center is a gray, shrunken bag, looking much like a deflated football bladder. The operator sets a green tire down over the bladder, into the lower mold half, and the press begins its cycle. Steam pressure expands the bladder against the inside of the green tire as the mold closes. Heated by the press, the tire softens and yields to the pressure, expanding. Buried in its rubber, the fabric cords resist, but slowly they migrate to allow the flat band to assume tire shape. The crisscrossing layers of cord scissor past each other in the plastic, flowing rubber as the tire deforms to fill the mold, whose inside is a perfect female replica of a finished tire. Mold gases vent through tiny holes in the tread area. The carcass fibers now stretch tightly from one bead, diagonally up and over the tire's crown, and down to the other bead. The tire remains like this for several minutes to complete its chemical transformation, heated from without by the hot mold, from within by the steam-filled cure bladder. At the proper time, the press opens and the finished tire emerges, its tread bristling with little whiskers—excess rubber which has escaped through the vent holes.

Let's consider how car tires produce steering forces and then turn to the special case of motorcycle tires. When you steer a car's front tires, the following occurs:

1. The tire treads begin laying down footprint in the new direction.
2. The car, because of its inertia, tends to keep going straight.
3. Something's got to give, and what does is the tire sidewalls, deflecting

between the footprints (departing in their new direction) and the rims (tending to go forward with the car).

4. The tension between footprint and rim is a side force on the rim, beginning to accelerate the front of the car sideways, making it turn.

5. Soon the tires and rims reach a steady state. So long as the wheels remain steered into the turn, the footprints will keep trying to track sideways out from under the car. This keeps the sidewalls permanently deflected and maintains their sideways pull on the front of the car. Under this pull, the car describes a circular path.

To keep the car turning, the side force between footprint and rim must remain constant. Because the tire is rolling, the deflected part of the sidewall between the footprint and wheel rim constantly escapes to the rear, while fresh, undeflected sidewall enters at the front. The result? The side force acts on the fresh, undeflected sidewall, pulling it to the side in turn. As the tire rolls, this steady deflection of new sidewall requires the rim to move steadily sideways over the footprint. Since the rim is already moving forward with the vehicle, the result of adding the forward movement to the slight sideways movement is a diagonal path for the rim as it moves over the ground. The car therefore moves in a slightly different direction from the way which the tires point—even though the tires are not slipping on the road surface. The apparent slip is just the sideways movement permitted by the continuous deflection of fresh sidewall as it enters the stressed zone between footprint and rim.

This angle—the difference between steer direction and vehicle direction—is called (just to keep us confused) the *slip angle*, even though there is no slippage involved.

As one of the very important tire variables, slip angle relates vehicle response to our steering input. Tire makers graph the side force versus slip angle, measured experimentally for each tire design. These curves rise steeply from zero, flatten to a peak, then slowly fall again. In the early steep-rise part of this curve, a linear relationship (in perfect proportion) exists between slip angle and side force; double the slip angle and you get double the side force from the tire. In this part of the curve, increases in slip angle (turning the steering wheel into the turn more) just increase the deflection of the tire carcass as it transmits more side force. This part of the curve is a straight line because the carcass is behaving like a simple spring, linking the footprint with the rim, but the footprint still is not slipping on the road.

If the tread's grip were infinite, this steep-rise part of the slip angle curve could go right on rising until the tire was torn from the rim. In fact, sliding of the tread against the road *does* develop at a point, beginning in the most highly stressed parts of the footprint first. As we have seen, tread distortion is least at the front of the footprint, and naturally sliding begins where side-distortion is largest, at the back, migrating forward until it becomes total. This sliding puts a gradual end to the smooth rise of cornering force with increasing slip angle, so the curve peaks gently, then falls slowly. Sidewall deflection is also present to some degree in the tread as it approaches and leaves the road, causing the tread rubber to squirm somewhat as it is pressed down and lifted up. This leads to some partial sliding even at the most limited speeds—but only at the margins of the footprint. Herein lies the major source of long-term tire wear, for this deflection produces some abrasion of the tread even though the bulk of the footprint is solidly gripping the road.

How great can the slip angle become before general sliding takes over? This depends on tire construction, but in most automotive applications a figure of 10 degrees is common. We do our everyday driving in the steep-rise part of the slip angle curve, an area of essentially no sliding. Racers must take their tires to maximum side force, the flat peak of the curve where sliding is a major effect. The stiffer a tire's construction, the narrower the transition between gripping and sliding.

In the case of motorcycle tires, the relation of slip angle to side force is supplemented by a steering effect called *camber thrust*. When a motorcycle is running upright, two circles drawn around the circumference of the tread, each through one edge of the footprint, will represent the same distance of travel. When the machine heels over into a turn, this no longer holds true. Now the circle drawn through the edge of the footprint toward the inside of the turn will be slightly smaller than the one drawn through the outer edge, and the outside of the footprint will advance slightly with respect to the inside as the tire rolls. This generates a torque on the footprint of the tire, steering it into the turn. This twist develops entirely in the tire carcass, and takes place without any steering movement of the rim. Steering itself into the turn this way, the footprint develops a side force just as though the wheel had been steered into a slip angle.

At small lean angles (such as at the beginning of a turn), camber thrust contributed largely to the side force required to steer a motorcycle. *Camber stiffness*, the rate at which camber thrust develops with lean, is determined by the carcass construction, which gives the footprint its slight freedom to twist and so steer itself in this way. The profile of the tire's tread also affects camber thrust, and so, the "feel" of the tire as it is leaned into a turn. Camber thrust must develop in concert at front and rear tires as the machine heels over, or too much steering effect may develop at one end, giving a feeling of oversteering or understeering.

The steering geometry built into your machine consists of rake and trail. Rake is the inclination of the steering axis to the vertical, and trail is the distance between the tire's point of contact with the road behind and the imaginary intersection of the steering axis and the road. Because the tire contact trails the pivot axis, steering deflections are self-correcting and your machine is (with proper design) stable and controllable. Even this, though, is not as simple as it seems.

The front tire doesn't and can't touch the road at a single point—the footprint is actually quite a large area. Moreover, the side force developed in that footprint doesn't behave as though it were originating at its center, but acts farther back where the carcass is stretched sideways by the deflection of cornering. The distance between the real point of action and the apparent center of the footprint is called the *pneumatic trail*, and this varies with carcass stiffness and with how hard the machine is ridden. In effect, the trail of your machine increases with hard riding—the more you deflect the front tire out of shape. In a car you feel this as the increase in steering force you must apply to corner more sharply. When the front tires have finally passed their maximum grip and you feel the steering "go light," what you feel is the pneumatic trail decreasing again as the stresses in the footprint are redistributed by the onset of actual sliding.

Because of this, motorcycles give neutral steering only when ridden in the manner intended by the designer. A roadracing machine ridden at beach-cruiser speed may feel cumbersome and want to fall over in turns. Ridden harder, the front tire enters the partial-sliding zone and the pneumatic trail relaxes to make the steering neutral near the limit. Obviously, such a geometry would be wrong for the street. Because different tires, traction conditions, and rider styles change these effects, racing teams carry several sets of front fork crowns, made in different offsets, so that their bikes' trail can be reset to compensate.

Most of us have very little understanding of tire construction—maybe we've seen a recap throw its tread rubber off on a hot day, or maybe we've seen a bald tire worn down to its cord fabric. Armed with this basic vocabulary, we are now ready to look at tire behavior as a whole.

# Tires: The Basic Vocabulary, Part 2

*I found books with titles like* Vulcanization of Elastomers, *and little monographs like* Friction and Lubrication *and* The Tire-Pavement Interface. *Each contains good stuff, obscured by the language of scientific priesthoods. When you learn things you think are cool, you want to tell someone. Here I try.*

*EDITOR'S NOTE: Last month, Kevin Cameron began a mini-series on tires, title, appropriately enough, "Tires, The Basic Vocabulary, Part 1." In the first thrilling episode, we learned that even though tires are useful because they are round, the most interesting parts of the tire are not round. Cameron identified the major parts of a tire, including tread, carcass, beads, crown, shoulders, sidewalls, and contact patches. This first installment came to an end with the discussions of slip angle, camber thrust and camber stiffness, and the revelation that the butler hadn't done it after all. Having completed his examination of the tire as a whole, Cameron begins our second installment.*

Now it's time to see how tread rubber, tire construction, and air pressure influence tire behavior. First, tread rubber and its relationship with the road surface: four generally recognized mechanisms of rubber traction affect our tire here—(1) cutting and tearing, (2) molecular bonding, (3) abrasion, and (4) hysteresis effects.

Sliding can't take place unless the infinity of mineral points and edges in the road *cut and tear* their way through the rubber. This is why traction can increase with increases in the tensile strength of the rubber compound.

Tires do grip even old, polished surfaces, like Daytona's Turn Two. How? As with other materials in contact, rubber forms actual molecular bonds to the road. The larger the area of real contact between tread and road, the more numerous these bonds and the higher the grip. Contact area depends not only on footprint area, but on the softness of the rubber. A hard compound bridges across the many hollows in the rough road surface, while a softer rubber is more able to fill the hollows and make contact in every nook and cranny. Surface contamination such as water, oil or dust reduces grip because it interferes with molecular bonding.

Abrasion is the actual removal of material by wear, and because it takes force to do it, it too contributes to grip.

Finally, we know from experience that tires have some grip in the wet, and even when covered with engine oil (not much, but some). How? Molecular adhesion doesn't completely disappear in the presence of lubricants, nor do tearing and wear, so some traction still comes from these. Supplementing these is a fourth traction mechanism, *hysteresis*, the internal damping of the rubber itself. As a tread slides against a wet road, the tiny wet hills and valleys that make up the road surface constantly push the tread's surface in and out. This cycles the rubber through compression and expansion, just like compressing and expanding a spring. While a spring may return 99 percent of the energy we push into it, a high-hysteresis rubber compound may give back only 30 percent. This means the road sliding under the tread must work harder to compress the rubber up the road's wet little hills than the road can get back again when the rubber springs back on the road's little downhills. This energy, taken from whatever force is making the tire skid in the first place, is stored in the rubber as heat. By absorbing energy from this force and opposing the sliding, hysteresis generates a traction force. Hysteretic traction works in the dry as well, but in the wet it becomes the major source of grip. A high-hysteresis rubber feels "dead" rather than snappy. When you stretch it, it returns gradually rather than snapping back.

The major sources of traction—molecular bonding and hysteresis—are closely dependent on temperature and on the pressure holding the rubber against the road. The rubber chemist tries to design his compounds to yield peak traction effects in the range of temperature and pressure expected in use, be they rainswept interstates or the Daytona banking in spring sunshine.

The sum of all these traction effects is the *coefficient of friction* (Cf) of the material, which is the ratio between the normal pressure (the pressure perpendicular to the surfaces) and the friction generated. If a tire carrying a 300-pound load finally breaks away on the skid-pad at a side-force of 275 pounds, its Cf is 275/300 = 0.92 for those conditions. It would be nice if this number were a constant, but, alas, such is not the case.

With normal solids, if you double the pressure between the surfaces, you get double the friction, but rubber behaves differently. Rubber isn't a normal solid at all, but a *visco-elastic* solid with characteristics of both a spring and a damper. For normal solids, the Cf is near-constant, but rubber generates a complex curve. This curve of rubber friction versus normal pressure begins at zero and rises steeply, flattens off to a peak, and finally falls again. The fast-rise part of this curve comes from the rapid increase of surface contact with increasing normal pressure. When the rubber has penetrated the road surface to its maximum, and no more surface area can be gained, the Cf tends to stop rising. As sliding begins, the rubber warms up, losing properties necessary for grip, so the Cf falls again.

This friction curve has important implications for motorcycles. Look at the front tire of a hard-ridden machine as it enters a turn. Because the machine is slowing, the front is carrying more than its share of the weight. The tire is likely to slide because overloading has driven its (Cf) past maximum and into the slowly falling part of the curve. If the rider now gets on the throttle, transferring weight back to the large rear tire, the front will grip again because the rider has unloaded it and allowed it to operate back near its peak Cf. If he gets on the gas *too* hard, he will unload the front so much that its Cf travels back down the steeply rising part of the curve to the much lower values. He may then lose the front end again, but

now for the opposite reason. Each little bit of tread rubber must be carrying optimum pressure against the ground; too much or too little and the Cf of that bit of tread will fall from its maximum.

Now we see why carcass design is so very important. Our rubber compound will perform best only over a narrow range of normal pressures, so if the stress of cornering, acceleration, or braking makes the footprint distribute pressure on the road in a non-uniform manner, part of its tread rubber will carry too

*Lee Klancher*

much pressure and part of it too little. Since the most heavily loaded parts of a footprint commonly carry twice as much normal pressure as the least-loaded, you can see that it is very difficult to get peak Cf across the whole footprint. The job of the tire designer is to get a maximum footprint area on the road and to put it there under uniform pressure, quite impossible because the carcass assumes a different pressure distribution every time we lean the machine over, open the throttle, or squeeze the brakes. A certain tire may give exceptional braking yet lack cornering power, or may be excellent entering a turn but dreadful coming out, all due to the designer's compromises. Any change made to the carcass changes all this again, so the tire designer must be a master of compromise who forgets nothing and who is satisfied with tiny gains.

Viewed in one way, it seems this problem shouldn't even exist. Isn't the air pressure inside the tire perfectly uniform, and isn't it the force that presses the tread down on the road? Yes, but that neglects the stiffness of the carcass in bending, and the tension in its fibers. If the tire were infinitely thin, with no resistance to bending and stretching, it would lie on the road at a normal pressure equal to its air pressure. Unfortunately, we can't tolerate an infinitely stretchy tire because we need some rigidity to keep the machine running straight, free from wobbles. We can't tolerate too thin a tire because the carcass cords must be thick enough to carry the loads. We can't eliminate the tension in the cords (too much lifts up the edges of the tread, too little lets it buckle) because that is the source of all rigidity in the first place.

A conventional bias-ply motorcycle tire has its plies laid such that their diagonally running fibers cross each other. The most fundamental variable in tire construction is the *cord angle,* or *crown angle,* or defined as the angle between any fiber and the crown centerline of the inflated tire. If this crown angle were zero, the fibers would run circumferentially around the tire and could never be attached to the beads. If the crown angle were 90 degrees, the fibers would not run around the tire at all, but would reach up from one bead, right across the crown and down to the opposite bead.

Early tires had a crown angle of 45 degrees, a nice compromise between these extremes. In the tread area, the crossed plies were describing an angle of 90 degrees to each other, just as do the interwoven threads in ordinary cloth.

In time, engineers found that changing this cord angle changed the behavior of the tire. A lower crown angle—say, 30 degrees—made the tire much stiffer. It gave more cornering force for a given slip angle, rode harder and, because it flexed less in rolling, was cooler-running. Increasing the cord angle from 45 degrees made a tire that needed a lot of slip angle for a given cornering thrust but was soft-riding and comfortable. Because such high-angle tires were so squashy, they flexed a lot and generated more heat. At high speeds, such tires would overheat and their treads might separate from the carcasses. Low-angle constructions were termed "hard" constructions, and vice versa.

Why? Consider how one cord fiber supports the bit of tread directly beneath it. This fiber is the only connection between that bit of tread and the wheel rim. If the cord angle is 90 degrees (the softest possible construction), then the cord goes straight to the rim at either side by the shortest path, joining it at only two places. Weak bracing.

Drop the cord angle to 30 degrees and we have two fibers crossing under our bit of rubber, running to join the rim in *four* places, meeting it on a diagonal. Reducing the angle further broadens the base of this four-point support system, making the bracing even stronger. The lower the cord angle—down to a practical minimum of some 23 degrees—the more rigid the tire becomes.

This makes a radial tire seem like nonsense, but in addition to its 90-degree radial-carcass ply the radial has a circumferential-stiffening belt of fibers running at a very low angle. Its tread is therefore well-braced, but in a different way than a bias-ply.

Not only is a hard construction stiffer under cornering loads, but it is also stiffer vertically. As the tire is loaded, it naturally yields somewhat. Its spring rate is just like that of a suspension spring—so many pounds per inch. A stiff construction has a higher vertical spring rate, so it spreads out less on the ground and tends to have a smaller footprint.

This isn't as bad as it sounds. A soft construction may lay down more square inches of footprint, but that footprint is poorly braced by the carcass. When driven hard, the footprint will lift up at the edges and twist and squirm more easily than will the footprint of a harder construction. A harder construction may lay down less rubber, but it uses that area more effectively, keeping it flat on the road rather than allowing it to deform and weasel out of its duties.

In addition to a vertical spring rate, tires have a lateral spring rate as well. This is important in vehicle stability, for too much freedom laterally allows the machine to yaw (point some direction other than the way it's going) and possibly weave.

Obviously, the tire carcass needs a certain strength to contain its inflation pressure and to tolerate vehicle loads. In the early days, all tires used cotton carcass fibers, as many as 20 or more plies to get adequate strength. All this thickness of rubber and fiber flexing constantly generated enormous heat—so much that in a car-racing tire, inflated cold to 50 psi, the air pressure in use would rise to 80–100 psi. Unless inflated rock-hard, such thick tires simply burned up in use. But under high inflation, footprint area dwindled away to almost nothing, leaving too little rubber to generate traction. The tires survived, but it was a bad deal.

Tire engineers knew perfectly well where the problem lay, but the weakness of cotton cord blocked them from making the tires thinner. In time, rayon, nylon, steel, polyester, and most recently Kevlar fibers have dramatically increased the strength in a single carcass ply. Thinner tires, well able to tolerate high speeds while laying down large footprint areas, are the result. Modern radial heavy-truck tires have only one carcass ply made of steel cord.

Since modern carcasses generate so much less heat, tires can tolerate hotter-running tread compounds without overheating—high-hysteresis tread rubbers that give good grip in wet and dry conditions.

With fewer plies, the heavy tread rubber must bond to less and less total fiber surface. Running the cord fabric through a bath of liquid rubber isn't enough, for this creates a weak bond. Current bonding systems use primers, able to adhere strongly both to the carcass fiber and to the rubber around them. Fiber-to-rubber bonding has had to keep pace with the development of stronger fibers too. A street tire may revolve 30 or 40 million times before it wears out. The number of flex cycles involved in such a long life is a terrible strain on the rubber-to-fiber bond. A racing tire may be thrown away after only 40–100,000 rotations, so even though it must stand high stress in use, it need not resist for long.

Now consider the effects of air pressure inside the tire. An overinflated tire puts its cord structure under more tension, raising its vertical spring rate and reducing its footprint area. The overloaded footprint overheats readily, slides easily, and wears quickly. The suspension system must work harder because the hard tire gives it little help. On the other hand, the carcass is stiffer and responds more positively to steering inputs.

In an underinflated tire, the vertical spring rate is low so the footprint spreads out. Flattening such a large, normally curved area of tire involves considerable distortion. The footprint's curvature makes it behave like the bottom of an oil can; it tries to pop up off the road in its center, reducing the pressure on the rubber there. At very low pressure, actual ripples may result in the footprint as it buckles inward, away from the road. The load it would normally carry now overloads the edges of the footprint, wearing the tire into odd shapes. With no part of the footprint under optimum pressure, traction is poor. The lateral spring rate of the underinflated tire falls, making it respond slowly to steering inputs, and offering less accurate guidance for the vehicle. In cornering, the tension in the fibers of the edge of the footprint on the outside of the turn increases, while on the inside edge it lessens. With low enough tire pressure or under extreme side-force, all the fabric tension can disappear along the inner edge, allowing the carcass to buckle there. In some cases, waves of such buckling can propagate under the footprint, making the machine feel as though it is riding on last season's beach ball.

Aha! All we need to do now is find an intermediate pressure between too much and too little—then all these nasty troubles vanish and we can ride smiling into the sunset. No such thing. The pressure distribution in the footprint is *always* non-uniform, so the tread rubber there can never display its peak ability. The deformation of the tire *always* puts stresses into the footprint that reduce traction and produce wear. The connection between footprint and rim is *always* flexible to a degree because it's impossible to separate that flexibility from the flexibility we must have for laying down maximum footprint area.

Although a slick, unpatterned tread lays down maximum rubber and is thus best for dry traction, when rain covers the road, the tire may advance too fast for the water in front of it to be pushed completely aside. The tread then rides up on a thin water film—an almost perfect lubricant—*hydroplaning*. Breaking up the tread rubber into ribs, blocks, or other elements divided by a network of drainage channels can push this occurrence up to a higher speed. Breaking up a slick tread into separate elements weakens it because the smaller the elements, the weaker they become in bending, tending to tip over under traction forces, riding on their edges rather than on their flat faces. This reduces traction in proportion with the loss of surface contact. The human mind cannot resist the obvious similarity between a gear and the toothed outline of a tread pattern, and concludes that traction is produced by these "teeth" cutting into the road. While this may be true of a knobby in the sand, we must cling to our sanity by comparing the hardness of rubber and asphalt.

One approach to give good wet grip *and* keep tread elements from bending under the high forces of dry traction is to employ "natural path" drainage channels which push the water diagonally ahead and to the side. Such channels become larger as they move from tread crown to shoulder, just as rivers become wider as they gather more volume from their tributaries. A parallel approach angles tread elements so they are strongly braced to resist primary traction forces and weaker at right angles to them. Front tire elements would resist braking combined with turning, while rears would be angled for combined cornering and acceleration.

To a point, pattern can control tread heating, for the drainage channels allow the tire to bend more easily, important if the reduction of rolling resistance becomes a consideration.

The tire designer can predict mathematically what cross section a tire carcass will assume when inflated. Reducing the cord angle gives a flatter contour, while increasing it makes the tire balloon out more. The final tread contour—so important in determining the steering "feel" of a tire—is the result of adding the thickness of the tread rubber to this carcass cross section. Severe limits exist regarding how thickly tread can be applied, because the more rubber there is under a certain area, the more heat that area will generate, and because thicker rubber is at more risk of pulling free from its bonds to the cord beneath. You can't make a tire of any arbitrary shape without careful consideration of how to make it stay together.

The *aspect ratio* is the relation between a tire's height off the rim to its overall width. A low aspect ratio combines a lot of tread area with lower sidewalls, and tends to produce a stiff, fast-responding tire that often needs to be supplemented by a very compliant suspension. A high aspect ratio puts more sidewall between tread and rim, tending to do part of the suspension's job. Such tires can lack directional control, traded away to get a low vertical spring rate.

Many tricks combine performance features. If the designer needs the comfort of a soft sidewall but needs a stable tread area for long mileage, he may wrap low-angle belts around the carcass, under the tread. These stiffen the tread against squirm, but hardly affect sidewall action. Or, if a tire works well as a traction generator but lacks something in directional stability, narrow sidewall stiffening plies, called chafers, firm up the sidewall. This raises the tire's lateral spring rate without too much effect on its ability to lay down footprint.

A revolution in motorcycle tires may emerge from the marriage of such tricks with the radial-tire technology developed for the automotive world. A pure radial tire, with its maximally flexible sidewalls, has a very low lateral spring rate and cannot supply the stability that motorcycles need to run in a straight line. On the other hand, the radial's extreme flexibility in laying down a large footprint is very attractive because motorcycles have very little footprint in relation to their weight and power.

Tire technology is almost invisible, and tire makers seem to like it that way. Unfortunately, this conceals the true importance of tires in the development of vehicle technology. Truly, today's motorcycles are what their tires permit them to be—whether on the track or on the highway. Without them, today's motorcycles would be only strange curiosities.

# Tires: The Basic Vocabulary, Part 3

*The basics of tires are still the basics, so it's useful to see how the industry has raised its game against the underlying physics over the years. A look at MotoGP lean angles shows how much has been accomplished, but heat remains rubber's enemy number one.*

The birth of the car and the motorcycle came at a time of unlimited belief in human progress, in the value of technology, in the future of industry. These vehicles grew from nothing, small seeds of invention irrigated by the money of wealthy sportsmen and eager investors. That world of 1885–1900 was rich with evidence of man's new power. Vibration-less steam turbines were taking over ship propulsion from hammering reciprocating engines. Lilienthal and Pilcher were soaring almost daily in their gliders; powered flight was only a matter of time. Trains ran routinely at 60 miles per hour. A powerful new explosive, dynamite, had just blasted the St. Gothard Tunnel nine miles through the Alps. An incredible steel bridge thrust 1,700 feet of free span across the Firth of Forth. Surely there was no limit to what might be done, and inventive people were busy proving it everywhere.

Despite all this optimism, early motoring required great strength of character. Everything useful in motor construction had to be created from scratch, and none of it worked for long. Tires blew, bearings seized, castings cracked. There were no dealers, no mechanics, no parts. There was no gasoline in the next town, and the road leading to it was full of hazards.

Who in his right mind would want gasoline around? It was a dangerous, explosive by-product of lamp-oil manufacture, but it could be ordered by anyone so foolish—in carefully crated five-gallon tins. Tires lasted to the next sharp rock, but the pioneer motorist loved his mechanical sport enough to repair tires 10 or more times in the course of an afternoon's run. And tires weren't cheap; in a time when butter cost five cents a pound, motor tires were $35 apiece. Motoring was not for everyman.

Everything the early motorist did was difficult—except enjoying the effortless machine propulsion that made magic out of the whole inconvenient, dirty, smelly business. Perhaps your motor-bicycle had hot-tube ignition and a wick carburetor. To start the engine, first light the burner under the hot-tube. Heat from the flame warms this tube until its other end, inside the combustion chamber, is hot enough to ignite the mixture. Too hot and the engine fires backward. Not hot enough and it doesn't fire at all. You'll need judgment and experience to get it right. Now the wick carburetor. It has no jets. The intake air picks up fuel by simple evaporation from a huge gasoline-soaked wick. There is an air shutter and a mixture lever. To start, you need a rich mixture; set mixture lever rich, air shutter at low.

Astride your machine, you place your feet on the pedals; after all, this is no more than a bicycle with a motor adapted. It weighs 110 pounds including its 800-rpm big single, belted with rawhide to the rear wheel's big grooved pulley. You push off, pedal hard for speed, and drop the exhaust valve lifter. The motor chuffs and pops raggedly, you fiddle with the air and mixture controls, and the popping begins to carry you forward. As the cylinder warms, it needs a leaner mixture, and protests by roiling out stinking clouds of partially burned fuel. You remember to stroke the hand lube pump to prevent seizure, and then lean down the mixture while easing the air shutter open. The chuffing steadies and you accelerate grandly, if gradually. This vehicle has no clutch and no shift. When the engine is hot and the air shutter fully open, you are at maximum—free from earthly care.

Free, except for having to adjust the inevitably slipping belt. Or attending to the mixture as the next hill pulls the engine speed down. Mixture control isn't automatic; *you* are the carburetor. Finally, at this wonderful speed of 15 mph, your tires will certainly fail, and you'll spend a good part of this afternoon seated in the grass by the roadside patching your tires and mentally savoring your moments of inexpressible freedom at speed.

Rubber has been known in Europe since the explorers of South America brought back the coagulated sap of the rubber tree, Hevea brasiliensis.

Europeans used it for erasers ("rubbers") or in children's balls. It was impervious to water and air—an interesting, suggestive property—but hardened into glass in winter and dissolved into slime in heat.

In 1839 Charles Goodyear found that long heating of rubber in the presence of sulfur changed it into a tough, elastic material of infinite uses—shoes, rainwear, any number of industrial applications. Indeed, solid rubber tires on wagons and carriages saved wear and tear on hard city streets.

One vehicle, the bicycle, lately come to huge popularity, needed something better than these solid tires. Because a human can deliver only a fraction of a horsepower continuously, the bicycle offers a valuable study in rolling resistance. When a hard tire hits a pebble in the road, it must either climb over it or drive it into the ground. Climbing over the pebble uses no energy but gives a shock. Driving it into the ground obviously consumes power. Bicycles riding on hard tires were uncomfortable and difficult to pedal on any but the smoothest surfaces.

Embracing the spirit of his age, John Dunlop of Belfast rejected the hard ride and rolling resistance of the solid tires on his son's velocipede. He made a test wheel of wood and fitted it with a rudimentary pneumatic tire, a handmade inner tube held against the rim by a cover of linen cloth tacked to the wheel on both sides. When he tested this pneumatic wheel side by side with the solid-tired wheel, bowling them with equal speed over various terrain, the pneumatic wheel rolled farther every time. This idea applied to racing bicycles was like magic—effortless speed. In France the Michelin brothers repeated Dunlop's work with the same wonderful result. Pneumatic tires became instantly necessary for every bicycle, and a large industry sprang up to supply demand.

Every one of the many companies vying for this market had its own idea of the best way to attach the cover to the wheel and contain the inner tube against the rim. They used glue, straps and buckles, lacings, and even bolts; repairing a punctured tube was a tedious job taking an hour or more. While the very first motor vehicles had used iron tires or solid rubber–tired wheels, there were very real advantages to pneumatics. In tests made in 1900, researchers compared the rolling resistances of iron tires, rubber solids, and pneumatics. The faster the vehicle went, the greater the power pneumatics saved, amounting to almost 30 percent even at 12 mph.

For motoring to progress, pneumatic tires were the only rational choice, as they had been for the bicycle. The Benz Velo rolled on air-filled tires in 1893, and the Michelins applied their pneumatics to a buggy-like Peugeot auto in 1895. These tires were extremely fragile, and the first solution was to protect them against puncture. One method called for riveting metal bars onto tires' heavy canvas or leather covers as armor, but these lacked the traction of rubber. The dominant form of tire, therefore, became the canvas cover (possibly made of more than one layer) with a rubber tread glued onto it and supported by air in some form of inner tube.

If armor was impractical, then why not simplify repair of the inevitable punctures? Instead of using bolts or straps, why not just lock the edges of the cover into the rim of the wheel in some way? The concept finally adopted for most bicycles (and later for many European and British motorcycles)—the Welch tire and rim—is the dominant type for all vehicles today. To keep the cover (even now some old-timers still call a tire a "cover") from expanding radially off the rim, tire makers molded high-tensile wire hoops into the edges, or beads, of the cover. Near-vertical rim flanges kept these beads in place laterally, while the center of the rim was depressed to allow the tire to be installed over the flanges.

Another concept, the Bartlett, or clincher rim and tire, used inward-facing rim flanges engaging a hook-like lip molded into each bead area—no wire. As the inner tube inflated, it pressed these lips tightly against the flanges, holding the cover in place. This clincher design, at first easier to manufacture than the Welch, dominated both motorcycle and auto tires for many years.

Tires were the most unreliable part of the new vehicles for two reasons: one, poor roads (travelers went by train); and, two, almost nothing was known about rubber chemistry except the rudiments of sulfur vulcanization, or curing. Tire carcasses were made of the best available materials—leather or heavy canvas. Those clever enough to see it knew motor vehicles would soon own the roads. They would need much-improved tires, and fortunes could be made developing and making them.

Out of the chaotic variety of patents and techniques that burst forth, one major process for making tires emerged. The tire was built up on the surface of an iron core form which looked like an inner tube. The strength of the tire came from layers of square-woven cotton duck canvas, impregnated with uncured rubber and applied on the form to the desired thickness. To keep all these layers, or plies, tightly together during the curing process, the iron form with the "green" (uncured) carcass on it was bandaged round and round with narrow canvas tape, then hung in a horizontal autoclave where steam provided the heat for curing. After some hours these rubber-and-canvas structures solidified into tire carcasses, and meanwhile tread rubber had been extruded into strips and partially cured separately. The cured carcasses were now unwrapped, the tread strips glued on, and the completed tires rewrapped and autoclave-cured a second time. Heating the tire on the heavy iron form, through all those thick wrappings, took a long time, and because these tires were made on male forms rather than in female molds, they could not carry sidewall lettering; they resembled canvas fire hose wrapped around a wheel.

Only easier production methods could make tires cheap enough to find wide sale. During this time motorcycles gained special popularity, and the motivation was economic—only the rich could afford cars. Consider that in the horse-drawn era, the average man did not drive horses. He walked. Who could afford the fine pair of animals, their stable, and the carriage house with its appointments?

The first "motors" were simply shod with reinforced bicycle tires, if they ran on pneumatics at all. A typical size was a 34 x 2, which meant that the tire outer diameter was 34 inches and the cross-section was 2 inches. Only such large wheels could handle the rough roads and deep mud of the time. And why not larger section? The stress induced in the walls of an inflated tube is proportional to its section diameter; the larger the tire section, the more a given inflation pressure tried to burst the cotton canvas of its carcass. To carry even the modest weight of a motor-bicycle these tiny-section tires had to be blown up hard, and to stand the stress of this along with the dynamic stress of rolling required many plies of canvas.

As vehicle speeds rose, a disagreeable side effect appeared: heat. Rubber is an imperfect spring. When you deform it with 100 units of energy, you will get back only 50–85 percent as it resumes its former shape. The remainder becomes heat, generated by the internal friction, or hysteresis, of the rubber itself. Contrary to common belief, most tire heating doesn't come from friction against the road surface. Certainly this generates some heat, but most originates *inside* the flexing rubber itself. A 1900 Benz motor truck on Kelly solid tires couldn't run higher than 10 mph or else the rubber

*Lee Klancher*

overheated and broke down chemically, reverting to a gum. The idea of pneumatic truck tires was attractive, but in use they were too large to be kept from bursting.

In 1902 Goodyear sent some tires to England for a horseless carriage race around the British Isles. These were thick "covers" built for the rough, slow going on U.S. roads, but because the English highways were fast and flinty the heavy Goodyears heated up and blew out. The competition— Dunlop and Michelin—built thinner tires that generated less heat and so survived speed better. These same three companies have been at one another in racing ever since.

In France a unique sport developed out of bicycle track racing. Enormous motors were attached to reinforced bicycle frames to make terrifying track "motorcycles." Tire makers struggled to cope with exploding speeds of 60–70 mph as engines reached a bloated 2,500cc in 1903. Then, as quickly, track racing died of overspecialization, to be replaced by tourist trophy races—endurance contests over public roads. England's backward speed laws slowed tire development there for a time, but with the completion of the great Brooklands Speedway complex in 1907, the pace again quickened. In that year the pioneer motor sportsman S. F. Edge put 1,580 miles into 24 hours at Brooklands, but his car used 100 tires in the process—blowouts, not punctures, were the problem. The Isle of Man motorcycle TT also commenced that year, and the following year motorcycle events began at Brooklands, stimulating development. The sizes of auto and motorcycle tires remained similar, with one 1907 Indian offered on large three-inch-section tires.

The destructive processes attacking early tires were these: first, the heat generated in the masses of flexing carcass rubber broke down the rubber, its bond to the fabric, and even the fibers themselves; second, early tires were laminated of layers of ordinary canvas, a material whose threads were interwoven with each other at 90 degrees. As this carcass fabric flexed in rolling, the threads sawed against each other at all of their thousands of intersections. Imagine a shirt inflated to 50 psi having to perform all the motions of a vigorous human wearer; it wouldn't last five minutes. The sawing inevitably unraveled the threads and the tire blew, tearing itself into long strips, wrapping around the axle, and locking the wheel.

How much heat did tires generate? A lot. In the first races at the Indianapolis Speedway (1911–12) cars used production tires because special racing tires did not yet exist. When inflated cold to 40–50 psi and run at 75 mph, they climbed quickly to 80–100 psi, implying a temperature of *at least* 400⁰ F. Since cotton fibers give up at 425–475⁰ F, and actually ignite at 500⁰ F, you can see how close they cut it. Tires determined all those races because constant blowouts stopped anyone who tried to run flat-out. The winner was the man who set a realistic pace and stuck to it.

Even with such difficulties, tire makers progressed. Pure gum rubber (the amber substance that makes such good slingshot bands) has little abrasion resistance and makes a poor tread. Lots of things were mixed into tread compounds to make them wear better, but the best of these was zinc oxide, a pure white substance. Tires made with zinc oxide–reinforced tread rubber were therefore white, as you can see in early motor ads. Apparently the surface properties of this pigment attracted the ends of the long, twisting rubber molecules, binding them together with greater tenacity yet not interfering with their springiness. Tire treads were made tougher without being made much harder—a valuable discovery.

In 1906 the excessive time taken for rubber curing was cut with the discovery that certain organic chemicals, added to the basic rubber-plus-4-percent sulfur mixture, dramatically accelerated the cure. At this time only three chemists worked in the entire U.S. rubber industry, but the proof that research was the key to progress generated jobs for chemists right and left. Technology!

Although better vehicles encouraged the adventuresome to try motor travel, in France the Michelin Travel Guide warned them to telegraph ahead to all destinations to ensure adequate supplies of the proper tire sizes were available.

Engineers considered the tire problem. Solid tires generated enough heat to limit speed, and rolling resistance was high. Though the current, very thick-walled pneumatic tires were better, they still ran too hot. Maybe the wrong part of the tire was flexing. The rubber had to be there to provide traction against the road, to seal in the air pressure, and to bind the carcass plies together. Solid tires don't work well because the *only* thing flexing is the rubber itself, which overheats and is destroyed. In thick-walled pneumatics, rubber and air share the flexing, and that worked better. Obviously the thing to do was redesign the tire to give the air a larger share of the flexing and the rubber a smaller share. Such a tire would run cooler because flexing air generates almost no heat at all. Take a look at a typical pneumatic of that time; here is a 34 x 3 tire with its 3-inch cross-section; of that 3 inches, nearly one-half is rubber, leaving an air chamber less than 2 inches across. What was worse, in the then-popular clincher tire, the beads came right together at the center of the rim, further limiting air volume. Men at

Goodyear and Dunlop looked at the other concept—the wire-beaded or straight-side tire. Its sidewalls ended at the bead flanges, leaving extra air volume between them. Such tires had appeared on motor-bicycles as early as 1897. By 1906 the few wire-beaded auto tires in racing proved to have a durability edge, and by 1908 Dunlop was building them for motorcycles. Goodyear staked its future on it, hoping a major automobile maker would adopt its version over clinchers.

Tire prices fell when makers stopped curing them directly on the iron building form in two steps. Now, after completing the carcass on the form, they added the tread and removed this green tire for curing *inside* a two-piece pot-heater mold. Instead of the tight bandages used to keep the plies together during cure, an air bag forced the green tire out against the inside of the new mold. Vertical autoclaves were stacked full of these molds for curing. And because the outside of the tire was now molded, sidewall lettering appeared for the first time.

There was more to come. The English Palmer Tire Company entirely abandoned the idea of using conventional canvas fabric as a tire carcass material. Palmer's tire fabric, called cord, consisted of threads running in one direction only, with *no* interwoven cross-threads at all. Laminating plies of this cord at 90 degrees to each other resulted in fabric as omnidirectionally strong as the ordinary interwoven fabric, but with one important difference: in the completed tire no thread could saw against its neighbors because there were no interweavings. Having no thread-to-thread friction greatly improved the fatigue strength of Palmer tires. Conservatively made, these tires had threads almost one quarter of an inch thick (hence the name "cord").

In the United States the Diamond Rubber Company (later B.F. Goodrich) licensed the cord process, calling its new tire the Silvertown, after the English city of origin. This new tire was safely much more flexible than a cotton duck tire at speed, but the new flexibility led to a special problem: Impact could force a sidewall against the rim, cutting it. Goodyear solved this by adding a narrow extra ply called a chafer just at the bead area to stiffen the sidewall there. Flexing then took place higher up and without cutting the tire. Goodyear researchers also worked toward smaller cords, experimenting a lot to get the best kind of fabric. How many threads per inch should it have? How heavy should each thread be? How tightly twisted?

Goodyear's belief in the straight-side concept won the company a large contract from Henry Ford, whose durable mass-market Model T greatly increased the demand for tires. Other auto makers gradually accepted this change, and the clincher tire died out by 1923.

Cord construction brought with it a new technique—flat-band tire building. Skill was important to building duck tires on the iron form, for each ply had to be carefully smoothed over the curved surfaces without the slightest bump or fold, which might lead to weakness or blowout. Cord fabric, with its all-parallel fibers, was infinitely more deformable than the old duck. Why not lay up the laminations on a plain cylinder where they could be quickly and accurately applied, and *then* forcibly deform this flat-band into tire shape afterward? It would take less hard-to-find skill to make a sound tire, would increase production, and cut down on defects. A bicycle tire builder in Providence, Rhode Island, had conceived this flat-band method back in the 1890s and then licensed it to Dunlop. Now its day had come.

In the new method the builder applied onto a drum one after another cut-to-length pieces of rubber-impregnated and rubber-coated cord fabric, angling the cords to cross those of the previous ply always at 90 degrees. Once the desired number of plies had been built up, bead-wire bundles were slid over them and the plies were folded inward over the bundles to lock them into the carcass. Last of all an extruded tread strip was applied down the center, with its tapered ends scarfed into a smooth joint. This green tire was then slid off the building drum and taken to another work station where it was bulged into tire shape, either by inflation of an internal air bag or by external vacuum. Once in tire form these were loaded into conventional pot-heater molds for autoclave cure, which took about an hour. It was fast, economical, and effective.

In 1913 Brooklands testing, Palmer cord tires lasted almost an hour at 100 mph. The following two years saw cord tires come to dominate Indianapolis racing for the simple reason that drivers on cord tires spent more time racing and less time changing blown tires.

Compounders now discovered a much better reinforcer than the old zinc oxide—carbon black. Mixed into rubber by masticating machines, carbon black greatly increased tread life. Tires have been black ever since. Though improved, tire rubber still hardened with time, developing tread and sidewall cracks that let in moisture to rot the cotton casing. Plenty of work in rubber existed for new chemistry graduates now.

In 1917 Firestone was producing only 25 cord tires a day, the rest being built the old way. A year later, 25 tires had become 1,000. The revolution was established.

The earliest tires, and indeed Grand Prix auto racing tires through 1908, had slick treads like those of the solids they replaced. When the era of metal armor and rivets ended, their traction on loose surfaces was, however, remembered, and many auto and cycle tires had rivet-mimicking button patterns molded into their all-rubber treads. Because these small unbraced tread elements wore quickly, their size had to be increased. The big-button tires that resulted became the trials tires of the 1920s. In the United States, where roads were all dirt and usually rough, a Trials-Universal-type tread pattern had become popular by 1910, with a block-shaped tread element. Better from the wear standpoint, especially on hard roads, were ribbed patterns, which acknowledged the danger of side-slipping on wet or loose surfaces.

A completed tire carcass should be more than just layers of strong cloth casually stuck together with rubber cement. The fibers should stretch straight and parallel so they can share loads equally, and all pore space in the fabric should be solidly filled with rubber. Voids invite ply separation and blowout. Each layer of cord fabric must be insulated from those above and below it by a controlled thickness of rubber to prevent fiber-to-fiber chafing. Because no hand technique could supply the huge volume of ply sheet required by industry, big fast machines were developed. They passed the fabric over rollers to stretch and align it, then passed it through baths of rubber and solvent to prime it, finally to receive thin skim coats of uncured rubber sheet emerging from mills. After rubber-coating, the fabric passed through thickness-control rollers.

Ply pieces to be used in cord tire construction must have their fibers running diagonally to their long dimension, so that as successive plies build up on the form, each ply's fibers lie at a 90-degree angle to those of the plies above and below it, and at a 45-degree angle to the centerline of the green tire. The easy way to make such pieces without waste is to begin with ply sheet whose fibers do run parallel to its length, cut strips from it on the diagonal, and then lay these strips end-to-end to make a new continuous strip with its fibers now at a diagonal to its length.

Even greatly improved by cord construction, tires remained unreliable because vehicles and roads were improving also. Faster machines needed always more flex from their tires to absorb greater shocks, but it was hard to combine increased flexibility with adequate strength, life, and cool running temperature. Still too much rubber. Engineers knew thinner tires ran cooler, but thinner tires also required much stronger ply fabric; a few strong plies must do the work of many weaker ones. What would be a better fabric?

By 1920 a synthetic fiber of great promise emerged—rayon. Made from wood pulp by a complex process, it cost five to six dollars a pound. No one was going to make tires out of that. How about woolen tires? Anyone for hemp or flax tires? It seemed the only alternative was to improve the old standard, cotton.

As the fibers grow in the cotton plant they are three-quarters to one and a half inches long. To make thread, spinning machines pull and twist masses of them together. Friction determines the strength of thread, as the twist acts under tension to bind the fibers against one another. Even though the strength of individual cotton fibers is high, thread made from them does not reach nearly that level. If the threads were fully impregnated with rubber during the preparation of the ply sheets, however, the liquid rubber should act as a glue to prevent slippage of the fibers in a single thread—much as epoxy resin acts to bind together the carbon fibers in a composite part. Why wasn't that happening?

Firestone researchers discovered the problem. As the cord fabric dried after being impregnated with rubber dissolved in solvent, the evaporating solvent carried most of the rubber back *out* of the threads, leaving them less rubberized. A better-controlled drying process allowed the solvent to escape more gradually, leaving more rubber to hold the threads together. Much stronger cord fabric resulted, and Firestone called the process "Gum-Dipping."

Now engineers had the fabric they needed to create the tire they had long dreamed of—a tire that was mostly air. Using far fewer plies of the strong Gum-Dipped fabric, each tire would contain less heat-generating rubber. Being thinner, the heat path from within that rubber would be shorter, and this tire would run cool. Firestone called the new development the "balloon tire" because its section was so much larger than before. For a given outside diameter, the balloon tire had twice the internal air volume of the old, high-pressure tires, which made it softer. It had half as many carcass plies, ran at one-half the inflation pressure, and laid down approximately twice the footprint area. Because of its low operating temperature, the tread wore very slowly, so a less heavy tread was needed. Cars on balloon tires rode more comfortably than before and yet had much improved traction. Industry response to this development was overwhelming; within three years the balloon tire had driven the high-pressure tire out of existence.

Except on motorcycles. When tire makers attempted to build fatter tires for motorcycles, the lateral flexibility of the sidewalls produced instability. On two wheels, the advantage of processes like Gum-Dipping (every tire maker soon had its own version of this) was the possibility of using somewhat lower tire pressures. With the primitive suspension of the time this was often important; competitors at Brooklands, for instance, were advised to run lower tire pressures than on the road because otherwise track roughness became unmanageable. Without the flex-tolerance of the new fabric developments, this advice would only have invited blowouts and injury. Stronger fabric really provided a supplement to rigid and semi-rigid motorcycle suspensions.

Dunlop was busy now researching. Using instruments designed in-house, they studied the heat-generating properties of various rubber compounds as they flexed, using the information to develop special low hysteresis compounds to reduce tire heating even further. They also made a pivotal discovery in tire construction: Until this time it had been assumed that alternate fabric plies should cross each other at 90 degrees, just as do the interwoven threads in conventional canvas. Dunlop engineers questioned this assumption, building test tires with plies crossing at other angles. This, they found, dramatically altered tire performance. As the cord threads were angled to run more nearly *around* the tire, it became stiffer riding, faster-responding in steering, more powerful in cornering grip, and cooler-running. Making the cords run more nearly across the tire gave a more comfortable, more sluggish and less grippy tire that ran hotter. Using its discoveries Dunlop produced a highly successful new generation of racing tires, and its production tires naturally benefited as well.

At the same time Michelin was running its own complete series of cord-angle experiments and drawing its own conclusions.

All was not yet blue skies for the balloon tire concept. With the larger cross-section, the rubber now made up a larger percentage of the wheel diameter, magnifying any out-of-roundness or lack of balance in the finished tire. As better vehicles and better road increased traffic speeds, this further magnified tire problems. Result? Wheel tramp and shimmy with the new, fatter tires—problems that better quality control, improved methods, and new kinds of vehicle suspensions would soon cure. The motivation was there.

In 1925 Pete DePaolo won the Indianapolis 500 on the new Firestone balloon tires, setting a new record. The larger footprint gave better car control and increased corner speeds by a solid five miles per hour.

By 1926 passenger-car tire life had increased to 12,000 miles. Furthermore, motorizing the tire-building drum and making it able to collapse to release the green tire had sped up tire production time. Now the labor content of a tire was only 10 percent of what it had originally been. Tires were affordable.

A better cure accelerator with the fine, mouth-filling name of mercap-tobenzothiazole, now prevented rubber from hardening. In fact, an entire range of chemical additives arose to better control curing and aging.

As drivers now trusted their vehicles in all kinds of weather and drove more often on hard roads, the rib-tread designs popular in the early 1920s yielded to further refinement; with more power and speed, vehicles needed ribbing across the tread as well as around it. The result was the popular block pattern treads of the mid- and late 1920s. Such rear tires often had two or more rows of blocks down the tread center, flanked by ribs. Cars and motorcycles from 1930 onward had much improved brakes, and operators began to brake and turn simultaneously, or turn and accelerate, putting *diagonal* stress into tire treads. Diagonal tread elements emerged, better braced to resist these diagonal forces without bending and wearing quickly. They also drained better in the wet; the German Continental Tire Company pioneered this particular development.

Indeed, high-speed motoring on wet highways made aquaplaning and skidding severe problems. The squeegee, or fine-groove tread patterns introduced by several European tire makers in the early 1930s, attempted to deal with them.

As World War II loomed on the time horizon, and the European community polarized into opposing sides, the intense motor racing competition of the time on two and four wheels reflected this nationalism. The era of unlimited supercharged competition was at hand, and the tire makers would be forced to a fever pitch of development to equal the pace. In short order, however, they would have to cope with a new possibility: When war cut off all supplies of natural rubber—of what would tires then be made?

# Cars & Bikes & Planes: Anti-Lock Braking

*Only now are ABS systems matching the braking of professional riders. Don't be disappointed! As* Cycle World's *test director Don Canet recently observed, "It took me five tries to improve on Honda's C-ABS. But in an accident situation, I don't think you get that many."*

In most panic-stop situations, steering is just as important as stopping quickly. With steering control, you can dodge objects you might otherwise hit. Unfortunately, the lateral grip available for steering diminishes as you ask more and more stopping force from the tire. As an overbraked tire locks completely, stopping force decreases and lateral grip vanishes; steering control goes away, and the operator becomes a helpless hostage of his own kinetic energy.

An experienced individual in a panic braking situation "pumps" the brakes—brings line pressure up high enough to provoke incipient locking, then releases it just enough to regain steering control—in a rapidly repeating cycle until he avoids the hazard or stops the vehicle. This is anti-lock braking at its simplest. Engineers, naturally, believed automatic devices could do it better. There were two goals; first, to preserve steering control, and, second, to shorten stopping distances, especially on slick surfaces.

Automatic anti-lock braking systems appeared first on expensive mass transportation equipment (aircraft, trains), filtering down to private vehicles only later. The higher the cost of smashing up, the fancier and more expensive the prevention can be. Aircraft anti-lock systems appeared in the 1950s to get fast-landing jets stopped safely on short runways built for propeller aircraft.

In the 1960s, American brake manufacturers offered simple anti-lock systems on some cars. These vacuum-powered systems operated only on the rear wheels of Ford and GM prestige cars, and on all four wheels of certain Chrysler products. More than shortening stopping distances, they were intended to prevent loss of steering control. Because proportioning valves (devices that automatically divide braking effort between front and rear brakes) did this job with greater cost-effectiveness, U.S.-made anti-lock systems did not develop.

European driving puts great demands on braking. Traffic is heavy, bad weather frequent, and speeds often double those in the U.S. in 1967. Bosch in Germany began research on automotive ABS systems, and by 1978 it was available on certain production cars. Again, the main goal was to prevent loss of steering control. Early systems cycled slowly between locked and unlocked states, so their braking effort averaged over time was no better than a skilled driver could achieve. Research continued, primarily in automobiles; being heavier, more complicated, and expensive than motorcycles, cars were better engineering and commercial subjects for ABS.

By 1985, the Bosch system was in use on 600,000 cars worldwide. At present, the Bosch III ABS is capable of cycling 15 times per second; instead of jumping back and forth between the locked and free states (averaging to a poor rate of retardation), it oscillates rapidly near the edge of tire grip and holds the average rate of stopping very close to the maximum attainable. This system improves on the stopping performances of even expert drivers.

The earlier Bosch II system was designed as an add-on for existing auto brake systems. The modulator unit (the device which varies brake line pressure to achieve ABS operation) could be installed between the vehicle's standard vacuum-boosted master cylinder and the separate brake lines to the wheels. Each wheel, which had a rotating toothed ring—the exciter—and a stationary sensor, could report its speed to the computer.

The Cadillac Allante's Bosch ABS III is an integrated system, combining the functions of master cylinder and ABS modulator in a single electro-hydraulic unit. ABS III does away with brake boost from engine-intake vacuum, replacing vacuum with hydraulic power from a pump driven by an electric motor. Should the engine stall, the system operates normally; ABS III also works on diesel vehicles which have no source of engine vacuum.

The pump charges a large-volume accumulator with brake fluid at high pressure, starting up when accumulator pressure falls below a threshold value. The system provides "power brakes"; that is, hydraulic pressure from the accumulator gives stopping power with low pedal effort.

ABS operation is as follows:

(1) The computer detects incipient locking of a wheel when its deceleration rate exceeds a certain level. The level chosen is significantly higher than any foreseeable peak deceleration rate for the whole vehicle.

(2) The computer closes a solenoid-powered hydraulic valve, isolating the fluid line to the locking wheel and preventing any further pressure rise from reaching it. The computer again monitors the wheel's deceleration rate; if the rate falls below locking level, the isolation valve re-opens. If the wheel's deceleration rate remains above locking level, the computer opens a dump valve, allowing fluid to escape from the brake line of the locking wheel. The dumped fluid drops into the modulator's sump, where it's forced back into the accumulator the next time the pump operates.

(3) With braking pressure reduced, the locking wheel's deceleration rate drops again below the set level.

(4) When this happens, the dump valve closes and the high-pressure accumulator injects fluid into the brake line. This initial shot is injected at a high flow rate, and for the most part restores line pressure. Then, a quick series of tiny shots adjusts the line pressure until the wheel's deceleration rate again exceeds the set level.

The computer counts how many of these tiny shots it takes to reach the set level of wheel deceleration, and compares the total with a value in its memory. If too many steps were required, the next cycle's initial shot will be increased in volume. If too few were taken, the first shot will be decreased. This makes system operation adaptive—able to optimize the size of the initial shot to make the system operate at its best rate on varied surfaces.

(5) The dump valve opens again and the cycle repeats.

On a very slippery surface, such as ice or packed snow, wheel lock-up may occur so gradually that wheel deceleration never exceeds the set level. A simple system would ignore this potentially dangerous condition. Bosch III calculates, from consideration of all four wheel speeds, an estimated vehicle speed. The computer compares each of the wheel speeds with this estimate, and if any wheel is slipping by more than a safe percentage, ABS operation begins on that line to bring the wheel's slip rate back to a safe value.

The system can accommodate differences in tire quality and road grip. The set level for wheel deceleration is chosen higher than any foreseeable combination of sports tires and high-traction surface could give. If this were not so, the system might unlock a wheel or wheels just because the entire car was stopping faster than the computer had been "told" was possible.

Because a car has two tracks, it's possible for its left wheels to have more grip than its right wheels, or vice versa. Such lack of symmetry in brake force gives rise to a yaw torque, and the vehicle tends to rotate toward the more highly braked side. ABS prevents this as follows: When the computer detects the beginning of a difference in ABS action on the two rear wheels, it limits braking of the wheel on the better surface to what is being used on the other rear. Because the rear wheels are several feet behind the fronts, the fact that they continue to turn gives enough lateral grip to prevent vehicle yaw. Since the front wheels account for most of the braking force in panic stops, sacrificing some rear braking power is acceptable.

Three channels control the four wheels of a rear-drive car. This is possible because the two rear wheels are mechanically connected in the differential. A single exciter-sensor can be mounted on the ring-gear or driveshaft, or a transmission-mounted sensor may share its information between the speedometer and rear-wheel ABS channel. On a front-drive car such as the Cadillac Allante, the rear wheels are not mechanically joined and so must be braked by independent ABS channels, as in front. This requires a four-channel system.

To prevent total system failure from master-cylinder defect or leakage, all auto brake systems have been split since the early 1960s. On a rear-drive car, half of a divided master-cylinder controls the front-wheel brakes; the other half operates the rears. Front-drive cars are more commonly split diagonally. Split systems are the rule with ABS as well. On a motorcycle, of course, front and rear systems are separate. One notable exception to this is the Moto Guzzi integrated braking system, which operates one front disc and the rear brake from the rider's brake pedal, and the second front disc from the right hand-lever. On Dr. John Wittner's Pro Twins roadrace Guzzi, there is no rear brake pedal, and the rear brake operates through a proportioning valve from the front master cylinder. These are both non-ABS systems.

In early 1988, BMW announced that delivery of ABS-equipped BMW motorcycles would begin, and that the system would add $1,200 to the bike's price. Developed by FAG-Kugelfischer with BMW, the K100RS's ABS is quite different from automotive systems. Like car setups, the BMW's uses exciter-sensor packages to report wheel speed, but instead of dumping fluid out of a locking wheel's brake line, the motorcycle has in effect a second master cylinder in parallel with the rider's master cylinder. When a wheel's deceleration rate exceeds the set level, a valve isolates the rider's master cylinder, and the second, computer-controlled master cylinder takes over braking. A powerful solenoid pulls back the piston—just enough to allow wheel deceleration rate to fall back to a safe level. Once this happens, the solenoid-powered master cylinder pushes the fluid back into the line—quickly at first, then gradually—until the wheel again exceeds the maximum deceleration level. This cycle repeats until the machine has slowed to 2.5 mph (or until the pressure signal from the rider decreases enough to terminate ABS action). The two ABS modulators are mounted one above each passenger footpeg. Each one, the size of a starter motor, weighs about nine pounds. The energy requirement is about 300 watts per channel during ABS operation.

In both the car and bike ABS, complete system breakdown is fail-passive. Coil springs in both types return all hydraulic valves to positions that restore normal non-ABS braking. In the case of Bosch III, the fluid stored in the accumulator will operate the system for a time after a pump failure.

Both systems are also self-checking. Bosch III uses a single computer which tests itself once when the vehicle is started, and thereafter monitors its input and output signals to verify that they are within proper limits. If there is a deviation, ABS switches off, a warning light comes on, and braking reverts to manual. The motorcycle system uses two computers, so the system is fail-safe even though one computer might go haywire. One computer is on ABS operation while the other is being tested, and the two reverse roles every 10 seconds. Should one computer fail, a warning light comes on and the other takes over. The use of fewer parts and greater electronic redundancy is appropriate to the motorcycle's greater need for stability.

Like the automotive Bosch III, the FAG system on BMW motorcycles also computes estimated vehicle speed and can use this as a reference in case of slow lock-up on very slippery surfaces. Since motorcycles are single-tracked, there are no yaw problems so long as braking takes place straight up.

Motorcycles have some unique braking problems: First, there's nearly 100 percent weight transfer during peak braking. Motorcycles are tall and have short wheelbases, so a deceleration rate of slightly over 1 G will transfer all weight to the front wheel. With little weight on the rear wheel, and with engine rotating mass and compression braking added in, ABS operation at the rear wheel becomes complicated. To prevent confusion, the computer compares deceleration rates of front and rear wheels during ABS braking, and adjusts rear slip rate to that of the front.

Another aspect of the motorcycle braking problem relates to a bike's large wheel mass compared to its total weight. When a wheel—especially the lightly loaded rear—has begun to lock and the ABS system has reduced its brake line pressure, there is a time-lag while that wheel accelerates. The heavier the wheel is in relation to the weight it carries, the longer the time-lag and the more slowly the system will cycle. This is especially important on low-traction surfaces, or, as noted above, at the rear during hard deceleration.

Automotive systems can be used during cornering, but owners of BMW motorcycles with ABS are cautioned against panic braking in corners. Because lateral grip drops as brake loading increases, a motorcycle that is overbraked in a turn—with or without ABS—will run wide or fall. For the moment at least, braking a motorcycle in a turn still calls for expert human judgment.

Automobile ABS systems are beginning to employ lateral acceleration sensors, which inform the computer of sudden loss of lateral grip. This grip loss may be at one end, causing the car to yaw suddenly, or it may occur at both ends simultaneously, in which case the car will run wide in a corner. In either circumstance, ABS operation would limit braking to a level that kept lateral acceleration within desired limits. Clearly, this higher level of function can also be applied to motorcycles, but the problem is more difficult. Motorcycles have very low yaw polar moments of inertia; once grip is lost at one end, the machine switches ends much faster than does a longer, heavier car. This would call for extremely fast ABS action to prevent a fall or a heart-stopping slide.

The reverse of ABS—traction or spin control—is relatively easily added once ABS sensors are in place. First employed on buses in snowy countries, such systems initially brake any drive wheel that accelerates faster than it should, then control engine torque in any variety of ways. Some systems use a throttle positioner; in others, ignition is retarded or made intermittent until the slippage subsides. Response times are of the order of 0.1–0.2 second.

Such acceleration control would also be a natural for motorcycles, whose power-to-weight ratios make them liable to spin or wheelie easily. An experienced rider might do better than even such a sophisticated system, however, because of his ability to learn and so anticipate conditions—rather than merely respond to them.

ABS has made little impression in racing. Porsche tested ABS on racing cars in the early 1970s but has not adopted it for competition. Racers are conservative where reliability is concerned; they want to see solid performance advantages from anything that adds weight and complexity. (Remember the Racer's Golden Rule: simplify, and add lightness.) Since race cars are operated by skilled drivers in top physical condition, who expect emergencies, there is far less need for ABS.

On the other hand, anyone with a license can operate a highway vehicle. Operators come in all ages, all physical abilities, all experience levels. Their behavior in emergencies is a consideration. A car driver, faced with an accident threat, frequently locks up all four wheels. ABS will make a difference for this driver, stopping the car quickly and under control. Accident statistics show a different pattern for motorcyclists: 33 percent of riders did nothing when faced with accident threat and a further 20 percent made a wrong response. The following points are noteworthy:

(1) ABS will not help the rider who "freezes at the controls" and makes no attempt to stop or maneuver during a collision threat.

(2) Riders who ignorantly use only the rear brake will find ABS of little help, though the system will prevent rear-wheel lockup and a possible fall. Use of the rear brake alone gives only 30 percent of peak braking power.

(3) ABS can't help riders who don't brake hard enough to trigger ABS operation. Most riders, according to a BMW-funded study, don't get hard on the brakes instantly when an accident threatens; instead, they gradually increase their braking, but only up to about 70 percent of the possible maximum. This type of half-hearted braking will not trigger ABS operation. BMW believes that riders using ABS will gain confidence in their braking, and so will commit to full braking at first threat of collision. It is essential for all riders—whether on ABS-equipped bikes or not—to practice hard braking frequently to maintain this essential skill.

For these reasons, ABS will have a less immediate impact on motorcycle accident statistics than on automobile. The machines on which it is being first offered—heavy tourers—are already ridden mainly by conservative and experienced riders. Human software, not advanced hardware, will remain the deciding factor in safety. A rider's proudest possession should be riding skills, and anyone, no matter what kind of machine he or she owns, can acquire and improve these skills.

# Two-Wheel Steering

*This is one of my favorites, for it promises to combine quick steering with a wheelbase long enough to brake or accelerate significantly harder than is possible with the present 54- or 56-inch sportbike wheelbase. I know an engineer who has made significant progress with this idea, so there's hope. But maybe the public, which knows what a motorcycle should look like, would find it just too weird.*

The subtle sensation of the Tokyo Motor Show was one feature of Yamaha's Morpho II show bike: two-wheel steering.

Do I hear a few "so whats" and "ho-hums?" I wouldn't blame you. The auto industry, with vast ballyhoo, introduced four-wheel steering a couple of years ago, but the results have been substantially less than revolutionary. Why should bikes with two-wheel steering be any different?

Here is why. When the driver of a car initiates a turn, he steers into the turn and the front of the car reacts almost instantly, being accelerated laterally by the side-thrust of its front tires. This swings the chassis, steering the rear wheels, and soon the entire vehicle is turning the corner in a steady state.

On a bike, the whole process is vastly delayed by the necessity of first rolling the machine over into its turning attitude—by countersteering. Only then can the front end "turn-in" in the same sense that a car does. To shorten this roll-over delay, motorcycles are given the lightest possible steering (minimum trail and rake angle, minimum gyro-mass front wheels) and extremely short wheelbases.

This works, but there is a price to be paid for it in reduced stability. Steep steering-head angles, reduced trail, and smaller front wheels all speed up steering—and they all make machines twitchier too. Conservative-minded English bike-dynamics researcher Geoffrey Rowe believes some modern sport bikes and all race bikes are too twitchy for most riders.

In any control system, stability and responsiveness are opposed qualities. If you make the system extremely stable (a 1970s Ducati, for example), then it resists the operator's efforts to control it just as strongly as it rejects undesirable inputs such as bumps. If you now make the system very responsive (a modern 400 sport bike), it responds not only to you, the rider, but to every little breeze and bump.

At their best, modern sport bikes are a tolerable compromise between responsiveness and stability, but the definition of responsiveness keeps changing. Last year's best becomes this year's third choice. Development—and users' preferences—alter standards. Just before World War II, full elevator control in U.S. training aircraft required 18 inches of stick movement. Any less and pilots complained of twitchy response. Five years later, 7 inches was regarded as generous. Twenty years ago, Ducatis with 4.5 inches of trail and 31 degrees of rake were considered to have sporty steering; now, the same machines are perceived as charming period locomotives.

As a motorcycle is countersteered by its rider, the front tire contact patch develops a side thrust. Because the patch is not directly under the machine's center of mass, but is ahead of it, this has the effect of both dragging the front of the machine sideways (out of the turn direction) and beginning to roll the bike over (into the turn direction). This lateral movement at the front acts on the wheelbase, using it as a lever to steer the rear wheel as well. It, too, begins after some delay to develop side thrust. Now both tires steer out from under the machine, causing it to roll over in the desired direction. The machine is stopped from crashing over on its side by reversing the side-thrusts of the two tires, balancing gravity against centrifugal force.

Note the importance, in this description, of the machine's wheelbase: It is the lever that steers the rear wheel. A given lateral movement of the front tire in countersteer will swing a short wheelbase through a bigger angle than it will a longer wheelbase. This is why, to make machines steer quickly, ultra-short wheelbases are used—wheelbases so short that sacrifices are made in other performance areas to achieve them.

What sacrifices? A short wheelbase limits the rates of both acceleration and braking. With grippy modern tires, twisting the throttle or pulling the brake lever too hard will stand the machine up—either on its rear wheel or its front wheel—and it can't accelerate or brake any harder than that. If bikes could be built on longer wheelbases and somehow still steer quickly, they could accelerate harder in lower gears and brake harder—without performing wheelies or stoppies.

Two-wheel steering will fix this. When the rider initiates a turn by countersteering, both wheels will turn in the same direction simultaneously, jerking the rug out from under both ends of the machine together, causing instant roll-over. Wheelbase will be completely irrelevant to the speed of this maneuver.

How might it work? (Yamaha isn't telling us yet.) Initially, both wheels will steer together. The rider will countersteer until the machine is snapping over as fast as desired, and then relax his pressure on the bars in normal fashion. The rear wheel will then follow the front in returning to center, but then lock there until the rider makes another large-amplitude steering movement. Turn-in will be manual, as with a conventional bike. In effect, both wheels will steer together for rapid roll maneuvers, while the front alone will control the machine for slower maneuvers or for fine control. With this system, wheelbase can be chosen to maximize acceleration/deceleration ability—without slowing the steering.

At the recent WERA Atlanta roadraces, I asked Kenny Roberts about the Morpho II and its two-wheeled steering. He instantly replied, "That thing could give Grand Prix bikes a whole new shape," and launched into discussion of the possibilities. There is a lot more to KR as team manager than being an avuncular riding coach. He has a finger in pies we don't even imagine.

Other solutions to the wheelie/stoppie problem exist. One that has been considered is variable-height suspension. When running on the straight—accelerating, cruising, or braking—the suspension will hold the machine at a low ride height, maximizing its resistance to standing up. Initial review of such a system shows that it might be worth as much as 2 seconds per lap at Daytona. And we all know what improved braking can sometimes be worth on the street.

As the rider rolls the variable ride height bike over for a corner, stored onboard hydraulic pressure will raise the ride height in proportion to lean angle, keeping the parts off the asphalt. Although this sounds upsetting and weird, if the height change occurs during roll-over, it will actually smooth the maneuver; as a normal bike rolls over, its center of mass falls, momentarily taking some weight off its tires at a very inconvenient moment. As the VRH bike rolls over, its suspension will extend, limiting this tire-unweighting.

Beyond that lies active suspension, which is no longer just a curiosity on Formula 1 cars. The Morpho II is so equipped, and it is a working option on such cars as the Nissan Q45.

Purists will write in, as they always do, complaining that the growth of complexity will take all the interest out of motorcycling. But is the human mind complex? Is it interesting?

# TDC: A Short
# History of Chassis Flex

*I'm staring at the last paragraph of this piece—the one about the computer generating N structures, providing X lateral compliance. I just now got back from BMW's S1000RR Superbike intro, where engineer Stefan Zeit described just such a process.*

Motorcycle chassis have always flexed. The earliest motorbicycles flexed so much that they broke their frames, so bigger and heavier-walled tubing was tried until durability improved. We've been experimenting ever since.

At various times, inventors hit upon the idea of building motorcycle chassis as bridges. These were built—as stiff, triangulated structures whose properties could be calculated. It failed to catch on, probably because the resulting stiff ride was so rough that no one could stand it. On the other hand it was clear that tail-wagging, occurring as chain-pull hauled the rear wheel to one side, was very upsetting because it destroyed stability. To counter this, "stays" were added—extra longitudinal members joining the rear axle to the gearbox. This made it clear that stiffness had its uses.

In the 1920s and 1930s, the girder fork was supreme—a pair of uprights made from small-diameter tubing, bolted to the front axle below, and moving up and down on four forward-facing swing-links joined to the steering head above. Such forks were stiff enough fore and aft but flexed laterally so much, especially in sidecar use, that the front tire might rub the

Lee Klancher

insides of the girders during hard cornering. Sometimes lateral stays were added to the girders, and sometimes riders just put up with the uncertainty.

Vincent guru Sid Biberman relates that one day in the 1930s a newly finished Douglas dirt track racer was found to hook up on the company's test track exceptionally well. What could be the cause? Measurements were taken but nothing was found amiss—until one practical person pointed out that the engine bolts had never been tightened! When they were, the mysterious handling excellence disappeared. This and doubtless many other such accidental experiences created a hazy idea that somehow, making a chassis too stiff might not be a good thing. It wasn't science, but it wasn't wrong, either.

Just before and after World War II it was clear that some kind of suspension at both ends would take over from the girder/hardtail frame concept. Bikes were now too fast to stay hooked up while their tires bounced and hammered over rough pavement. Rex McCandless gathered up the best of the possibilities into the chassis he built for Norton's 1950 TT effort. This chassis—later named "Featherbed" for its smooth ride—employed hydraulic damping at both ends with a swingarm rear suspension and telescopic front. The soft, bump-eating qualities of this classic design would obscure the chassis flex issue for a long time. Suspension flex was king!

Specialist frame-builders in England retained the idea that chassis flex is hard to avoid, and that it's usually better to let at least some occur than try to brace a chassis so much that it fails instead. Yamaha's illustrious TZ750 roadracer underscored this point by always cracking its frame tubes in the same places. If it didn't, your rider wasn't riding hard enough! Meanwhile, the slick-tire revolution took place and grip shot up, obsoleting flabby pipe frames by making them wobble. Stiffness to the rescue! During the 1980s, chassis stiffness increased rapidly, first in Grand Prix racing where it seemed to be the key to stability, and then on streetbikes. Occasionally, disturbing things happened to confuse the issue. When one of Yamaha's 250cc Grand Prix bikes refused to hook up at an early 1990s event, a crewman who remembered the murmured truths of the past took a hacksaw to the frame. On that particular track, the result was good. Elsewhere? Not so good.

Through the 1990s, talk about chassis flex was limited to whispers, and when highly paid handling consultants in desperation sawed through swingarm bracing or deleted a cross-tube here and there, no papers were published in learned journals. Destroying the stiffness all had worked so hard to create seemed somehow shameful, a sacrilege.

In the late 1990s, Honda took up the cause with its customary enthusiasm, producing some test and race bikes that seemed like Jell-O to riders raised on rigidity. Team managers spoke cautiously to journalists about a search for "good chassis flex," as opposed to "bad" flex.

Was a hooked-up chassis to remain a happy accident forever? Would there never be an underlying theory that could tie all wishes and suspicions together? As recently as 2002, major companies seem to have been still at the level of the 1930s Douglas dirt-tracker—finding accidental value in loose or deliberately missing engine bolts. But the secret work was gaining respectability as it discovered more things that worked, and even some inkling of why. Single-sided swingarms have a killer high-tech look that's hard to reject, but when they flexed they also did some unpredictable steering of their own. Upsetting! And so old, uncool-looking twin-beam swingarms were brought back. When these flexed sideways, their symmetrical beams acted like parallelogram links to keep the rear wheel on a constant heading. Stability! Now it was possible to think about increasing their twist resistance by making the beams deeper vertically, while controlling their lateral "spring constant" by varying beam lateral thickness.

I think we are now moving into an era in which the front of the main frame will provide the same lateral compliance for the front wheel. This is more complex because the large leverage of the long fork tubes greatly complicates the avoidance of twist. This may be an ideal problem to be investigated by Finite Element Analysis, now a well-developed technique with an established cadre of "FEA jocks."

Computer, please generate for me a family of N structures which provide X lateral compliance, while keeping steering-head twist within Y tolerance. And now I hit Return, and begin to think vaguely of where to go for lunch.

# *Part 3*

# GEARHEAD GENIUSES

*John Owen*

# Morbidelli: On the Cutting Edge of Two-Stroke Technology

*This particular battle is now history. Two-strokes rose and now have fallen, victims of not having invented direct injection quite soon enough to save them from their own considerable emissions. I've enjoyed the whole process, all the same.*

I maneuvered the van into a space in Connecticut's Thompson Speedway pits and shut off the engine. A breathless face appeared at the window.

"Come quick!"

The owner of the face turned and started to lope off across the parking area. He looked back impatiently at me over his shoulder.

"A Morbidelli in that van over here! Come on!"

I swung out of the seat and sprinted after him.

A moment later we peered through smoked windows at a tiny machine, enshrined in the gloom. Certainly a Morbidelli 125 roadracer. There were the distinctive tank, the gold magnesium fork sliders, and Campagnolo magnesium wheels, the tiny twin front discs. The fairing bulged suggestively to clear the carburetors jutting unseen from the sides of the engine.

Presently the owner appeared, Peter Grufstedt, who has been variously a competition rider, a public relations specialist for Suzuki's European roadrace team, and a gentleman farmer. His new $5,700 Morbidelli was bound for Bonneville for record attempts, and here only for running-in and familiarization. Would I like to do a story about the machine? Yes, please.

Morbidelli is hardly a household word for Americans, for this Italian company manufactures woodworking machinery. It has also won the World 125cc Roadracing Championship the last three years with its sophisticated twins. Grufstedt's machine was a privateer replica, one of a limited production run by the factory.

When you think of success in Grand Prix motorcycle racing, what images do you conjure up? Automated production lines spewing out untold number of machines to world markets? Rows of test cells, ranks of saluting technicians in company caps, singing the company song? And perhaps on top of all this, the works racing team, the bright banner of image-making, the creature of sales policy?

Such may be the rule, but there are exceptions. Morbidelli is an exception. Giancarlo Morbidelli is a mechanical designer whose work created the company that bears his name. His machinery is used in the production of furniture, and it must work well indeed, for he is prosperous. The racing motorcycles? Only a sideline. There is no related product line to advertise on the racing circuits of Europe. None, that is, unless you can imagine potential buyers of woodworking machinery doing their shopping at the Italian Grand Prix.

The traditional economic motivation for racing must somehow be missing. Like the long tradition of racing success at MV Agusta, racing at Morbidelli is the result of one man's will. He likes to build racing motorcycles.

Morbidelli has one dynamometer and one racing engineer, whose only computer fits into the palm of his hand and runs on batteries. There are few technicians and it's doubtful if they do very much saluting. The 125cc Grand Prix racers they have built are simply the best in the world today.

Pete Grufstedt agreed to a track test by rider Richard Schlachter and to a tear down for measurement and photography by myself.

Richard rode the machine in practice at the spring Bridgehampton club races. Performance was very impressive, approximately equal with a decent private Yamaha 250, with the engine coming clean at 10,000 rpm, continuing to the power peak at about 13,500, then cutting off sharply at 14,000. You might expect this from a 35-horsepower machine that weighs only 176 pounds. It had very powerful

*John Owen*

brakes, no handling vices (though for obvious reasons he didn't press too hard), and generally confirmed the European experience, where Morbidelli 125 lap times are frequently as good as those of the 250 class.

The machine had been conservatively supplied from the factory with very cold Champion N80-G spark plugs, and it was a tribute to the clean combustion and sharp carburetion of this machine that it was able to clear and run on such cold numbers.

The real fascination began for me when I got the engine into my shop. Almost without exception, each part removed showed deliberate thought at the hand of experience, a great contrast with the "Shotgun R&D" evident in mass-produced articles. Although a piece of machinery's national origin can often be identified by an experienced person, these Morbidelli pieces were not discernibly German, English, or Japanese. They were just very, very good. The engine teardown was a gourmet delight.

The 57-pound powerplant is ordinary in its simplicity. There are no design surprises, no radical deviations from current trends—just tremendous quality and harmonious use of available technology.

The engine is a side-by-side 44 x 41mm twin with separate water-cooled cylinders inclined forward at a steep 45 degrees. From either side of the crankcase projects a shortened and reworked 28mm Mikuni carburetor, each serving its own rotary disc intake valve. Ignition is by battery-powered Kröber total-loss CDI. Power passes by strong straight-cut primary gears to an impressively over-designed dry, all-metal clutch, then back into the case to the 250-sized six-speed CIMA gearset. This engine gives 35–36 bhp at 13,200 rpm for a BMEP of more than 140 psi, higher than the best of the complex Grand Prix racers of the 1960s. And this is not even the works engine—just an over-the-counter production-racer replica. The works engine gives an additional 6 or 7 horsepower.

Before removing the heads, I measured the compression ratio. It was 8.5:1, measured down to the top of the exhaust port, or 17.3 on the full stroke. This is a very high ratio, yet the heads were unmarked by detonation even after 250 miles of running on local gasoline. The heads are unexceptional in that they have conventional circular geometry with a gentle transition from a thin squish band to a shallow combustion chamber.

The cylinders are perfect jewels of excellence, made by the very experienced German Mahle firm, and coated for wear resistance not with the usual chromium plate, but with the new nickel/silicon carbide matrix called Nikasil. A single large exhaust port opens at a very early 77 percent ATDC with a width of 32mm. (This is 73 percent of the bore—remember when 65 percent was considered radical?) The four transfer ports open 32 degrees later at 109 degrees ATDC.

An extremely critical area in a two-stroke cylinder is the top edges of the transfer ports. Here, the bore plating often piles up in manufacturing to leave irregular ridges which can and do skew the transfer flow and reduce power. The Morbidelli cylinders are carefully handworked at the factory to eliminate this problem.

The two main transfers are backflowed at 25 degrees and hug the piston crown until their flow meets on the cylinder centerline. The two back ports are steeply inclined up and forwards.

The Mahle forged pistons showed almost no wear after their 250 miles of running. The original machining marks were intact over the entire piston surface. A single conventional 1mm piston ring is used on each.

Removing the cylinders revealed the crank, which advertised its designer's care by the striking slimness of its connecting rods. Bearing loads are proportional to the weight of the reciprocating and rotating parts, and to the square of rpm. The 41mm stroke and moderate peak rpm give this engine a modest 3,600-feet-per-minute piston speed at peak, and the tiny rods and light pistons keep the weight to a minimum.

This crank is an expensive item—$630. Obviously the company subscribes to a much different philosophy than most makers of production racers. These Morbidelli cranks are guaranteed for 20 Grand Prix races, a far longer lifetime than other racing engines enjoy. There is design everywhere here—the crankpins are smaller than usual, which is possible because the reciprocating parts are so light. Small pins also mean small, light bearings which resist the skidding that kills two-stroke big-end bearings.

The working space for the conrods is smoothly accessible to the incoming fresh charge, with the inner edges of the flywheels chamfered, as though the designer considered the crank a part of the transfer ports. It is.

All the bearings are made by the German INA firm. The ball bearing mains have fatigue-resistant plastic cages rather than the failure-prone riveted steel separators that have caused other brands so much trouble. The rod bearings are the Dürkopp pattern, with tiny needles separated by light, silver-plated M-section steel cages.

The rods are perhaps two-thirds the weight of those in comparable machines, show much handwork, and are pierced with by two huge cooling slots in each big end. They are nice pieces indeed.

The aluminum crankcase halves give strong support to the crank, carrying it in non-magnetic hard metal inserts. Crank support has recently

*John Owen*

been identified as a real source of power, for flexing and bending of engine and crank lead to measurable losses. The cases are cast in sand by Ferrari (yes, the very same Ferrari) and they are sound. Much of their internal surface is machined, and in all this shining expanse of finished metal there is not one defect or bit of porosity to be seen. Sensibly, the finning of these cases runs front-to-back, parallel with the direction of air movement.

Fitted compactly behind the crank is the CIMA gearset. Every gear has tapered teeth to reduce oil churning losses, every set of engaging dogs is undercut to make certain of gear changes. The finish is outstanding. All of the free-spinning gears run, not directly on the shafts beneath, but on needle rollers. Below, the conventional shift drum drives Yamaha shifter forks to select the six speeds.

Perched atop the gearbox and driven from it is the small water pump. Since this engine is cooled by the same aluminum radiator supplied to Yamaha for their TZ250/350 racers, there is plenty of cooling capacity. The thermostat is in a separate housing spliced into the water lines.

The thin, steel rotary valves are held to their hubs by high-tensile screws, then to the crank by heavy keys. These have been problem areas for other brands, but not here. Opening comes at 150 degrees BTDC, closing at a late 79 degrees ATDC. The discs seal crankcase pressure against their covers which are cast in solid, heavy bronze. The reliable, wear-free seal of steel on bronze is more important than weight.

Nestled under the left-hand carburetor is the pulse-generator assembly for the Kröber ignition, sending firing impulses to the remotely mounted control box.

The clutch uses friction plates of a sintered copper alloy coating, much like those used in Suzuki and Kawasaki 750 racing clutches. There is nearly as much area here as in a 750, and the spring pressure is very heavy. To deal with this pressure, the release mechanism is an expensive and precisely made ball screw. As a result, the bullet-proof clutch is easy to operate.

The conventional chassis is made for Morbidelli in chromium-molybdenum alloy steel tubing by Benelli Armi. It is isolated from much engine vibration by rubber inserts in the crankcases. The front fork is a very light Marzocchi, as are the gas pressurized rear shocks. Brakes are Brembo, wheels are narrow WM-1.5 Campagnolo magnesium castings, and tires are Michelin M-38 block tread design for lightweight machines.

It's all very well to recite this litany of praise for dimensions well-chosen and concepts well-thought-out, but how has this happened? Why a woodworking machinery company?

During the classic years of European Grand Prix racing in the 1960s it was impossible for a small firm to make any impression. The Japanese Big Four had the resources to pursue horsepower without reservation, and at the end the dominant machine in the 125cc class was the four-cylinder, disc-valve Yamaha, making over 40 bhp at 17,600 rpm, delivered through a 10-speed gearbox.

By 1969 it was all history. The big companies had withdrawn and the FIM had limited 125 and 250cc machines to two cylinders and six speeds, 50cc machines to one cylinder and six speeds. The smaller companies could now hope to make their contribution to the sport.

Giancarlo Morbidelli tried his hand at racing on a Benelli 50, then funded development of his own 50 and 125cc machines through the early 1970s.

The trend of design was fixed by history, for when the FIM axe fell, the only available twin-cylinder machines were a few ex-works Suzukis and Kawasakis. These were adapted to run with only six speeds, and as parts supplies dried up, these old works bikes were gradually reborn as local products with improvements and improvisations. One such Suzuki 125 twin came to Morbidelli about 1971 and served as a basis for future Morbidelli roadracers.

Considerable ingenuity had to be exercised to get these old narrow-powerband engines to work well with the reduced number of transmission speeds, but championships were won and engineering lessons were learned. Morbidelli pressed on, always promising, but with real success just out of reach. Something more was needed.

The Dutch firm of Van Veen had long been the importer of the German Kreidler mopeds and had been involved in Kreidler's 50cc Grand Prix racing program. The new FIM rules were less of a handicap for them because their engines had never enjoyed more than one cylinder. With the departure of the multi-cylinder Japanese opposition, the Van Veen Kreidler emerged as a potent force in 50cc Grand Prixs, and the man responsible for its engineering was Jörg Möller. This man was thus at a strong focus in the transition from the old era of 10, 12, or even 18 speeds and ultra-narrow powerbands to the new era of only 6 speeds with the need for much wider powerbands. Möller's work with the 50cc Kreidler Renn-Florett transformed it into essentially an all-new machine, giving the colossal total of 20.5 bhp at some 16,000 rpm, driving the tiny racer at over 125 mph.

This is a specific power of over 400 bhp per liter of displacement, better than the best ever achieved in the classic years. This unprecedented power was also achieved over a wide range suitable for use with only six speeds. It's clear that this man Möller had formulated some rather interesting new ideas.

How could the Japanese factories have overlooked any such thing? Racing engine design, like biological evolution, seems to track a single line of development until an accident forces a change. The great Japanese racing machines of the 1960s pursued higher and higher power through more and more cylinders at higher and higher rpm. Their narrowing powerbands (with few exceptions) required ever-more gearbox speeds. There was no need to question the validity of this line of development since it was successful right to the very end. Then the FIM acted, forcing engineers to think again.

What is the powerband, anyway? It is the envelope of the efficiencies of the engine's three systems for pumping air in or out. These are: 1) The intake/crankcase system; 2) The crankcase/transfer port system; 3) The exhaust port/exhaust pipe system. These systems interact, of course, and when all have their peak efficiencies at the same rpm, the power can be very high. This is especially so when each system is very sharply tuned to a narrow range of effectiveness. On the other hand, when each system has a broad range, or if the efficiency peaks are offset, the power will usually be lower, but delivered over a much wider range.

It might seem a simple matter just to broaden out the tuning of the systems to get a narrow-band engine to run with only six speeds. This is true, but a power loss would result. The accomplishment that distinguished Möller was that he not only broadened the power, he raised it as well, to a level never before achieved. Even Suzuki's fabled RP-38 three-cylinder 50cc racer never made as much power as Möller's Van Veen Kreidler.

There are some clues. Engines of the classic years used high crankcase compression ratios, for theory showed that delivery of fresh charge should rise with the ratio. High power could indeed be obtained in this way, but at some expense to width of the powerband.

As an example, a TA125 Yamaha I worked with had a powerband from 8,500 to 13,500 rpm with the low stock-case compression ratio of 1.28:1.

When I raised this ratio to 1.35:1, the peak power was little different, but now power came in later, at 10,000 rpm, making the powerband narrower and less useful.

Using case pressure as the only means of transferring charge from case to cylinder means that gas flow is permanently tied to piston motion. There is no changing the timing of the flow. There will be only one speed range in which a maximum charge is transferred and retained. Below that speed, the transfer charge squirts out so fast under the high pressure that it reaches the open exhaust port too soon and is lost. Power falls off. At speeds above peak, the ports soon become inadequate and again, power falls off. A narrow powerband results. What was needed was a way to make transfer flow more proportional to rpm.

Designers knew that a lower case pressure would indeed broaden the power below peak, but this trimmed off too much power on top. To supplement the fall-off in transfer flow at high rpm, they began to rely more and more heavily on *exhaust-pipe-generated suction* to supplement the action of crankcase pumping.

The divergent section of the exhaust pipe sends back a wave of low pressure to the cylinder which can be timed to arrive at any desired moment. This low pressure wave "sucks" on the top of the transfers as the crankcase pressure "blows" on them from below. Either action or both will produce flow. The designer could now use low case pressure to give good power at lower speeds, then bring in the pipe pumping at higher speeds to give desired top-end power.

There was another benefit to the low-pressure case. It was much larger than the tight, high-pressure cases formerly used. It's as simple as this; you can draw a deeper breath of air out of a 55-gallon drum than you can out of a milk bottle. Exhaust-pipe suction, which can be prolonged at will, could pull an increased volume of air through the engine out of the larger case. The piston displacement was no longer an upper limit on air delivery to the engine. This greater airflow scavenged the residual exhaust out of the cylinder that much better, raising the BMEP and the horsepower without sacrificing band width. Twelve-speed gearboxes weren't necessary after all. All this, and heaven too!

At the same time, other changes had taken place. Carburetion had improved steadily since the classic era. The importance of strongly supported crankshaft bearings had become appreciated. Vast improvements in ignition had come along, replacing the monster "radar-set" ignitions so often seen on the old Japanese racers. All these could contribute to horsepower, but only if they were properly used together.

The classic designs tended to have single exhaust ports with three moderate-sized transfers. As time passed, there was considerable refinement of this time-honored concept. The entire cylinder wall, except for the exhaust port, was devoted to a ring of transfer ports. These were so aimed and sized as to produce a coherent column of rising fresh charge in the rear of the cylinder, far from the exhaust and safely stuck to the back cylinder wall so it couldn't suddenly detach and head for the pipe. This rising column occupied approximately one-half the bore area, shooting up to the cylinder head and being deflected across the spark plug and then down in the direction of the now-closing exhaust port.

The smaller transfers of earlier designs tended to squirt in tiny fingers of high-velocity gas that penetrated into the cylinder, mixing with the exhaust residuals there and being diluted by them down to a low purity. The solid column of transfer gas in the modern engines tends to act more nearly as a piston, pushing the exhaust ahead of it with little mixing. This leaves the cylinder well filled with a high-purity fresh charge, and BMEP can then rise up into numbers usually associated only with four-stroke engines.

It appears that Möller's success with the Van Veen Kreidler used these concepts, and it is certain that he drew heavily on all available advances in other areas as well. He orchestrated all of this into a complete success. That success was noticed by Giancarlo Morbidelli, whose racing hobby had burgeoned into a full-scale attempt on the 50 and 125cc world titles. Morbidelli offered Möller a blank check to design a machine that would take the championship, and he accepted.

Möller quickly got the power up so much that the original primary gears had to be redesigned.

In two outings at the end of the 1974 season, Morbidelli riders Pileri and Bianchi knocked out the opposition, serving notice that Yamaha would never again win this class with their water-cooled YZ623, an adaptation of their TA125 production racer. Racing in the 125cc class had suddenly become serious business.

Just how serious was realized the following spring when, one by one, the lap and speed records set by the superpower Yamaha and Suzuki square fours of the 1960s were destroyed by the Morbidelli twins. At the very fast Spa-Francorchamps circuit in Belgium, the electric timer caught the Morbidelli at 151 mph. Horsepower rose to the 41–42 bhp level.

The Morbidelli as designed by Möller not only had tremendous power—it had reliability as well. In interviews, Möller has stated that his construction philosophy is to have components built to his design by specialist firms, in the best available materials, without regard to price. Giancarlo Morbidelli had asked for the world 125 title, and he got it, thrice over. He didn't quibble over the cost of returning every development cylinder and piston to Mahle to further refine both. With success like this, who would whine at the cost of vacuum-remelt steel alloys to make cranks that never stop, gears that never break? Möller's job was to get the title, and he did that job.

In 1977, racing at Morbidelli became even more ambitious. Their prototype 250 racer, ridden by Mario Lega, has now clinched the 250cc world title as well. There is a 350 machine, and talk of a 500cc racer to come. There are the 125cc replicas for privateers, with the possibility of larger displacement offerings in the future. Despite Jörg Möller's having left the company (to Minarelli, where he is aiming for 48 bhp) the will to race remains as strong as ever.

The machine I saw that day at Thompson Speedway is good, solid evidence that people can and do pursue excellence without succumbing to the enervating drag of economy and mental laziness. The Morbidelli is a machine for winning races. It is also an assertion that the mind can overcome its circumstances. And that is art.

*July 1985*

# Buell: The Other American Maker

*Erik Buell is still at it. His greatest weakness—stubborn-ness—is also his greatest strength. He keeps at it. Now a part of Harley, the Buell Company nevertheless continues to nourish advanced ideas that puzzle or annoy Juneau Avenue. A miraculous marriage.*

Erik Buell has a problem. He, personally, is a motorcycle manufacturer. In a small shop next to an old farmhouse in rural Wisconsin, this fellow Buell is making engines, chassis and brakes, is putting all these parts together into complete motorcycles for roadracing—750cc, square-foot, rotary-valve, two-stroke motorcycles with close to 150 horsepower. Last year at Talladega his prototype RW750A was clocked by Harley-Davidson personnel at 178 miles an hour. Buell's adventure is not just a plan or an ambition; these motorcycles are in stock and available for immediate delivery.

Let's start at the beginning. Buell was a privateer roadracer for many years. The only real goal in this game is a factory ride, and because factory rides are few, there are correspondingly few winners. To play, you trade your real life for an artificial one lived out in vans and midnight truck stops, rushing from one national race to another. You race and crash and heal and race again. You break a mountain of parts. You fight with cranky track officials. You hand out your money as greedily as others earn it, hundreds of dollars at a crack. Gotta have cranks. Gotta have tires. The game is all-consuming, but no one doubts its worth even though no one wins. It turns into something done for its own sake, something nice to have done, but not always nice to do. Buell played this game.

He raced not only as a rider but also as an engineer and builder. Motorcycles irritate engineers because they aren't pure products of intellect. They irritate people like Buell because they are full of senseless tradition. Every time Buell ran his Yamaha production racers he tried his damnedest to express *right thinking* with a growing array of his own handmade innovations. But often the mind leaps laughingly ahead of the hands that must translate ideas into hardware. Buell put in the hours necessary to learn to operate precision machine tools. He learned to make clear engineering drawings anyone could read. And he was wounded every day by the painful slowness of converting ideas into reality. It took hours of careful work to make one correct pair of brake caliper mounts—hours taken from a normal job, from his family, from sleep. And how long would it take a solitary man, working 24 hours a day with milling machine, lathe, and TIG welder to make a motorcycle?

The job had to go. In its place he put a small business distributing the English-made Dymag racing wheels. He also conceived a bimetallic brake disc made as a heat-bonded sandwich of two thin stainless sheets with light aluminum between. At least one major manufacturer has taken an interest in these discs, but in the meantime Buell nibbles them from flat sheet one at a time to fill customer orders. The imagination, though, goes hungry on such work, and the money eked out clearly would never have underwritten real racing.

Fate decided to punish Erik Buell for having ambitions that extend beyond the possible—it decided to give him what he wanted. Would you, Erik Buell, care to buy for a song all the design drawings, parts, and existing castings to build the engine of your dreams? Would you, backyard innovator, pledge all your earthly energy to build your own racing motor-cycles, your own way, whether possible or not?

Yes.

Understand this: Racers don't look at their projects with accountant's eyes. They don't write slick business plans for each racing season, listing cost of machines and spares, fuel, lodging, van payments, and help. The total would be so big that no one would ever try to race. So they don't add it up. They just order the machine, put all their stuff in the van, enslave their friends as helpers, and split. The money isn't always there when it's needed, but there's almost always another way. So, when confronted with his fate, Buell accepted instantly.

This engine that Buell took over was made originally in Wales, in a converted church, and it started life as an All-British Project to build a world-class 500cc roadracing engine which any racer—not just the factory stars—could afford. To understand the emotional climate that created this project—the Barton 500—you have to know something about England and its romance with motorcycle racing. The English believe racing is their creation despite the hard truth that a British engine hasn't won a world title since 1952. The British motorcycle industry was on its way down even before then, but with every factory closing, more and more "underground" shops sprang up to supply English racers with what they needed to keep racing. Little specialist shops made forks, frames, tanks, even engines. All the skills needed for making gears, castings, and elegant chassis were flung about the English countryside, not distilled and immured in factories. Even this, however, never slowed them down or damped their vigor. The English are, as they say, keen for racing.

Then there is the English press. When the Grand Prix results are reported in their magazines, the coverage goes: SHEENE NINTH IN FRENCH GRAND PRIX! (Roberts, Spencer, Mamola 1-2-3). You get the idea. When fog covers the English Channel, their national weather service reports: CONTINENT ISOLATED. The results of this nationalistic reporting style are many, and whenever one of England's tiny race-ware specialists decides to make almost anything, the trade papers scream, WORLD-BEATER PLAN SLATED! ENGLAND WILL PREVAIL! Over the years, the British press has announced so many world-beater plans that you would expect the readers to harden into cynicism, but they haven't— it's still fun. England's small specialists can't stop thinking up these projects any more than our own U.S. riders can listen to their accountants' wise advice and give up racing.

One of these specialists was Barry Hart. Having made many custom parts for the English-based Suzuki team and rider Barry Sheene, he was very familiar with the design of the Suzuki RG500. He had already made most of what goes into an engine, so when he decided England needed a good 500 racing engine of modern design, he made one. A "documentary" film was planned around this creation. The new Barton 500 engine was fitted with an English-made chassis and dubbed "The Silver Dream Racer." The movie was execrable, and the dream racer was never to achieve any fame. Hart couldn't make his engine competitive because the largest development expense is reliability development—hundreds of hours of testing. English racers continued to pay high prices for proven Japanese raceware.

Meanwhile Hart had produced an enlarged version of the 500 for sidecar racing. Bigger cylinders accepted 66.4mm Yamaha TZ750 pistons with the 54mm stroke of the factory Suzukis to make a full 750. An American auto racer tried these Barton 750s in D-Sports Racing, ultimately buying eight engines and building them out to 850cc. Never trouble-free at 500cc, the engine was a handful at 750, and impossible as an 850. The car racer put his Bartons on the shelf.

Now we return to Erik Buell. Having raced Yamahas for years, with a short break for a Harley RR250 and its unique problems, Buell wanted a fresh start. At the end of 1980 he had to replace his aging Yamaha TZ750 because chassis design had passed it by, and he had rejected the Yamaha 500 as a piston-port design in a rotary-valve world. The Dymag wheel business was doing well enough to justify a trip to England, and while there he visited Hart's little factory and decided that the Barton 500/750 was what he wanted—a serious design capable of real power. Buell ordered a 500 engine with early delivery of 750 parts promised. He also bought the Silver Dream chassis.

The engine was awful. It broke a crankpin in five laps, wrecking the crankcases. The pins were hollow like the crankpins of 10 years ago, and were only a light press-fit in the flywheels. Looseness led to fretting, and fretting to fracture. Fine, Buell could fix the crank. He knew how to specify surface finishes, dimensions, heat treatment. With better pins he was able to get two club races per crank. Then the disc-valve drives broke—a common rotary-valve engine problem. Buell could cope; he designed new parts and made them.

The chassis was awful. Small-diameter tubing, used in irrational ways, was the cause, but Buell would have to soldier on for the moment. Part of the Silver Dream Racer's design was a tiny nose-mounted radiator, and the engine was overheating as a 500. What would happen with 50 percent more displacement? Crankcases were a problem now, damaged as they had been by crank breakages and disc valve seizures. Buell wrote to Barry Hart, requesting more parts. The reply came: Barton was being taken over by Armstrong; parts for the square four would cease to be available immediately.

"Somewhere along the line I got this insane idea," Buell recalls. Although it would take eight months of negotiation, he bought everything Hart had for the Barton 500/750. Now he was in the engine business. The deal was made final in the winter of 1982, with the parts to come in early 1983. In fact, with Hart's move to Armstrong, no parts came until July, and

*Lee Klancher*

even then with no finish-machined cases. There went the possibility of running a complete '83 season. With redoubled effort he readied a running engine for the Pocono AMA National. He qualified the machine and went from 25th to 12th in four laps before pulling in with rapidly tightening gearbox. Hmmm . . . no oil in there. Where'd it go? Measurement showed the crank's main-bearing support rings had improperly dimensioned O-ring grooves. The resulting leaks allowed the engine to inhale the gearbox oil. Buell added bearing rings to the growing list of self-sourced items. He was sliding in faster, deeper all the time.

Now another step. Anxious to avoid further use of the dangerously flexible Silver Dream chassis, he cobbled up a frame of his own design, using "the miracle of jigless construction." This means clamping the wheels, engine, and other parts to a table in the chosen positions, then joining all parts with frame tubes tacked into place. With this chassis working quite well thanks to its stiff straight-tube design and largely TZ750 Yamaha geometry, Buell entered the Brainerd national but got no result. The jigless frame was now used as a buck around which to construct a proper jig, and a new frame was built.

In August 1983 Buell talked to Harley management about his Barton/Buell racing program, and they were interested: *anything* that could bring in more points to a hard-pressed H-D Grand National team was a matter of interest. Harley indeed had its own plans at the time to build a new racing twin. But how to test the square four? Pending such a test, it was proposed that Buell supply four machines, two spare engines, re-fueling tower, and support equipment—all on a contract—rather than a buyout-basis. If this program received approval, it would commence October first at a low but workable funding level. The plan was to rent the Talladega track and run a 200-mile test with a recognized rider. Doug Brauneck was picked to ride, and in preparation H-D lent Buell its carburetor specialist.

The Talladega test was set up rather optimistically, beginning on a Saturday afternoon and extending through Sunday. Buell appeared with a broken-in engine, ready to run. Brauneck did one warm-up lap on a tall-sidewall Goodyear tire, and on the next lap bored past start-finish at

11,000 rpm, pulling the tallest gearing Buell had in the box. The Harley radar gun showed 178 mph, and everyone was terribly excited. Moments as delicious as this one don't come often. Brauneck continued to do 10 to 12 laps in all and then came in to report that in addition to being very fast, the machine handled well.

Now Harley wanted to run their engine test, and this would require a hard-compound tire for prolonged use at high speed. Brauneck's tire choice was the Michelins he normally races with, but the only French tires on hand were low-sidewall models—much smaller in circumference than the tall Goodyears of the first run. Achieving the same speeds on the smaller-circumference Michelins required the engine to overrev— remember, the bike was already carrying its tallest gearing. Human momentum carried the test forward, and the run began. Now, turning beyond its natural power peak, the engine tightened, filling the lower end with gritty, crumbled piston. Buell stripped, cleaned and reassembled the engine overnight. Sunday morning it seized again. And again. Time up. The test had failed.

Back in Wisconsin, Buell found the immediate cause: the rotary-valve cover of the seized cylinder was admitting air—incorrectly machined. He would have to add valve covers to his list of personally produced parts. Nothing could be trusted. The engine had probably been comfortably rich in the first test, pulling at its power peak of 10,500–11,000 rpm, even with a bit of extra air getting to one cylinder. When the bike was overrevved, overall carburetion leaned out as intake pulses became less vigorous, and the leanest cylinder tied up.

"Harley's disgust wasn't total, even so," remembers Buell. The discussions continued, but now they were saying things like 'go win a race or so, and then we'll see.'"

In December, Brauneck rode the Buell Motor Company machine at West Palm Beach, lapping faster than he ever had before on his own TZ750 Yamaha, significant especially since West Palm is such a tight, slow circuit—ill-suited to the sudden power characteristics of a rotary-valve engine as it makes the transition from below the power to on the power. In the first race Brauneck started cautiously, but he had the lead in two laps. Then the Harley-type front antidive unit suddenly lost air pressure, allowing the fork to collapse. After Buell spacered up the helper springs to give a fork travel of only two-and-a-half inches, the bike went out again and came in second in the second race.

Over Christmas Buell's dialog with H-D continued. Now he wanted to sell them his entire operation for a modest, loss-cutting sum. Clearly, every part was going to have to be personally made by Erik Buell, and the job was just too big for one pair of hands. He'd be better off without the promising square four, no matter how invitingly it beckoned. Harley didn't want to own the machines, however—Milwaukee just wanted to rent them, and by January, H-D was out of money for new projects. Buell was stuck. He now alternated between wild optimism (Everything is *right here!* Just a little capital and some extra people working and we could...) and "informed despair" (I should just junk all this stuff. Besides, now the AMA is trying to do away with Formula 1 altogether. Get a job. Live a normal life again.)

He also knew the telephone could ring at any time and the caller could be, just maybe, a person with racing ambitions, a desire to do something different, and some money. But more likely it would be just another brake disc or wheel customer with normal concerns like price and delivery.

Last fall a visit to Buell's operation showed two completed machines in the center of the shop on workstands. They run. Their parts are right. Buell controls all dimensions. In the true sense, they are his creations. On the big tilt-top drafting table was a detailed drawing of the crankcase set. The machine tools at the far end of the shop were in use turning out Buell brake discs. In the farmhouse basement, not far away, is the parts department. Dymag wheels in shipping boxes are ready for delivery on one side, and in steel shelving on the other side are the thousands of parts for the square-four engines—flywheels, crankcases, cylinders, pistons, ignitions, gearsets.

Why doesn't Buell just go racing himself? He knows what that would mean. Instead of earning income, he would be spending, spending, spending, with no hope of ever clearing a dime. AMA prize money doesn't allow even the most gifted privateer to do more than break even. For Buell to race would be a pointless exercise. It will take more than one man to push this project forward.

Let's take a look at what he has done so far. The engine is 66.4 x 54.0mm bore and stroke, and weighs what a TZ750 engine weighs— 140 pounds. Although AMA Formula 1 rules limit the class to 500cc two-strokes and 750cc four-strokes beginning in the 1985 season, a grandfather clause permits older engines, designed before 1978, to compete without intake restrictors. This lets owners of older designs still run their equipment. The 750 Buell engine, as well as the TZ750, is eligible for the class under this rule.

The RW750A is a square-four design with two twin-cylinder crankshafts, one ahead of the other. Each crank has a central gear meshed to the large jackshaft gear below. The outer end of the jackshaft carries a small pinion driving through a needle-bearing idler gear to the large clutch gear on the input shaft of a conventional six-speed gearbox. The engine has two levels: the upper split is between crankcase cover and main case. Four separate cylinders crowd closely in square array on the top cover. Removing the cylinders and then this cover gives access to the cranks without disturbing the gearbox, and without removing the engine from the chassis. In the lower split lie the jackshaft, idler shaft, and the two gearbox shafts.

The outer face of each crank is bare except for its rotary-valve disc, carried immediately outboard of the outer crank main bearing. All accessories—the Suzuki RG500 retard ignition and water pump—are driven from the jackshaft, located where they can't interfere with cornering clearance. The four 38mm Mikuni carburetors project out from the sides, two on the right, two on the left. Because they feed the crank chambers through ports *above* the outer main bearings, they too are out of the way in cornering.

Like other engines based on a smaller-displacement design, the cases and cylinders provide conservative transfer-duct entry area at the cylinder base level. In this the Buell is like the Yamaha OW69. Another legacy of the 500cc past is the small 93mm-diameter flywheels. These are Buell-designed with special rotary-valve drivers on them, and are 8620 case-hardened steel. Solid crankpins press in with 0.003-inch interference to give solid grip in the wheels.

The pistons are now of Buell design, made in England, and have the usual subtle contour designed to become a true cylinder at operating temperature. The Buell-designed heads give a compression of 7.6:1. This high a ratio is possible only with the retard ignition: Were the timing fixed, the engine would destroy itself at peak torque rpm because flame travel speed is so fast there that premature peak pressure would result, and the engine would overheat, begin to detonate, and destroy the pistons and heads. With the RG ignition, there is plenty of advance at low rpm to give peak pressure just after TDC, and it pulls back spark lead as flame-speed builds. Two exhaust pipes sweep forward, down, and back under the machine, and two more shoot straight back up to cross in the streamlined seatback, emerging from the rear.

Bit by bit, drawing and vendor by drawing and vendor, Buell has built up his control over the engine's crucial parts and dimensions. Now he feels it is solid. He knows the power is there from his own riding, from

Brauneck's; and from the dyno runs made by the car racer in the recent past. An 850 version gave 165 bhp, so it would be reasonable to expect little less from Buell's much more developed 750s.

After mechanical reliability Buell's chief goal has been a better powerband. Carburetion work has gained much here, and Buell has been through three changes of exhaust pipe design as well. He has on hand chrome-bore cylinders in two styles: the high-horsepower, sudden-powerband type with Rotax-type exhaust ports (one main port and two boosters), and the moderate-horsepower, broad-band type with one main exhaust port only.

Another of Buell's concerns has been aerodynamics. Most racing fairings are just covers, with no streamlining effect. (Proof? In 1979, while tire-testing at Daytona, Mike Baldwin ran quicker *after* removing the entire lower fairing of his TZ.) When a vehicle moves through air, the air must speed up to flow around it. This takes energy. If the energy is recovered from the air by decelerating it again, smoothly closing the flow *behind* the vehicle, then the air drag will be low. But if this fast-moving air just drops off the back of the machine in the form of turbulent eddies, its energy is wasted, and the drag is high. It's a common mistake to think the front of the vehicle must be smoothly contoured and to ignore the back. Buell's fairing is widest at the engine, and then begins to taper inward again. The flanks of the large seat continue this taper, nearly closing again at the back. Tuft studies make sure the flow remains attached all along the fairing surfaces. If the flow is attached, little woolen tufts glued to the skin will lie down flat. If the flow is separated and turbulent, the tufts stand up and oscillate. The basic shape of this fairing began in 1969 in Harley's Cal Tech wind tunnel study, but Buell has built upon it. An example of this fairing ran at Bonneville on a TZ750 and added five mph over the stock TZ fairing—equivalent to an 8 percent horsepower increase on the top end.

Cooling drag is another Buell concern. Air passages through a radiator are small and tortuous, and it takes a goodly amount of pressure to push the flow through. Thus, the pressure at the front of the radiator will be higher than at the back, producing a drag force that can be as much as 20 percent of total drag. Buell prefers to look at a radiator as a jet engine. A jet engine takes in cold air at low velocity, heats it to make it expand, and expels a high-velocity hot stream to produce a net thrust. To function as a jet engine, a radiator needs carefully shaped intake and exhaust ducts to preserve the air's velocity. Carefully ducted aircraft radiators have been made to produce actual thrust in this way. Make that waste heat work for you! Buell's fairing has just such intake and exhaust ducts to control airflow through the custom-built copper-and-brass radiator.

A straight tube is far more able to bear compression or tension than a curved one, and most of the Buell frame's tubes are straight. The solid-mount engine is set well forward to give an unloaded weight distribution of 52 percent front, 48 percent rear on a 55.5-inch wheelbase. Wheelies may be fun to watch, but they do nothing for acceleration.

Front suspension is a 38mm tube Marzocchi, adjustable in both compression and rebound damping. The load is carried by

Brian J. Nelson

light steel springs plus internal air pressure acting through the patented H-D electro-pneumatic antidive system. When the brakes are off, the volume of pressurized air above the fork oil is large, and so the spring rate of this air volume is soft. When the brakes go on, a switch closes a solenoid valve that isolates much of this air volume, reducing the air volume to be compressed above the fork oil. The fork is now much stiffer, more resistant to bottoming. Twin 310mm Buell bimetallic brake discs are used at the front, gripped by a pair of Lockheed calipers on quick-release mounts.

One Works Performance two-hose damper/spring unit controls a triangulated rear swingarm. Designed into this rear geometry is inherent rising rate, accomplished without linkages; the ratio begins at 2.2 and ends at 2.7. The front of the damper attaches to a special boss on the engine cases, low enough not to interfere with the 24-liter fuel tank. The two-hose feature means that oil displaced from the damper flows out through one hose and is drawn back in through the second hose. Because of this, oil circulates rather than just panting back and forth in a single hose, and better cooling results. Rear travel is six inches.

Why are axles so small when so much of a chassis' stiffness depends on them? And why, if an axle measures six inches between its supports in fork or swingarm, are its bearings only four inches apart? This allows a full inch of unsupported, overhung axle to flex over every bump. Buell uses a large 20mm front axle, mounting the wheel bearings right against the inside faces of the fork sliders. All of the axle is supported, and the 20mm part is 60 percent stiffer then the normal 17mm piece. The rear axle is 25mm instead of the usual 20 of racing designs—a stiffness gain of 95 percent.

The chassis is mainly 1 1/16-inch chrome-molybdenum steel. Why not trendy aluminum? Buell isn't trying to make a statement about maximum technology; rather, he is trying to build a real product a racer can own and operate. Steel can be welded anywhere. Steel is survivable.

The 16-inch front Dymag has a 3.5-inch rim width and is carried with a conservative 4.5 inches of trail to ensure stability despite the small wheel size. The fork angle is pure TZ750—26 degrees. The 18-inch rear Dymag is 4 inches wide, with a 4.5-inch rim optional.

Where are the radical, far-out features? Where are the bottom-mount fuel tanks, the carbon-fiber frame, and the hub steering? Where are all the places magnets won't stick? You won't find any of that here—Buell wants to build machines that can actually be raced. He's stuck to solid, sensible engineering with available materials and technology, and hasn't wasted his time on futuristic projects beyond a one-man shop or beyond a privateer racer's budget. And he has running motorcycles, not just paper projections. This project is not art; it's engineering.

Buell has done an unbelievable job, understanding and correcting a tangle of problems. He has prepared drawings, has found proper sources for specialized items like pistons and crankpins and flywheels, and has put his engine into a complete motorcycle of his own design. Think of the administrative headaches alone! Contracting for special parts is much more than a phone call, a set of clear drawings in the mail, and beautiful parts by next Wednesday. Suppliers prefer to make things incorrectly and, if possible, too late to be of any use. They like to whine about tolerances that can't be measured with a ruler, or simply ignore them. Often, the best way to get parts that work is to go to the supplier and live there until they come out right. Drawings seem clear and unambiguous when they leave the board, but in the supplier's hands they become mysteries which must be explained in endless and expensive telephone calls.

Large companies have separate departments for every major group of parts: a wheel and brake group, a chassis group, a fits and tolerances group—all working hard. Buell had to embody all these in one man. He made the drawings, measured the incoming parts for acceptance, performed the assembly and test functions.

What chance does he have? Well, the phone *has* rung twice now, once with an order from the racing group of the Machinists' Union (who operate an Indy car and have for years wanted to roadrace an *American-made* motorcycle as well), and once with a private order from an individual racer. Nineteen-eighty-five may be the year of vindication for Erik Buell, his wife, and his single phone line.

In a world of $27,000 Honda 500s, and of painstakingly resurrected TZ750 Yamahas that are really U-Build-Its, Buell's RW750A makes sense at $15,900. And if all that isn't enough, here's what may be the RW750A's greatest asset: its chief engineer speaks excellent English.

# April 1990

# Silent Hero:
# Erv Kanemoto

*Today, the top racing machines either work or don't work—no middle ground. They work for Casey Stoner, Valentino Rossi, and Dani Pedrosa. They don't currently work for Nicky Hayden and Loris Capirossi. Isn't there any step-by-step process by which to make them work? Or have race bikes assumed the nature of electronics, which either work perfectly or emit smoke? Erv Kanemoto's analytic methods extracted order and function from hardware and chaos. Where is he now? Thinking about drag racing.*

Grand Prix racing is a constant struggle to make machines handle, to get the most from tires, to fit the most effective experiments into the tight format of four 40-minute practice sessions. To do this, each rider uses multiple motorcycles. He tests one machine and its setup, comes in and comments briefly, then saddles up on the next. Almost before he's out of the pits, mechanics are hurriedly reconfiguring his first bike. With the rider almost continuously on the track, the 160 minutes of practice are most effectively spent.

Because Erv Kanemoto has always seen information and time use as the keys to racing, his 500cc Grand Prix team maintains a hectic practice pace. The work had many levels—technological, interpersonal, political. The pistons must be out of each practice machine after every test for his examination of combustion in each cylinder. When engines are started, he must watch and listen attentively. The response to throttle and the nature of the sound reveal much of the engine's character even before it reaches the track. The results of tests must be logged. The right tires have to be on the right wheels, and clearly marked.

Beyond the technical, Kanemoto must hear both the spoken and the unspoken parts of what the rider has to say; he must be a student of the rider's personality. He must also understand the workings of the rider's style, and the demands it makes of the machine combination. Where Erv feels an advantage can be gained by a change in that style, he must find an acceptable way to present it. When Freddie Spencer found the Honda three-cylinder lacked a wide enough powerband to hold the back tire loose through a long sweeper at Silverstone, Erv worked out an effective substitute: Take a polygonal line, steering with the back wheel only at those points where the engine has the torque.

VIPs are a fact of life, and political matters are every bit as important to survival in racing as safety wire. There are constant conferences—with Honda engineers, with suspension, carburetion, and chassis people. Extra tests may have to be scheduled, which means renting tracks, arranging air tickets, and routing equipment and people. Running a race team is an exercise in almost infinite complexity.

During the season, Kanemoto also has the design of next year's motorcycle in mind. Although his views will receive respectful consideration, the major design decisions will not be his. Therefore he must deal with the decision-makers most diplomatically. From time to time there are meetings in Japan—technical reviews, planning sessions, or business negotiations. That Erv is unfailingly and instinctively courteous, and able to see problems from viewpoints other than his own, surely makes such meetings and relationships easier and more productive.

Kanemoto has no university degree, but Honda Motor Co. puts him in charge of multimillion-dollar racing budgets working with multimillion-dollar riders. Corporations, Japanese or otherwise, don't foster independent people like Erv or even quite approve of them. Yet the complexity of roadracing makes them necessary. Despite his accomplishments and the trust Honda places in him, he will always remain in some degree an outsider to the organization.

Erv, like both his parents, was born in the U.S. His education began with a family that wholeheartedly supported its children's interests, and continued through working with his father, Harry, once an avid outboard racer.

"The end came, or maybe it was the beginning," Harry told me, "when I brought home a go-kart. After that, the outboards were all finished."

At first, Kanemoto drove the kart himself, but was disappointed in his own driving and transferred that task to his sister. Kart racing was an ideal education. Engines were cheap, and preparation time was short, so Erv was able to cram hundreds of experiments into each season. In time, his father would ask him if he wanted to go to college, but Erv, despite the likelihood of being drafted, decided to continue racing.

A stint in the National Guard came with this decision, and Erv was attached to a unit doing acceptance testing of new tanks in the desert.

"You sit there on night duty for hours," he said, "and if you didn't have anything to do you might drink too much coffee. So, we got to working on those governors a little bit [the tanks were diesel-powered, and speed-governed]. And you know what? Those things would go over 70 mph. You can slide a tank, just like a dirt-tracker.'

In the late 1960s he went to Daytona with a motorcycle team and promptly forgot about karts. He would go wherever the game was played the hardest, with the greatest opportunities to learn. In 1972, he built Kawasaki 500 triples for an AMA Junior. A year later, working with Expert-class rider Walt Fulton Jr., I saw him in a brightly lit garage at California's Ontario Speedway at 1 a.m., surrounded by H1-R engines and chassis. A helper had just brought him four Quarter Pounders with fries and drinks.

"How can you eat all that?" I asked, wishing I'd had such a helper myself.

"Got to keep up my strength." He cast an ironic glance at the work remaining.

For 1973, Erv struck a deal with Gary Nixon to run the old warrior on jointly owned semi-factory Kawasaki 750 triples. It would be a strong combination; they would win more races than the factory team that year.

They showed what they could do at Atlanta: Nixon set the fastest time, but Erv was still searching for a running combination. The big triples made their power through revs, and pistons and rods were breaking. Engine after engine scattered. Erv built one after another, using an upended oil drum as an open-air table. In the tension and heat Erv developed a nosebleed, but kept at it, blood streaming down his face as he worked with one hand. They didn't win that one, but developed the ingredients for the next. By Loudon, Erv had a working combination. This time the pistons broke-in perfectly, detonation was kept at bay, and Nixon won going away.

As Gary began his last two laps in winning the 1973 Pocono National, Erv stood on tiptoe on the pit wall, craning to see the machine all the way around the track. Someone else jumped down, saying, "Well, he's won another one."

Erv stayed on the wall, straining to see. "No, there's another lap and a half. . . ." He doesn't like to tempt fate by showing too much confidence a lap and a half from the finish.

The next year, Erv had a similar deal with Suzuki. This time he extended his control by designing his own chassis, very short and stiff, with the engine forward, and with adjustable steering geometry. When Nixon won Loudon on this machine, there were no official pats on the back from the factory team; in their view, the Kanemoto/Nixon special wasn't a Suzuki at all. Factory teams are like that: They want to win, but they want to do it their way.

No matter how productive an individual is, he's not a factory team. He needs skilled help. Erv subtly enslaved the machinists, fiberglass workers, painters, and welders of San Jose. He enslaved them by needing their help so much, and by being able to project that help into victory circle. Erv's certainty put him in debt. When he needed wheels, or cylinders, or titanium stock, he ordered enough. Sliding into the hole to the tune of half the price of a nice house was OK with him; what was not OK was to lose the edge because of not having the parts. The good years recouped the bad ones, and there were some of each.

Erv never became a hardware freak. Special titanium screws or machined-all-over fork crowns meant nothing to him unless they worked better than some alternative. He didn't form emotional attachments to motorcycles; they were just the current expression of his thinking. Hardware can't be built as fast as an agile mind can conceive it. In the privateer years, this year's bikes were always sold to finance next year's. As manager of a Grand Prix team, Erv returns his bikes to the factory at season's end for what is euphemistically called "disposition."

Time has always been short for Erv. Therefore, even when there was not money, he flew to the AMA races, using plastic money. Why? "Because I can work those extra days. Maybe do a couple more cylinders." A smile flickered across his face as he said this. Years later I would hand him a cylinder of my own, of which I was somewhat proud. Handing it back to me after examining it, he asked only, "How long did it take to do that?"

Time became a central preoccupation; every procedure he contemplated was evaluated according to how much time it would consume. Once, as he and I discussed this, he said to me, "Kevin, you make racing impossible for yourself because you not only want to know how, but also why, when there isn't even enough time to find out how."

From the beginning, Erv was racing against time. The big gamble was to bet that ideas, skill, and good riding could win enough races to attract the right kind of support—before terminal bankruptcy set in. So many try, only to end up selling insurance. It is one of the mysteries of Erv's character that personal modesty co-exists with an evident, enormous self-confidence that he will win such bets. He describes how, on a business trip to L.A., he asked himself, "Why don't I just give up? What makes me, a single person, think I can compete with whole factories?"

Then, in detail, he listed for himself all the many areas being over-looked by factory engineers in the early 1970s. There was enough scope in exploiting them, he decided, to constitute a potential winning edge—for a while.

"Of course," he went on, "once a factory really wakes up and begins pushing everywhere, there's nothing you [an individual] can do."

Finding and using that edge has been Erv's driving force. A new idea is a risk, a gamble with self-esteem as well as with physics. When the idea works, there is no greater satisfaction. Even when it fails, something is learned. Almost 30 years of engine development, and 20 of motorcycle chassis experimentation, have brought him not only detailed knowledge, but also remarkable intuition: He knows things he doesn't know he knows.

Though the edge depends on information, Erv doesn't wall himself in with secrecy. This expresses his confidence; he wouldn't say this, but the truth is that he will conceive fresh ideas, so guarding yesterday's supply isn't a top priority. Even so, when you visit his shop you somehow never find any pipes or cylinders in plain view. If you commit the gaffe of asking him a direct question on a technically sensitive matter, he never refuses to answer; he just finds a socially agreeable way to redirect the conversation.

Non-racing alternatives have presented themselves to Erv—sometimes very desirable ones—but he has always had the hardness of character to refuse in favor of continuing the big gamble.

Erv and Gary Nixon began their association in 1973, winning three Nationals that year as part of Kawasaki's "B-Team." Later Nixon would come tantalizingly close to winning Daytona on a Suzuki. In 1976, with Kawasakis again, the two men would win the Formula 750 World Championship, only to have it taken from them by an FIM technicality. None of this made funding the next year's racing any easier. They were losing their race against racing. Kawasaki pulled out after 1976, so Erv and Gary ordered a new TZ750 Yamaha.

In a country that largely ignores motorcycle racing, where was the money to come from? Erv did what had to be done; he gave the motorcycle tuner's equivalent of piano lessons. At first, the small extra income would come from providing support services to a rider/protégé of airline pilot Jim Doyle. The protégé's name was Randy Mamola. Later that year, Erv was approached by the father of a promising young WERA racer, interested in having a better sort of 250 built for his son. The son was Freddie Spencer.

Erv and Nixon would consume enough experimental cylinders in 1977 to pave a small patio. If you could visit Erv's garage and the sheds behind it, you would see the price of admission he paid in the 1970s: stacked crankcases, pipes, cylinders, and chassis. The hours of work are incalculable. No amount of pay could have motivated this outpouring of work.

But were they succeeding? The 750 was now extremely fast, but critics could dismiss it as unreliable and overtuned. Only the wins are counted. In this business, when the wins don't come, you disappear. These were the hardest of times. Not only was there no reliable U.S. support base for racing, not only was the action moving to Europe, but now Gary Nixon was in his final riding years. Quitting the sport is difficult—it was especially so for Nixon, who had returned to its top level more than once after reaching the depths of unfashionability. Who could be sure that such a remarkable man was finally in decline?

Erv, for one, could not. They had worked so successfully together on a basis of trust that for a long time they pretended all was well. Yet slowly, painfully, Gary Nixon struggled with eclipse as teen-aged Freddie Spencer emerged as a new star. Because Erv was long in doubt as to which part of their combination had ceased to function, he redoubled his preparation efforts, and also closely studied riders on the track. He began to understand that in Freddie he had discovered someone truly exceptional

When Freddie first came to Erv, he was riding all WERA classes—mainly on street bikes. Therefore he relied more on the powerband than on the gearbox. Erv set to work to re-educate him toward the realities he would soon confront. The first of these was Erv's 250, whose power began at 10,500.

In 1978, Spencer won the Loudon 250 race, setting a new lap record in practice (1:10.19) that would stand for seven years. Clearly, something outstanding was happening. The race Erv most wanted to win—the Daytona 200—eluded him through the 1970s. Finally, in 1980, his day seemed to have come: There was Freddie on Erv's special Yamaha, leading Daytona by more than a minute, just before the second fuel stop. Then came the voice of Fate, personified by race announcer Roxy Rockwood: "The race leader, Spencer, has stopped in the chicane and is walking back." Driving the knuckles of his two hands against each other, Erv said only, "Damn," and began packing the pit equipment.

Racing deals hard disappointments, but offers only two choices: quit or go on. There's no point in going on unless you build for the next event with all your knowledge and energy—hard to do when you're in debt, in doubt, and battered by events. There was no certainty that they were winning their race with racing, but success came often enough to keep them struggling.

Not only was racing shifting from the U.S. to Europe, but the FIM now killed off Formula 750. When Freddie ran Erv's 750 Yamaha against the new 500 Grand Prix bikes in the Transatlantic Match Races, he was outclassed despite having a clear power advantage. The new chassis were too good—and they weren't coming to America.

They would have to go Grand Prix racing. Erv prepared a Yamaha TZ500 for Freddie, cutting cylinders, making test pipes, and shuttling to and from a distant dyno. The need to meet expenses had converted part of the two-car garage into a production facility for Yamaha RD400 street pipes. Not enough money, but enough time.

Still the job offers came, from teams large and small, and from industry. Nevertheless, Erv's desire for independence remained. The TZ500 ultimately produced 126 horsepower, but Freddie rode it in only one Grand Prix, retiring after a start-line accident. This was more proof, as if it were needed, that without money—lots of it—racing is an endless and chilly range of Everests. And then came the final blow; Freddie was hired away by Honda to ride four-strokes in U.S. races.

With no attractive possibilities opening up, and his brilliant young rider snatched away, Erv changed plan. Whatever the future might bring, it would bring it in Europe, so he'd better be there to meet it. He finally accepted one of the offers that had been so numerous over the years—this one from the notoriously difficult-to-work-for Barry Sheene, to prepare his semi-factory Yamahas in 1981 Grand Prix races.

A year later, fortune reversed itself. Freddie was going Grand Prix racing on Honda's new two-stroke NS500, and he wanted Erv to join him. Ideally suited to Spencer's new style, this machine was light, and made sudden, narrow power. It was, in effect, a 100-horsepower 250.

The timing was perfect. Erv had consumed his personal resources and understood that only with factory-sized help could he make any impression in Grand Prix racing. There was no more massive help possible than Honda. And there was Freddie, the rider he had himself chosen, returned to him.

Amid predictions that the (initially) 108-horsepower Honda couldn't survive among the dominant 135-horsepower rotary-valve Suzukis and Yamahas—and despite doubters who thought Spencer somehow not tough or independent enough to deal with the likes of Roberts, Sheene, or Lucchinelli—Freddie, Erv, and Honda went Grand Prix racing in mid-season 1982.

The Honda team was new to Grand Prix racing, and flouted many established conventions. Honda personnel were openly hostile toward the other teams, and flaunted their money, resources, and status. Perhaps such behavior is understandable as the reaction of a proud company reduced to underdog status, but it must have been trying for Erv, with his humane views, to be seen as part of this. Nevertheless, he and Freddie were able to win the German Grand Prix that first year. Uncini, on Suzuki, became World Champion.

If Spencer's German win was a surprise, the following year was astounding. Nineteen eighty-three was the closest, hardest competition seen in the Grand Prixs in 20 years, a one-to-one battle between the two Americans, Spencer and Roberts, and the two great factories, Honda and Yamaha. It became a contest between Roberts's analytical style, and Spencer's intuition and improvisation. Roberts showed great versatility, remaking his own style to match or exceed Spencer's performances, while Spencer himself went repeatedly to the edge of his capabilities. The detractors had said Spencer would need years to learn the circuits, that he would fall apart in the strangeness of Europe. Those predictions didn't reckon with the special nature of Erv's and Freddie's working relationship. The two men handled problems collectively, pushing aside distractions. When Freddie awoke out-of-sorts, wishing he were home in Shreveport, and full of misgivings about the upcoming race, it was Erv who created around him a supportive atmosphere of confidence and certitude. Erv, who hates to be away from San Jose and his favorite chair, knew firsthand the uncertainties and loneliness of living abroad. He therefore knew what Freddie needed, and worked hard to provide it. He saw to it that Freddie was, when he needed to be, well-insulated against all disturbances. Within the cocoon of professionalism, Freddie performed miracles.

If Erv saw that Freddie responded badly to being told by a stranger about another rider's faster lap time, he arranged to provide the news himself, at a carefully chosen time. It became Erv's job to anticipate and head off bad surprises. Nothing is so comforting or confidence-inspiring as a meal with one's own family, and Erv often cooked for the two of them, standing in as a sort of older brother. Through all of this Erv made clear his deep respect for Freddie's professional ability. No other rider could do the things Freddie did—pushing hard into corners, losing the front end, recovering it with bursts of throttle, and continuing—all with unbelievable fluidity. If such astounding performances were only possible with the closest attention to Freddie's moods, his meals, and his company, Erv was willing to do whatever was necessary. By the end of the 1983 season, Spencer was World Champion.

This opportunity to operate at the highest level brought with it the need for Erv to think of everything, to provide against all contingencies, and to constantly review all arrangements. This kind of endless concentration is extremely fatiguing, and Erv used himself hard. Beyond that, the hours were long and the stakes were always high. By the end of each of those early seasons, he was sick and worn out. Returning to his family's home, relaxing in his favorite chair, and talking to friends on the phone turned out to be the best medicine. More recently, knowing himself better, he has taken some control of his own intensity, and so is able to maintain a kind of strategic reserve of personal energy. When the racing season ends, the negotiations with manufacturers, with sponsors, and with riders are just becoming most intense, and require every bit as much energy as do the Grand Prixs themselves.

The year 1984 was less than perfect. The new NSR500 V-4 Honda was ill-balanced. A carbon-epoxy wheel collapsed in South Africa, putting Spencer behind Eddie Lawson in points. It was a hard year for Erv—especially so since Freddie so strongly dislikes the unforeseen. Erv had worked hard to establish some separation for Spencer and himself from the main Honda team. Partly this was simply Erv's old desire to have the fewest eyes on his work, and partly it served to put more barriers between Spencer and the unexpected. Lawson—formerly Spencer's nemesis in U.S. Superbike racing—became 500cc World Champion in 1984.

In 1985, Freddie ambitiously determined to ride two Grand Prix classes—500 and 250. Although 1983 had pushed Roberts and Spencer close to the limits of what humans can stand in the form of voluntary and repeated exposure to extreme danger, Freddie now elected to bite off more yet. To an outsider, his performances appeared seamless, perfect. He won again and again. Erv, however, saw that not all was well. Eddie Lawson cannot tolerate second-level status, and was harrying Spencer at ever-closer distances, taking his measure. Spencer's mood responded to every tenth-of-a-second improvement in Lawson's practice times. He remained always able to push harder yet, maintaining the appearance of perfection, but it must have cost him dearly. Racing at Spencer's level, in two classes, was consuming Freddie's substance. Continuous exposure to extreme concentration and anxiety—even though voluntary—cannot be tolerated indefinitely. Kenny Roberts used to say that a man has 10 years in this sport, no matter how early he begins, because "something gets used up."

This left Erv in a dilemma. He knew that continuing to support Freddie as friend and confidant was tantamount to encouraging him to continue taking major risks. He was obliged to ask himself, "Is it right to do this? Is it right to do whatever it takes to win races? Or should I attend strictly to tire and gearbox choices?" Erv's morality was seeing a dilemma where in fact there was no choice. He could no more withdraw his personal support from Freddie than he could give him a motorcycle with square wheels. It had been hard to witness Nixon's struggles with himself. Now it would be harder yet to witness Freddie wrestling with his demons at the very peak of his career, and to find that nothing could help him. Nevertheless, Spencer won both 250 and 500 World Championships in 1985. It had never been done before.

In 1986 and 1987, Freddie occasionally rode as brilliantly as ever, but more often was stopped by a recurrent wrist problem or other difficulties. Race fans who seem to believe their heroes owe them endless, godlike perfection cruelly turned away from Freddie when he displayed human frailty. In 1988, Erv worked with Scotsman Niall Mackenzie, and Freddie announced his own retirement.

In Erv's years in Grand Prix racing, he has edged ever closer to his goal of personal independence. For 1989, he formed his own corporation, which then contracted with Honda, with sponsors, and with rider Eddie Lawson. Though motorcycle makers prefer tight control, Honda has come to accept that Erv must be Erv. As so often in business, personal trust counts more heavily than do contract terms.

As soon as the last Grand Prix of 1989 had run, the game of musical saddles instantly began. When the dust cleared, Erv was without a rider and none of the first rank remained unsigned. He was back in the soup.

Honda's choice, already contracted, was Wayne Gardner, who had an existing, organized, experienced team behind him. Presently, feelers went out from Honda, inquiring whether Erv might somehow work with Gardner. Erv couldn't act on this because he already had his own staff, familiar with his way of working. One rider couldn't be supported by two teams, and Erv did not want to push Gardner's men aside. Now, Honda has found ways to align the team it wants for 1990: Gardner, Erv, and Erv's team.

Will the struggle be perpetual? Erv believes, as Kenny does, that "something is used up" over years of racing. So far, in himself, that something is still plentiful, and the problems of racing still strongly engage him. Erv is looking forward to working with Gardner: "Maybe I can find out something about why he rides the way he does."

Erv was racing engineer and team manager to Freddie Spencer through his three roadracing World Championships, and to Eddie Lawson during his 1989 championship. Yet despite being effective in a hard business that requires experience and cold calculation, he remains the most pleasant of men—interested in people and courteous to all. He desires success or he wouldn't work so hard to achieve it, yet his response to it is simple pleasure. With only his parents and sister as family, racing is quite literally his life. For nine months out of the year, he is at trackside, on airliners, in meetings, or on the phone—in pursuit of his goals—to win races using his own ideas, without becoming the creature of any person or organization. Erv Kanemoto is the most remarkable man I know.

*November 1991*

# Soichiro Honda: 1906–1991

*We might not have liked working for this complex man, who surely found it difficult to live in several contrasting fast-changing cultures at once. But he got things done!*

Soichiro Honda has died at age 84 after a remarkable life. His name is known everywhere today as that of a man who created in 25 years a manufacturing empire as powerful as any in the world. It is correct to say that he was rude, unconventional, difficult, and an extremely original thinker. This is all the more remarkable when we recall that he was born in a nation that reveres formality and tradition. Soichiro Honda burst the bonds of traditional Japanese life, never fearing to offend anyone, never giving up an idea because experts said it wouldn't work, always respecting people, not for their degrees or positions, but for their originality and character.

Born a blacksmith's son in 1906, Honda entered an impossibly split world; private life went on in the mannered ways of medieval Japan, but industry was fast changing everything else. As a boy, Honda was intoxicated by the strangeness and power of the first automobile he saw. Later on, he did an unthinkable thing, disobeying his father to travel to a nearby town—to see an airplane. It would not be the last time he broke with tradition to follow his own path.

Moving to a faraway city to work in the auto trades, Honda lived through a numbing apprenticeship, unable to show his special understanding of machines. But when the Tokyo earthquake of 1923 hit, real talent was suddenly more valuable than seniority. Honda was quickly made branch manager. Machines made sense to Honda, and he was soon able to live well and drink deep of life's pleasures.

It wasn't enough. Honda wanted to build his own ideas. At first, this meant constructing and racing automobiles, but even this was simply Tinkertoys to his powerful imagination. Brashly, he entered the piston-ring business, but discovered quickly that raw enthusiasm and a knack with machines wasn't enough. The business came close to failure, but Honda rescued it by finding people who understood metallurgy and casting, and by experimenting relentlessly.

Then came the war, ending in devastation. It is now legend how Honda bought surplus generator engines, attached them to bicycles, and sold cheap, basic transportation. With gasoline strictly rationed, he and his few employees made a turpentine-like fuel for their customers—out of evergreen tree roots.

Honda Motor Company rose above its many competitors by constant improvement and creative marketing. The primitive generator engine was replaced by better Honda designs. Honda franchised dealers all over Japan in an era when motorbike brands were only sold locally. The Korean War pumped capital into Japan's economy, but the war's end brought recession. Honda somehow survived it. Many other motor companies did not.

Racing was always central to Honda's marketing, but success was slow to come. The company struggled with racing's special problems until success came—first in Japanese national racing. In emphasizing the importance of racing, Honda was surely recalling the power of the excitement he had felt as a boy, seeing his first self-propelled machines.

In 1954, Honda took another great step; he left Japan to tour Europe's motorcycle and machine tool producers. He wanted to know what the world standard was in these areas, and what he learned was hard to swallow. The most powerful Honda 250cc engine developed only one-third the power of similar-sized German engines.

Honda knew the power of research and development; he had saved his piston-ring enterprise by finding correct answers in a sea of wrong ones. Through research and development, his products would achieve high quality. Through marketing, Honda would become a household word. To establish the name, he set an ambitious goal: to defeat the best motorcycles in the world at the Isle of Man TT roadraces. At this time, Japan was derided in Western countries as a maker only of toys and cheap cameras. Westerners laughed at Japanese engineering, calling it uncreative copying.

Honda proved otherwise. His company equaled the power of European racers by 1959, then out-powered them decisively in 1962, when the Honda factory team won its first 250cc world championship. Honda personally attended the presentation ceremony and told the world it could no longer dismiss Japan as "a nation of copyists." How right he was.

Having launched his company on post-war demand for transportation, Honda needed a new market. He would create it. Motorcycles had been sold as cheap wheels, a substitute for a car, but Honda had seen the West and knew of its affluence and leisure. He would sell motorcycles to Americans, and they would ride them because it was fun. We did. The coming of Honda motorcycles to America created the biggest motorcycle market ever known—and it created a generation of riders who have kept motorcycling in their lives ever since.

Even as this market was expanding, Honda entered the automobile business. Early models failed to click with the U.S. market, but the coming of the Civic coincided with the first oil crisis. Small, economical, and reliable, the Civic made Honda owners of millions more Americans. More sophisticated models followed. By the 1980s, the Honda Motor Company was recognized as one of the most powerful and innovative auto makers in the world.

In the production of motorcycles, Honda showed the world that high quality in a sophisticated product need not be expensive. Honda models brought to market features previously found only in factory racing machines: overhead camshafts, multiple valves, liquid cooling. His factories showed that rational production methods—not cheap labor—were the key to all this. When Honda automobile and motorcycle factories were built here in the U.S., high quality and reasonable price continued to be achieved with highly paid American industrial workers.

Honda always emphasized that failure is an essential ingredient of success. If you haven't the stomach to push confidently through failure, eliminating the wrong answers, one by one, you will never succeed. Only through this creative struggle can success be reached.

Despite his position, Honda was never a remote figure locked away in a boardroom. He wore the company cap and jacket or coveralls when he joined in problem-solving sessions on the factory floor—and when he attended meetings with high government officials. He believed that work, not clothing, gave dignity.

He was impatient with muddled or stereotyped thinking. There is a story of his having entered a lab where two technicians were struggling to remove the cylinder head from a prototype machine: it was too close to the frame. Honda helped with the removal, then summoned the engineer responsible. When the frightened man arrived, he had to duck a flying cylinder head, personally hurled by the president.

After his retirement in 1973, his presence and influence continued much as before. When the Gold Wing touring bike was in development, he quietly appeared one night at the test track, where under bright lights, an untried prototype was being readied for the morrow's testing. Without a word, he eased the heavy machine off its stand, and rode smiling into the darkness. Returning some hours later, to the great relief of apprehensive employees, he parked the machine, said, "Pretty good," and went home.

Throughout his long and creative life, Honda went his own way. But it was our way too. We who are motorcycle enthusiasts share the wonder and excitement of that little boy, so long ago, who ran after the first motorcar he had seen. We are fortunate that he had the combination of fascination, unconventionality, patience, and knowledge to give those powerful feelings solid form in the machines we have enjoyed so much.

Thank you, Soichiro Honda.

# Forging A Future:
# Michael Czysz

*The powerful State of California, hotbed of U.S. auto culture, said, "Let there be electric cars!" Nothing much happened. Sometimes that's how big ideas turn out.*

Some suggest that only large companies can innovate because only they can afford original research and the development that exploits it. Others claim only small companies can innovate because of their agility and tolerance for the creative personalities who sicken in large organizations. It's also trendy to say, "genius ships product." The latter view observes that ideas are plentiful, but genius is their translation into accounts receivable.

Three years ago I went to Portland, Oregon, to see what Michael Czysz was up to. He runs a successful interior and conceptual building design firm (see his work in Las Vegas) and is an enthusiastic amateur motorcycle racer. He also has strongly held ideas about motorcycle design and has succeeded in finding $20 million in start-up capital to build novel machines. That has enabled specialists to be hired away from Cosworth, Ducati and Kenny Roberts's GP Motorsports to translate those ideas into metal. I felt three years ago that he had a reasonable mix of promising and not-so-promising ideas for street and/or racing motorcycles of radical design.

Two years later I feared the public side of his work shared too much with past Indian revivals—too much drum, not enough melody. Now I've returned from another trip to Portland. In brightly lit premises I met the new staff and saw them at work with modern modeling and CAD software, about to cut metal in a shop full of new equipment. I saw the initial main casting for an engine of original design and many rapid-prototyped plastic parts—engine and chassis—in full scale. I saw a dedicated dyno room containing new units, plumbed and connected, ready for business. Great things could be accomplished in this dream shop, which is similar to facilities I saw at Roberts's place in England. Just getting this far is a serious accomplishment.

Here is what they are up to.

The machine you have seen in magazines and videos is a trial-of-concept test mule, powered by an engine made from reworked Suzuki parts. It does, however, embody many of the ideas that will be carried forward into the next machine, whose powerplant is designed by the new professional staff.

The engine appears at first to be an inline-four, oriented the long way in the chassis. Then you see that it's split in the middle—two 180-degree parallel-twins, rotating in opposite directions. In the test mule, this was accomplished by placing gears on the inner end of each twin crank, then raising the front "half engine" to enable the two gears to mesh. Because it would be difficult to machine step crank-bearing bores and insufficiently strong to fasten cases together as they are in the mule, the new engine is different. All its crank-bearing bores are in line, and the central gears mesh not with each other but with gears located on the axis of a jackshaft running alongside the cranks. One of these connects through an idler, thus allowing its crank to turn opposite to the other as both cranks drive the shaft.

What does this accomplish? Instead of presenting the engine's broadest profile to the wind, it presents its slimmest. The goal is not the cancellation of engine gyro effect; Yamaha and Suzuki also had twin contra-rotating cranks in their two-stroke 500cc Grand Prix engines. Instead, the purpose is to permit lengthwise mounting without disturbance from crank inertia.

Clutch and transmission axes parallel the crank, with final drive turning 90 degrees via angle gearing, passing to the rear wheel by conventional chain drive.

Front suspension is by a single spring/damper unit integrated into the steering head, rather than by separate dampers and springs in each fork leg. While current sport bikes and MotoGP designs provide supplementary in-corner front lateral suspension by allowing steering head and forward chassis to flex sideways, Czysz commendably moves the flexure closer to the tire. The lower legs of his fork are oval, giving large twist and braking stiffness combined with enhanced lateral flexibility.

To ensure supple fork action both under heavy braking and during acceleration when tire load is light, the fork sliders move on linear roller bearings rather than on the usual lubricated Rulon bushings. The sensitive feel that results is a best-liked feature among those who have ridden the bike.

In the words of the song, "An' if that ain't enough to make you flip your lid, there's one more thing . . .," the lower fork crown attaches to the stem via a pivot that allows the legs to tilt slightly from side to side in response to mid-corner bumps. That motion is opposed by a compliant link between the top crown and the top of the stem. The stiffness of this link can be—and has been—varied, and a damping medium can be included if that is found desirable.

The engine presents other interesting features. Its bore/stroke ratio of 1.75:1 is beyond the 1.5 usual found in modern-say sport bikes yet short of the higher ratios that lead to Formula 1's cramped combustion chambers and sluggish flame speeds. At the 7,500 G peak piston acceleration now accepted in sport bike engines, that yields peak revs of 15,000. Given combustion pressure usual in early development, that becomes just over 200 horsepower, which is comparable with what is claimed for 1,000cc fours in World Superbike. The engine has four valves per cylinder set at an included angle of 21 degrees and driven by conventional inverted-bucket tappets.

To continue the theme of reduced frontal area, the engine could not have its intake system project to the sides in conventional fashion. Therefore,

*Lee Klancher*

Czysz resorted to some trickery. Cylinders 1 and 3 are angled slightly one way from the engine's central plane, while cylinders 2 and 4 angle the other way. This permits the intakes (two per side) to be folded in against the engine to minimize their contribution to width. It also places all four intake bells within an airbox of reasonable dimensions. This angling of the cylinders also offers the option of a staggered "big-bang" firing order. With this narrow-angle V-4 layout, three camshafts are necessary. The center (intake) cam and one side (exhaust) cam are driven by spur gear train from the rear of the engine, while the second exhaust cam is driven by gear from the front of the center cam. Engine intakes are fitted to pass down between intake and exhaust cams on both sides, making the result quite narrow. If necessary for drive stability in the racing application, a Cosworth-style compliant drive element can be built into the cam gear train.

Oiling is by end feed of the cranks in F-1 style, from what is at the moment a wet sump. If the engine is raced and requires it, this may become four separate dry sump crankcases (again, F-1 style, to eliminate cylinder-to-cylinder air-pumping loss), each with its own scavenge pump. The water pump is to be electrically driven, allowing its speed to be matched to actual need and saving some power.

Familiar geometry prevails at the rear of the machine, allowing squat/antisquat suspension forces to be conventionally adjusted by changes to swingarm pivot height. This supersedes an earlier version with concentric front sprocket and swingarm pivot. To provide supplementary rear suspension at high lean angles, swingarm beams are compliant laterally but stiff vertically as seen in conventional racing machines of the past five years. Czysz calls his focus on such lateral eompliance "2D suspension." This gives a name to the need that appeared so dramatically 13 years ago when Wayne Rainey's super-stiff Yamaha YZR500 failed to hook up in corners in the first Grand Prix of 1993. It was then clear that future motorcy-cles would need two suspension systems: the conventional vertical one of dampers and springs, plus a new lateral one, currently of engineered flex-ibilities, at right angles to it.

To avoid the width and drag of a typical "square-rigger" radiator (in conventional bikes, it is the full width of the fairing), the Czysz machine has two narrower radiators—a front and a rear.

Start-up capital has provided a spacious, well-lit design office equipped with the usual computers running a wide range of Ricardo design software. Next door, a machine shop stands ready to cut metal with Haas machining and turning center, a surface grinder and other tooling. Adjacent are engine and chassis assembly areas and a 3D shape-development shop centered on a giant CAM router. A dyno room contains a new Superflow 902 engine dyno and also a chassis unit. At the time of my visit, some machined parts had begun to arrive from suppliers. Pistons, cranks, and rods will be sourced from Cosworth.

In the design office stood the first main engine casting, produced in a mold generated directly by a computer-driven, sand-layer deposition process akin to that of rapid prototyping, This potentially allows delivery of a metal casting as little as one week after receipt of the computer file. The four canted cylinders and the head are made in one piece, eliminating not only the sealing problems of a head gasket but also the distortion and weight associated with conventional bolt retention of a separate head. Valve seat machining can be carried out with straight-on tooling through the cylinders, thanks to the short stroke and narrow valve angle. This cylinder/head unit secures to the crankcase by long studs which pass through case and main bearing girdle.

The prototype phase of engine development is undergoing important changes thanks to short casting lead time. Instead of preparing 20 or more prototype engines as is normal, evolution of the design can begin from the very first casting, leading to adaptive changes in the second and later castings.

The really fascinating part of my time in Portland was the interplay of Czysz's conceptual aims and the hardware experience, and factual understanding of powertrain engineers (and Cosworth "graduates") Simon Jackson and Adrian Hawkins. They said this job caught their attention because it offered a change from the standard implementa- tions that are the usual fare in specialist firms such as Cosworth, Ilmor, and Lotus Design. Engineering—race engineering, in particular—is very conservative, favoring refinement of existing architectures over exploration of alternatives.

These engineers say they enjoy the challenge of finding practical ways to implement the novel priorities that Czysz insists upon. Reshaping the engine into a new architecture has required solutions for unusual problems. Who can argue with reduced frontal area or with the idea that sport and racing motorcycles need both conventional and "sideways" suspen- sion? Czysz believes that by shifting his focus away from expensive refine- ment of the conventional toward identification and solution of neglected problems, he can create a vehicle with abilities unique enough to make a place for itself in the market or on the track. His backers clearly agree. His plan calls not only for early limited production of the machine now in work, and possibly for entry into racing, but also for other production types to follow, including a 600.

Motorcycles have more drag per square foot of frontal area than do cars, because a bike's wake cannot be closed within its short length. This is part of why a small four-door sedan may achieve better fuel economy than large-engined sport bikes.

Therefore, the obvious strategy for motorcycle drag reduction is to minimize frontal area. Japanese 1,000cc sport bikes have measured 21 inches across their fairings, with the classic Ducati 916 sveltest at 19 inches. A year ago, Kawasaki's ZX-10R split the difference at 20 inches. Is this width the fault of the transverse engine? If you transversely line up four big 87mm bores in a row separated by 5mm of metal and add 25mm on one end for a gear cam drive, you get an engine width of just under 16 inches—the hip width of a human and that of the transverse engine in Yamaha's MotoGP YZR-M1.

At present, the trend of chassis design is to concentrate engine and gearbox mass far forward, loading the front tire to hold line during off-corner acceleration and allowing use of a swingarm 24 or more inches in length. Czysz's longitudinal engine reverses this trend in hope of a drag reduction from reduced width.

Czysz's ducted rear radiator is much like that seen on the Saxon Triumph of a few years ago. This can be highly effective because it takes in high-energy air from near the front of the machine, converts that energy into pressure to push air through the radiator core, and then discharges the heated air into the low-pressure region behind the machine. Properly executed, a ducted rad is a low-grade jet engine that can combine good cooling with low (or even non-existent) drag.

I very much like Czysz's devotion to his 2D suspension concept, and I believe the rolling-bearing fork may give a useful jab to makers of conventional sliding-bushing forks. Nikko Bakker built a single-sided roller fork some years ago but it was not adopted. Chassis lateral flex was hailed in the late 1990s as a means of improving tire grip in bumpy corners, but today its lack of damping facilitates chatter and "vibration." Thorough analysis and novel solutions are needed. This is an area in which a modest investment plus effective thinking could produce significant results. I hope to see it.

Unlike some Internet pundits, I am unbothered by the 1–2 percent power loss that occurs in the right-angle drive between Czysz's engine and front sprocket. Every rear-drive car has exactly this kind of right-angle gearing, and Czysz is in any case not part of a horsepower race.

I'm not easily persuaded by radical projects. Success is expensive and it seldom happens by accident. Ducati estimated its price of admission to MotoGP at $32 million—and it already had established design and development groups, prototype shops and long rows of dyno cells. Conversion of ideas into performance requires testing. Cam drives develop parasitic oscillations. Oil defies gravity. Torsional vibrations not found on the drop-down menus devour shafts and gears. Recursive testing and redesign settle such issues, but their costs can be punishing. This is where the majors shine. Their resources and experience trample such problems to death. Therefore, what Michael Czysz proposes is ambitious. Aprilia, with experienced racing personnel and 18 race department dyno cells, failed in MotoGP despite a powerful F-1–based engine and wind-tunnel studies. Ducati, dominating World Superbike for years, has won only four MotoGP races.

Czysz must not compete with the majors at their own game, as Aprilia did. As the late rider/engineer Al Gunter told Dick Mann years ago, "You can't beat your competitors using their methods. They had them first and will always be ahead of you. You have to find something new that's yours alone."

I hope Czysz will spend wisely on crucial issues like lateral suspension, whose solutions may maximally improve performance at minimum investment. That is his wager—that carefully targeted development can raise the game significantly. We await the product.

# *Part 4*

# RACING REVEALED

John Owen

# The Racer
# as Tourist

*For once, what we explored was not race tracks. Was it perhaps Renaissance palazzos? No. The Museo Moto Guzzi, wood pattern-making at Morbidelli, and dynamometer testing at Minarelli. With always wonderful food.*

Racing will make of you an international Philistine if it can. You get a start money offer at a foreign circuit, pack madly, grab your passport, and fly. You arrive out of breath and short on sleep, force your way through the language barrier, buy your way to the circuit, race, and finally get out, thankfully, win or lose. Back on the airliner you can remember in fitful torpor that you have completely ignored an entire different people, culture, and history. Wasn't I within 50 miles of where Caesar crossed the Rubicon? But there's never time. Crankshaft in, crankshaft out, weld that crack, tote that crate.

After the AGV Cup at Imola, Italy, in the fall of 1978, it was different. The race came at the season's very end. With nothing else to do, we could stay out the full 14 days of our economy flights, a full week to spend after the races. We rented (or did we buy it?) a tiny car and set off to start a second career as tourists.

My first trip to Italy had been in 1972 and it was a classic, a trans-Europe mad hustle in a 24-horsepower van of no known make. Refused at one German border point for lacking the green insurance card, we tried another, less businesslike frontier and sped on. Practice was a nightmare of hurry and anxiety. Even dinner at the hotel was a fright. We tried to order, searching desperately for cognate words the waiter would understand. Aha! Spaghetti! The tired man was using a kind of passive resistance towards our ignorant babble. They want spaghetti! I'll give them spaghetti. Here it came, a big steaming plate of plain, tasteless, boiled spaghetti. Sauce? Meat? Incomprehension. Salad? Maybe. Much gesturing. Here he came back again with a plateful of plain lettuce. We eat this. This is our dinner.

The 1978 trip was a revelation. We stayed in an excellent provincial hotel far from the track and staffed by friendly people. Much of the time we had an Italian-speaking guide who liked to eat and drink, and saw to it that we all did too. Every meal was a leisurely and civilizing affair of several courses, each of which was brought around in advance for our inspection. Yes, please, I'd like some of these and some of that and a little of those. Wine and water bottles lined every table. There was time to talk over the day and digest its events, to relax completely. Each course followed imperceptibly and was often unusual as well as very good. These were not the war horse favorites made familiar by U.S. dining Italian restaurants. Afterwards, if we liked, an evening in the sitting room, sipping something agreeable from the bar.

All the little details of life were rewardingly different. Really, it was a matter of sparing the energy required to open my eyes and look at things. Wonderfully worked wood is everywhere. Windows were fastened with graceful and effective cast bronze fittings. A remarkable variety of ceramic tile and rock surfaces promised to last forever. The ordinary parts of things seemed to have commanded respect in the

*Lee Klancher*

making. The well-cared-for land showed the same attention, miles of neat grape arbors lining all the roads. After the racing, our itinerary called out a trip to the Moto Guzzi museum near Lake Como in the northwest, then a visit to Minarelli in industrial Bologna, where the great racing engineer Jörg Möller is engaged in a 125 Grand Prix program. Then we would run down to the Adriatic coast and see the Morbidelli factory where Grand Prix machines for all classes are in preparation.

We already had plenty of *autostrada* experience from the many trips to Milan airports in search of missing bikes and tools. Each of these 600-kilometer round trips had cost us $96 in truck rental, fuel, and tolls, carried out at a steady, governed 107 km/hr. The extremely noisy open-chamber Fiat diesel had given us an amazing 20 mpg at near-70-mph speeds, pulling this very large vehicle. I wish I had one now.

Our little rented Opel hummed along marvelously on the flat but detected the slightest hill by slowing depressingly. I curled up in the back among the piled luggage to enjoy my post-race headache. Richard Schlachter drove while Jeff Cowan, Wes Cooley's mechanic, puzzled over the pleated pieces of paper which we had been told were maps.

Giant, unfamiliar-looking Saab-Scania and Fiat trucks with strange wheel arrangements rule these roads, and the usual German and Swiss businessmen bear past at 80 and 100 mph. The service plazas offer gasoline at nearly two dollars a gallon, together with faster-paced and less tasty versions of the meals we had enjoyed at the hotel. Our *lire* left us quickly wherever we went. Onward to the bank!

An early start got us up to Lake Como in the morning. The lake's three arms lie among the feet of the Alps, where great fractured masses of limestone cliff towered up in the electric morning sunlight. The rock itself was creamy and glowing in the light, but here and there streaked with dark gray, as though years of dingy smoke had been imperfectly washed away by rain. My headache made it all a bit unreal—the rock walls didn't seem to me hard surfaces that I might climb so much as interesting apparitions of light.

The shore road passes through tunnels, some cut through solid stone with no inner facing of masonry and no lights. Others had crude windows blasted through to the light, making us inhabitants of an ancient fortress, armed in imagination with terrible bronze bombards. People have been doing clever things in these parts for a long time. Other tunnels are really roofed roadways with rows of heavy columns supporting the earth above, providing a shaded secret view of the lake from within.

Here in the new sun were the grand closed-up summer places and the former estates, perhaps staffed until just recently by servants able to remember more opulent times. Architecture ascends the hillside on one side of the road and a solid row of matching formal boathouses fronts the lake on the other. Each boathouse has a sundeck caged in wrought ironwork to keep out less-fortunate citizens. Various neglected boats are still in the water. In one place a heavy stone breakwater many feet high shelters an ancient cabin cruiser beyond repair. Its owners are interested in other things now.

*Lee Klancher*

The destination is Mandello del Lario, the home of Moto Guzzi on the eastern leg of the lake. In the boom years of the 1950s Italians were eager for cheap motorized transport, and Guzzi turned out just what was needed. To nourish the imaginations of moped owners there was roadracing. A great era of racing flourished, with the many makers pushing technology forward quickly in rapid developmental strides. From Guzzi there came a remarkable series of machines, concentrating at first on a single exquisitely simple theme, then spreading out into wide innovation. The pre-war machines had been horizontal singles; the new Grand Prix racers were developments from them. The center of gravity of these powerplants was actually below the axle centerlines, contrasting strongly with recent multi-cylinder engines whose crank centers are 15 to 18 inches off the ground.

These Guzzi singles were remarkably efficient for a variety of interesting reasons. Their cylinder heads faced straight forward, so direct cooling air had a straight shot at the hot, troublesome area between the valves. This excellent cooling allowed engineer Carcano to narrow the angle between the valves for better entry to the cylinder and reduced short-circuiting of charge from intake to exhaust during overlap. The horizontal cylinder also allowed complete freedom in locating the intake tract. On the contemporary Norton Manx and Matchless G50 singles, the intake angle could not be raised too far without interference between carburetor and fuel tank or seat. On these Guzzis, a steep downdraft angle contributed to good breathing, putting the carburetor bell just below the lower steering race. There was room for everything, and Carcano exploited every means to make the result handy and light. Power was never staggering, but the good torque spread and extreme light weight made a potent package on all but the fastest circuits.

By concentrating on this simple design, Guzzi was able to win and defend their championships for a long time. Eventually, despite the 210-pound weight of the 250 and 350 Guzzis, the horsepower of multi-cylinder competition from Gilera, MV Agusta, and others, was beginning to tell. After sporadic adventures with V-twins, in-line threes, and fore-and-aft fours (looking for all the world like miniature Offys), Carcano decided to go straight to the heart of the matter. If cylinder multiplication was the technology required, he would master it. The new Moto Guzzi would be a water-cooled V-8. Transverse fours and sixes were too wide. Air-cooling could not scoop out the heat from the many recesses of such a complex engine. So it was done.

Two questions remained: really high rpm was still a mystery, and there were troubles with crank and rod bearings. Handling had been worked out a long time before for the remarkable singles, but with eight times the cylinders there was no place for the weight to go but up, both in pounds and in height off the ground. Traditional geometry and the tires of those times put engine and rider at the extreme rear of the frame, and the frames themselves were none too strong. Suspension was just emerging from the friction-damper era. There were too many problems to solve all at once, though the eight was moderately successful. After much development and a rising tide of expense. Guzzi was ready to withdraw from racing. It would be left to the growing Japanese company, Honda, to continue the struggle with the problems first defined by Carcano's design, and even they would need lots of help.

The Guzzi offices turned out to be cool, humid, and nearly empty. There was in their dark corridors the atmosphere of a severely run school, or even of a convent. The floors were of the inevitable stone. An austere graph on the wall lectured the visitor about reduced stopping distances with integral braking, a modern Guzzi feature. There was a woman under glass in a kind of office. My tentative questions about the *museo* provoked a telephone call. Moments later another woman, clad in a seminary uniform and thick, rope-soled sandals, arrived to assess our request. She in turn summoned yet another level of judgment, a thick-lipped young man in a white, turtle-necked sweater. He looked very like the men in the scooter ads of the late 1950s: foppish, sleek, and self-conscious. Please come back at three. The "please" was not his goodwill, but his training. He should be happy if we came back on Doomsday. Apparently the museum is not a walk-in, but only to be seen by appointment. We have no appointment, but perhaps. . . .

All right then. We can drive down to the lake and look around. I would like to find a quiet place to leave my headache. Good fortune showed us the way to a fine little park. I walked down to the water's edge and looked out to the far shore. Maybe that's what's so nice about the ocean—it has no far shore. Yet this lake was extremely pleasant, misty and blue in the distance. Somewhere behind the trees a harsh mechanical chattering came from a gravel separator. This was strange because the area is so obviously populated by the rich, their private hoardings all protected and fenced. Here is noisy work invading every preserve.

An empty gravel streambed led down to the water nearby, crossed by a caged and padlocked bridge. This dry run must thunder and shoot in the springtime because it is pointed right at the mountains above, already topped with new snow.

I can't cross the bridge, so I walked along the park road where a wounded bronze soldier was subsiding pitifully on a stone plinth. Dead men are listed there, officers first.

Here came a Guzzi three-wheel truck, right out of the 1940s, its single-cylinder 500 engine thudding so heavily I fancied I could almost feel the combustion shock reverberating through the connecting rod at each power stroke. It was massively loaded down with gravel.

Back at the factory, we rousted out the young fashion plate, who listlessly led us through the offices and out into the unusual courtyard of the factory complex. This could easily be a small provincial town, for the buildings are tile-roofed and of a relaxed and almost residential character—unlike any factory I have seen. Big open wooden doors revealed high-piled steel baskets of fresh castings, and dark shapes moving within the rooms beyond suggested people at work. We entered another building and came to yet another metal cage, this one enclosing a stairway. It was like the rare-book section of a library. The man unlocked the wire door and we made our way up a stair, which by now had the character of a luxury private apartment—modern banister, genteel stone steps, steep but definitely not industrial. At the top, another door, another key. He entered and switched on some lights. We were there.

I sized up the room as the fluorescents blinked. It was a long hall with racing machines to the left. On the right were the many commercial products that had paid for them.

I turned to the left and thought no more about my headache. Here were the legendary singles, not on paper in a book, but right in my face. The cylinders were enormous! The finning of the 250 must be 8 inches across, and that of the 350 perhaps 10. How did they get those machines down to 210 pounds? These engines look very solid. The early ones carried magnetos on their backs and the later ones are evidently coil and battery. That must be the influence of the V-8—since no one could conceive a compact magneto to fire so many cylinders, they were forced to use coil and battery, just as Maserati did with their V-12 at nearly the same time.

Here is the in-line four. There are the ponderous-looking transverse triples. Most of these machines have short leading-link front ends, the ones I used to see in the pictures. Friction dampers! Here are two of the venerable and successful 120-degree V-twin 500 racers with their exposed hairpin valve springs.

I noticed considerable wear on the footpegs, the seats, and the handlebar grips. All these motorcycles had done thousands of miles of hard racing all over Europe on a busy, vital schedule 25 years ago. Under a long bench were more engines, looking as though they had been pulled from their frames after their last races and just never made it to the rebuild shop before their programs were cancelled. Here were two more, black with oil. These things are all frozen bits of a departed life.

And here was the V-8. There were several of them, complete machines and engine units. Here were the eight tiny Dell'Orto carburetors, inter-locked like the fingers of two hands. The sweaterman wasn't looking so I took the throttle linkage in my hands and made the phalanx of throttles rise and fall. Years before I had read the hero-worshipping accounts of the eight and of Dickie Dale, Ken Kavnaugh, Bill Lomas. The machine that was greater than anything that could be conceived. Staggering complexity, incredible engineering. Well, I was glad enough to be here looking at it now. Back then they needed that much machinery to get 75 bhp from a 500, and it is a nice piece of work.

On a table was a scale model of the Guzzi *galleria del vento*, the special wind tunnel which tamed all the little eddies and turbulences into the improbable but effective bird-beak fairings used then. To my question, the guide answered that the tunnel is still active today.

The only racing equipment of recent construction to be seen was all based on the transverse V-twin Le Mans, long-distance speed record versions. Though they look a bit like masquerading police bikes, each one has its neatly lettered little card proclaiming the records set. No more exotica. That's all over with. The company's business is limited and well-defined now—no more wildly expanding post-war market, no more vast sales to justify the cost of racing. This isn't 1953, and these are prosperous people whose currency is rising against our own. These Europeans are buying cars and fancy ones at that. Their motorcycle boom is over, it was over way back in 1957 when the big Italian companies signed the secret protocol which ended factory racing. The costs had become too great and the returns, in a world that wanted cars now, had become too small. Only the maverick upstart, MV Agusta, continued to race, establishing a great reputation against scanty opposition. The great machines are put away now in places like this museum and they have been for a long time. The great riders of that era are paunchy and balding if they are with us at all.

But think of it—the 1950s, the many companies, some very large and some little more than garages full of tools, all producing scores of designs filled with ideas. Fabio Cesare Taglioni and his springless valve gear, Giulio Carcano and his subtle singles, all the incredible Morinis, Mondials, Gileras, Benellis.

That particular set of conditions is over, its hopes have been hoped, flags have fallen, tracks have closed. Genial older men, former racers, builders, and designers, still come to the events to see the Japanese machines perform the latest steps. We had seen the hills around Imola solid with people the previous Sunday. Big-time factory racing has simply moved to other places, where it flourishes.

The guide was obviously getting restless. Time to go. We all thanked him and filed out down the stairs. Outside, Mandello del Lario was still a lovely place of trees and reposed buildings on a lakeshore. In Italy can anything truly be over with entirely?

We had a long drive back to Bologna and stayed again at our race-week hotel, where the staff greeted us with surprise and pleasure. The next day a short drive and some good directions got us to Minarelli, quite near the Ducati factory. Via Melozzzo da Forli is a dead-end residential street. Just up the way, exclusive shops rub shoulders with an aluminum foundry and old men in flat caps totter past with their groceries in their arms. It would be unthinkable to find an engine factory in such a neighborhood in the U.S. But here is Minarelli. Through this arched brick gate pass thousands of sturdy, unexciting cyclomotor engines, power for a dozen or a score of little-known moped brands. These engines look like smooth aluminum eggs, each with a finned cylinder projecting from one side. Here is steady, if minor, industry, supplying transport for those who cannot or will not afford cars: students, pensioners, people with other uses for their money.

Because of that strange spark which glows here and there, Minarelli has sought speed records from time to time. Italians, it seems, can convince themselves that racing makes sense; to hear that records have been set by a Minarelli means to this public that the company is healthy and the management is still interested in something. Under the heading of reminding the public of this and no doubt because it pleased him, Sr. Minarelli contracted with Jörg Möller to design a 125 twin for Grand Prix roadracing. This machine came a whisker's distance from the World Championship in its first year, running off from the reigning Morbidellis (Möller was previously with Morbidelli) with comparative ease when all was well.

Here was the door to the race shop. The secretary was opening it, and we were meeting the man Möller. He was a fit, stylishly dressed figure in his mid-30s with a large face. The shop resembled a small railroad terminal in the grand style with its broad arched roof and clerestory windows that offered a light, spacious work area. Here was the big Mercedes diesel transporter emblazoned, MINARELLI REPARTO CORSE. And a big solid new lathe. Lots of cylinder detailing equipment. There was a row of small offices, then a gap, and at the end, the test house. Running along the wall above, a row of drying, curling victory wreaths. Motorcycles, unique handbuilt factory racers on work stands, tiny and purposeful.

We introduced ourselves as well as language permitted. Möller's English, he explained, was 14 years old and unimproved by time. It was not, he continued, technical English. We must excuse any difficulty on that account.

His small office was largely bare. A drawing board stood up at a bold angle bearing a print of a new frame. He has found that frames are too important to be left to the "experts," those well-publicized frame salons we hear so much about.

I felt badly to have invaded his operation on such short notice. I had fed nearly a pound of telephone tokens into the instrument at the hotel, trying to make this appointment. May an American journalist and two racers come by for a few minutes of your time? It is possible. Come tomorrow at two.

Here was a clean desk with nothing on it but two magnesium center-float Dell'Orto carburetors and a hand-held calculator. He must, I thought, do a lot of work at home.

As our fitful conversation staggered along, a terrible noise assaulted us; an engine test! Unable to talk, we went out into the shop. The test technician, with ear protectors clamped to his head, was slowly and rhythmically revving the tiny twin against the dyno load in warm-up, the torque meter needle of the Borghi & Saveri eddy-current brake swinging sharply up and back as the frightful noise advanced and died away. The engine spoke a single mindless syllable each time, "OUANGGN! OUANGGN!" and the room vibrated with the three or four very loud pure tones from the exhaust pipes, dissonant in the extreme, and multiplied by the hard walls of the room. It was a very unusual sound. Just what I had come for.

The technician was waiting for water temperature. The moment he had it, he snapped the throttle open and the engine spun up quickly to near maximum rpm, the heavy load of the dyno slowing the rise near the top, the insistent resonance drilling into and permeating everyone and everything. Möller walked over to the open test house door and leaned there watching the torque scale as the engine sang its hideous huge notes unrestrained for a full 75 seconds. Just try a 75-second full-throttle run with your production racer engine sometime. I was impressed.

The test over, the throttle sides closed and the notes tapered steeply away to a popping idle, a sound from the familiar world. Then another run and another. There was a white flash from beneath the engine, bright and sudden like a magnesium fire. The technician and Möller paid it no attention whatsoever. Fuel or oil apparently was dropping off the engine onto the very hot pipes.

I had approached the door myself, and could see that the test was probably concerned with efforts to broaden the powerband. The pipes on the test motor had two-stage baffle cones, and it appeared that this unit might be equipped with extra-large intake disc valves. The bigger the disc, the shorter the time taken to open and close the port. Suzuki and Morbidelli are also testing engines with this feature. There was another set of the special magnesium Dell'Ortos here, but these had enormous intake bells.

Later, in the office again, Möller showed us one of the pistons, very thin, light, insignificant things with the narrowest ring grooves I have ever seen. There was little to ask Möller not already covered in the European motoring press. Did he have interests in engineering outside racing? Yes, and in perhaps five years he would turn to them for his livelihood, but for now, well. . . .

We had expected to see something like a silver-gray Mercedes somewhere in the compound, his personal car. Where was it? No Mercedes, he answered smiling. A Ferrari. The smile became a bit sly. I think this man is having a very good time. He is doing distinguished engineering work, verifying the results in international racing, and is always in demand. The rumor of a tie with Honda for future projects? No, but certainly a major company.

Technical questions were harder. Did he think there was any present barrier to two-stroke brake mean effective pressure? (Four-stroke BMEP has been as high as 200 psi, while that of two-strokes has been limited to some 135 psi.) Now Möller and others have pushed it beyond 165 psi. No, he did not see any limit thus far, except that there appears to be some critical crank speed for each cylinder size, placing a ceiling on delivery from case to cylinder. Yes, perhaps BMEP might rise as high as that of four-strokes. Hopes for four-stroke engines in GP racing? Where there is money there can be hope, and four-stroke power requires only money, not ideas.

Machines for sale soon? No plans. The horsepower of the present machine—42 to 43. What about the 48 predicted last year? Not necessary just now. How many ports? Enough. A smile. Thank you very much.

He was visibly restive towards the end of our conversation. Are these people staying forever? I, however, could not keep myself from smiling just to be there, and I told him so. We left.

An interesting man. He had been affable and interested in his guests but within limits. He was sure of himself and of his results—no need to say much. Better to just get the power up and let the engine do the talking.

The next day we discovered the Morbidelli factory in an industrial section of Pesaro, near the Adriatic. We were given a factory tour by a deputy in the absence of Sr. Morbidelli, and saw a large assembly floor covered with automatic furniture panel positioning and drilling equipment. All this impressive activity was the result of the founder's determination as an apprentice craftsman years ago to eliminate meaningless repetitive work.

After touring the public side of the factory, we were taken to lunch at a local hotel. This is the sea coast, we were told, and there are many seafood specialties; perhaps you would like to sample some of them? Yes, we would. Course after course of fish, clams, mussels, and more was brought, all wonderful and impossible to refuse. All the while the talk was racing, a small window with a big view of the European scene.

Vastly full, we drove down to the sea. On this warm and sunny afternoon the perfect Adriatic beach was almost empty. Europe takes its vacation in August—no other time, so all these many resort hotels were now closed. Impossible to get a room. All that beautiful beach was ours.

Later we were led around behind the main Morbidelli operation to a connected series of small shops—the racing department. In the first a pattern-maker was at work, using a special chisel to refine a wood pattern for the upper case casting of the new 500 square-four. Dark green against the walls was the expected row of wreaths, victories memorialized in the manner of the Caesars. A second room was full of 250 activity, two technicians fitting components to a prototype chassis. Morbi has had endless trouble with 250 and 350 handling. The combination of massive power and conservative geometry has been as hard for Morbi as it was for MV Agusta before them.

Two dynamometers were bolted to cement and steel mounts in the next shop, and on one of them was the latest 250 prototype engine, said to give nearly 75 bhp. Though designed originally by Möller during his stay here, this one is now the personal project of Sr. Morbidelli himself.

The last room had been Möller's office, and contained evidence of the recent occupant. A dark and cheerless place from which to plan World Championships, I thought. Rather like an army installation—regulation gray filing cabinet, regulation drafting board, regulation potted plant, one small window high up on the wall. Never mind. Results! There have been lots of small offices like this one, especially in Italy. Small operations like this, directed by one man, have their strengths. There is more than one way to build fine racing machines. One man who truly knows his business can concentrate the work on the real problems according to a flexible plan that quickly changes to take account of field conditions. He doesn't try to cover every useless case, such as by testing two-stroke exhaust pipes that are fat on the ends and skinny in the middle (would they work?), or by trying hopeless aluminum shift forks in the gearbox. His experience can be worth more than entire graduating classes of Magna Cum Laudes. He can leave the nonsense for the time-serving general-purpose engineers in the giant companies, whose drawings must first be initialed by J, then approved by B, revised by M, and then filed for study. Those men can go home at night to dinner and forget the whole thing.

Not Möller. Not Taglioni, not Kaaden. You can be sure that as they work on the daily problems of this year's machine they already have most of the features of next year's effort well in mind. These brains are pregnant all the time with ideas, not just when they have been inseminated with corporate money, not just when the time clock is running. Because they are genuinely engaged by the problems and are living that life. The victory wreaths are more important perhaps even than the coveted key to the executive washroom.

Not that the big budget approach of the giant factories isn't supremely productive. Guzzi had been a giant in its time and scale, and it had the results. A mature factory with an experienced and well-financed racing department is the most powerful possible force in racing. Their three shifts of engineering task groups will ultimately solve any problem, develop any necessary technology. It's just that for their results they are inefficient and wasteful compared with the one-man operations. Very few companies can afford it for long. When they get tired and go home, the one-man shops continue; the Möllers, the Villas, the Bossaglias find ways to stay at it.

Only economic necessity can muster up the real money. Only when the image of a big company needs freshening do the lights stay on all night and weekends in the race shops. That is reality, however much as we like to remember the wonderful accomplishments of Guzzi, Gilera, BMW, or Norton in the years of their greatness. The money simply isn't there for them now. It has moved on to the Japanese industrial giants who dominate world markets today.

The Guzzi *museo* was full of thought-provoking mementos of a long-gone era of factory racing. At Morbidelli and Minarelli I had seen two important proofs that racing doesn't die when the giants get out, that important and original work still gets done because there are always people who like to do it, who find ways. And fresh from the knuckle-cracking and wide-eyed running of the Grand Prix wars, it was comforting for us racers as tourists to know that long after the Castrol clouds and cheering crowds are gone something of racing still remains.

*July 1984*

# TD1: A Personal Remembrance

*It doesn't seem that long ago that I sat cross-legged on the right side of this 1965 Yamaha production racer, watching the needle of the Okuda Koki meter jump as I rocked the crankshaft back and forth past the firing point.*

Innocent events sometimes punch through time into the past, leaving us fascinated, surrounding us with the vapors of forgotten feelings. On my way back from Daytona this spring I picked up a 1965 TD1-B Yamaha production roadracer—the ancestor of the sophisticated TZ250 Yamahas which dominate 250 racing. I ran a B-model many years ago, and my friends all had them too. I've half-wished to find and restore such a machine, but it was no big thing or I'd have done it long ago, right?

New England mud season greeted me at home, and the old Avons on the bike left wet grooves in the soggy lawn. It was a hard push to the shop, where I leaned the tattered machine against a bench still strewn with Daytona preparations. Then I carried in three sets of exhaust pipes and several moldy boxes of parts. One of the boxes broke, spreading pieces everywhere. Never mind—I'd deal with it later. My Daytona coverage beckoned from the typewriter inside the house, setting me firmly back in 1984 with its water-cooling and radial tires and 180-mph speeds. In the evening I told my wife, "I have to go up to the shop to check on a part." This is something I say often. With the wet earth threatening to suck my shoes off, I trudged toward the TD1—it was the real reason for the excursion.

I turned on the shop lights and looked at the mess, then squatted down to pick up the pieces from the burst box. I began to recognize them. This little slotted brass slug is part of the throttle cable junction box. This is a remote-float Mikuni M-type carburetor—they didn't release the superior VM center-cloat carbs until late 1967, and then only to factory teams. M-types flooded under braking and, conversely, leaned out under acceleration. Seizures. As I hunkered over the parts pile, I remembered all the schemes for preventing this, schemes we had hatched and coveted and later shared 17 years ago. What difference did it make now? This junk is obsolete. Mikuni would be embarrassed even at the mention of these zinc hazards to navigation.

All the same, my mind hurtled back through time. I stood up and looked over the other boxes of parts. I might as well spread this stuff out and go through it, I thought. An hour later I was still pawing through the mess, setting grimy pieces in little piles. Each part had a nature and a story, and I remembered them all. These linen-and-varnish-insulated magneto coils used to short across to the rotor, leaving little black spots and then quitting. The sand-cast, vertically split cases required a special Yamaha jack to separate them. These forks had what we had called "joke damping" and would blow the seals in two or three races. Replacing them was a machine-shop operation, requiring the drilling out of steel pegs, the pulling of a bushing, the making and fitting of oversized pegs, or the use of Allen set-screws. Warm up the engine too fast and the cast-iron piston rings would break, in turn chipping the chrome off the cylinder walls above the exhaust ports. I remembered waiting at the parts counter with needs that didn't help the dealer one bit. Waking up in the van after an all-night 600-mile trip from Boston to Harewood Acres in southern Ontario, hearing the rumble of a Manx Norton started by an early bird intent on having his oil hot before breakfast. Cold-water shaving in the van's side mirror. Standing stiff and hungry in the sign up line.

We left Boston after dinner on Friday nights, having loaded the van with bikes, parts, and tools. Everyone put $10 into the gas kitty. Somewhere on the way, maybe on the New York Thruway or 95 South to Virginia, we were transformed in the sweep and glare of interstate headlights. That morning we had been nameless big city working stiffs, but now we were motorcycle racers. Perfect trip-timing would put us at sign-up with no time for a nap. The adrenaline rush that had sustained us through all the driving could continue unbroken right through Saturday practice. Pure energy, pure enthusiasm. It was fine.

This was the dying time for the lightweight racing four-stroke. The special Ducatis of Charlie Ingram, the Motobis of Amol Precision, the Sprint H-Ds of the national circuit all had to bow under the terrible pressure of the maturing two-stroke. Yamaha had found ways to stop the constant seizures of the TD1-A and had broadcast the message in hundreds of AMA-legal production racers, bringing this awful truth to every racetrack. The four-strokes were still very good—light, responsive, and highly developed—but the Yamaha powerplant was steadily squeezing the life out of them all. The B-model was the turning point.

My friends with TD1s urged me to prepare my racing rivals properly; pull up in the four-stroke's draft, flick out to pass, sit up, and pretend to adjust my goggles while riding one-handed.

Our Boston-area TD1 stars, Frank Camillieri and Andres Lascoutx, had other humiliations for their opponents. Frank would roll out of his truck on practice morning, slide a kickstart lever on his bike, and start it *with his hand.* Lascoutx was always first onto the false grid and first out to practice. He won everything in 1966. In those days you could enter your 250 in the 350, 500, and open classes in club racing. Camillieri won them all one year, and the big-bike riders went out on strike; we won't race any more unless *he* is out of here. They compromised: Camillieri could ride, but would not be scored except in 250. After that, he would build up a big lead and stop out on the course, waiting for the big four-strokes to come toiling around. He would pull out after them from a standing start and catch and pass them down the straight. Or he would build up a half-minute lead and wait playfully a few feet short of the finish line on the last lap. When the smoking bored-out Triumphs and Nortons came wobbling into view, he would grin at them and push across the line—first.

Why so vindictive? Before the Yamahas came, you had to belong to a clique to win races—a clique centered around one of the specialty shops that did secret porting and could (most important of all) put needle bearings in your rocker arms. You couldn't just *buy* this work—that would be too crass. You had to *qualify* for it, and that meant spending hours, weeks, and years hanging out at these shops, buying lunch and hoping in time to be accepted as one of the elect. Then they might take your money and put the all-important needle bearings in your rocker arms.

The Yamaha was the great equalizer in racing. To win, all you needed was the ability to ride and $1,147 plus destination and setup. No more rocker arms. No more buying lunch.

At this point I had been standing in my shop, staring at the piles of parts, for quite some time. I was startled by my wife's voice: "How *is* that part, Kevin? Did you know it's dinner time?" Yes, it's not 1967 any more. I drifted back to the house.

I had surprised myself. I have never been able to understand the "vintage" or retro-fashion impulse. I'm not interested in repeating my own mistakes no matter what the style. But here I was, backsliding in the same way. Somewhere in that pile of parts was a catalyst, acting mutely to send me back 17 years. Would I become foolish like those fellows in their perfect 1968 Camaros, antique Motown blowing out of the eight-tracks, while both their drivers' licenses and their hairlines say they are all 40 years old? Our lives are here in 1984, aren't they?

But I still have my pale-green Okuda-Koki points checker. I could sit right down to worship my TD1 with it as I did back then—cross-legged at the right side of the engine, rocking the crank with a 12mm open-end, watching the needle, tapping on the points arm. I know these crank-mounted clutches—you have to service them after every fast start or they will slip next time. Save time by flopping the bike on its right side so the oil falls away from the clutch. Pull the cover, pull the clutch, compress it, pull the snap-ring, and you have hot, warped clutch plates in your hand. Slick. Also obsolete nonsense. Yamaha made those crank-speed clutches small because they had only one-third the torque to transmit. Seems like a neat idea until experience teaches that clutches must be sized not so much for the torque but for the heat of slippage.

Events floated into mind. We did a double weekend—Mosport up in Canada and Nelson's Ledges in Ohio, leaving after the Mosport final, tired zombies, humming through evening into dark with our eyelid hooks in place, changing drivers often and pouring much coffee. It seemed to take a long time getting to Buffalo, and when at last we saw the sign, "Bridge to USA Ahead," it didn't look right. It wasn't. This was Detroit, not Buffalo. Following the white line like robots, we had missed the turn, driving an extra 180 miles west. Rugged racers, stupid but tough. The famous Detroit riots began shortly after we had whistled through the empty early morning tunnels and vacant interchanges.

The following week I had collected everyone's magneto rotors to have them re-magnetized. When I failed to return one rider's rotor on time, I found a poem on my bench.

*Urban uproar, Black ghetto*
*I care only for my magnetto*

My TD1 never started well and I never figured it out, although in the process I learned to rebuild cranks, port cylinders, and do other fancy things that didn't help either. My worst start was at Mosport. No doubt my calves bulged in my $100 Lewis leathers as I pressed forward against the locked front brake, looking at the starter's flag. Push-starts were still in vogue then. The flag was up! I lunged hard, heaving the 236-pound machine ahead, dropping the clutch on the third step. There was no answer from the motor. I heaved, clutched, and heaved again. Riders streamed by me on both sides as I tried to keep from falling over my bike in my struggle. No reaction from the engine as I spun it over. Push! Now I was the last rider, for even the most recalcitrant Ducati had fired and left. I could hear the hollow EEEEOOOOEEEOOO of my intakes as I searched unavailingly for that perfect throttle opening, the one that would bring the engine up with a shriek. At a faint pop-pop-pop I snatched the clutch in with hope. But the noise died away. My legs were very tired now, and I noticed a great need for air. I began to worry about being ridden down by the riders coming around the circuit behind me. Lapped in 200 yards! How long had I been pushing? Long, I was sure. Turn one, where the track turns downhill— gravity will help me now. As I pushed out of sight around turn one, a ragged cheer went up from the few spectators there.

That was humiliating, but worse was to come. I sold that machine to a Vespa mechanic who saw instantly what I had overlooked—two different needles in the carburetors.

*Lee Klancher*

It wasn't all like that or I never would have continued. There were fine moments. My best race centered around a lecture I gave myself. I had just fitted a set of 1967's latest tires, Dunlop Triangulars, and I engaged in this self-directed monologue: I am a novice, my corner speeds are slow, but now I have these fine tires. At such speeds, on these tires, I am as safe as if at home in bed. Just snap open the throttle in turns and nothing will happen except I will go faster. In the event I followed a Ducati 250 into Gunnery Corner, a long right-hander, and I opened up. I closed on him quickly (the throttle is a great thing, isn't it?), and he, hearing the crack of my exhaust, tried to escape. Accelerating, he leaned over farther and farther, but I pulled up easily on my lovely tires. Presently his peg struck a long stream of red sparks from the tar and then dug in. He slid and tumbled off the course while I continued, elated and confused at the same time. Certainly my idea about the tires had been proven, which was nice. Overcoming fear is valuable. I had passed one of the highly touted Ducatis in a corner, and that was nice too. There was also something else more valuable—I had felt that sudden elation and clarity of mind spoken of by mountain climbers, motor racers, soldiers in battle, that state of grace in which it seems you have become perfect and cannot possibly make any error, cannot be touched by events. I had, for a moment, become a perfectly relaxed passenger in the back of my own skull, looking out with calm detachment as my actions unfolded. It was a tremendous feeling. It was also a dangerous one, as any drunk on his way home from a party well knows.

I gave up racing at the end of that year, turning to working on other people's machines instead.

Now here is this old TD1-B in my shop, asking me to find the missing parts, to sandblast and paint, to renew bearings, to re-create. It has already paid me well for these services by turning my thoughts back to the big, gnarled roots of my enthusiasm for this sport, back to the silly romantic notions, the elations, the round-the-clock enthusiasms. I think it's a fair deal.

# Breaking Away:
# Doug Chandler

*Like actor/writer/humorist Peter Ustinov, Doug Chandler
had great strengths in multiple disciplines, and like Ustinov,
he never quite became supreme in any of them. Yet for a man
who could do anything, to focus in one area means giving up
so much. Who could do that?*

At the June 10th World Superbike round in Brainerd, Minnesota, Doug
Chandler challenged the best four-stroke racing teams and riders in
the world. He led the first leg, only to slow with engine problems. In the
second leg he simply rode away to the win.

Chandler's performance at Brainerd began one of the most impressive
displays of roadracing talent since 1977—Kenny Roberts's last year in the
U.S. Aboard his Muzzy Kawasaki ZX-7, Chandler went on to dominate
four of the first seven AMA Superbike Nationals, clinching the 1990 U.S.
title with one round remaining.

Two years ago, only Rob Muzzy was gambling on this outcome. He had
hired Chandler for his Kawasaki team at the beginning of 1989, both men
having been employed by Honda—Muzzy as technical manager, and Chandler
as a dirt-track and roadrace "B-team rider." Because Chandler finished few
roadraces on the Hondas, he attracted little attention, but Muzzy—the man
who had been instrumental in title-winning Superbike rides for Eddie Lawson,
Wayne Rainey, and Bubba Shobert—liked what he saw.

Doug Chandler, 25 now and a California native, looks like a rangy
Midwestern farm boy who hasn't quite got his full growth yet—slender

still, but stringy and tough. You might expect to see him out stretching fence wire with his granddad. Deep creases at the sides of his mouth give him a deceptively grave, serious look. It may be that on the Grand Prix circuit, riders have speech coaches (as politicians have) to improve their projection in press conferences and interviews, but Chandler's language is richly dotted with ain'ts and dropped g's. Dirt track is where he's from and he doesn't pretend otherwise. Like other trained athletes, Chandler moves with tight springiness, but as with Wayne Rainey, there is grace besides.

That grace and Chandler's impressive dirt track performances—between 1983 and 1988, he won eight Nationals—may have been what piqued Muzzy's interest. But in 1989, the initial unreliability of the Kawasaki, like earlier mechanical problems with the Hondas, concealed Chandler's developing roadracing skills. Once problems with the Kawasaki's valve control and minor oil leakage were solved, Chandler's promising but short rides extended into decisive wins at the end of 1989—but too late to affect the championship. His first National roadrace win did, however, place him with Dick Mann, Kenny Roberts, and Bubba Shobert as only the fourth rider in AMA history to accomplish The Grand Slam—scoring victories in mile, half-mile, TT, short track, and roadrace Nationals.

Great things were expected at Daytona in the spring of 1990, but Kawasaki has a long and unfortunate tradition of ruined engines and mysterious problems at the speedway. This time, unresponsive carburetion nearly kept Chandler out of the top-10 qualifiers, and no one gave him much chance of success in the 200-miler. While the leader, Dave Sadowski, dueled the last few laps with Randy Renfrow, Chandler moved unobtrusively up the leader board into third. More interested in championships than in races, he squeezed valuable points from his poorly carbureted machine. I thought of Wayne Rainey, who began a winning season here with similar persistence not so many years ago.

At Atlanta, Doug Polen returned from Japan to win on a Yoshimura Suzuki, but Chandler's close second place took maximum points because Polen rode on a Japanese license. The long-awaited Keihin flat-slide carburetor, promised to Muzzy before Daytona, had finally arrived to end the Kawasaki's carb problems. Things would be different now.

The U.S. World Superbike round at Brainerd was next. Chandler's cautious ride to a third and a first there showed the level of his skill, and the performance of the Muzzy Kawasaki. There was more to come.

At Loudon, New Hampshire, Chandler won with confident ease on a redesigned racetrack. He made time on the fast sections; on the slow corners, he visibly refused any temptation to push, satisfying himself with braking on the approach until the rear wheel showed daylight. Across the pavement jump onto the front straight, where other riders lurched heavily, Doug already had his machine sliding; his well-set-up suspension ate the bump, making it invisible. By comparison, the pursuing riders looked overworked. Chandler, responding to pit signals, cruised out of reach, leaving his pursuers ragged under the strain of his pace.

Two weeks later he repeated the win at Elkhart Lake, Wisconsin, a track where top-end power is invaluable. Chandler and the Kawasaki had now matured into a combination with everything. At Miami—a slippery, bumpy street course new to all the riders—Chandler went faster and faster through practice and race. Although teammate Scott Russell would achieve the fastest lap of the weekend, Chandler's quick early laps were decisive. Learning fast can be even more important than being fast. At Mid-Ohio, Chandler won again.

These four back-to-back wins and his title-clinching third place in Topeka (after leading most of the race) establish that Chandler has little more to learn from the U.S. Superbike scene; he is racing only against himself.

Nor was the win at Brainerd against world competition an accident, a one-time affair. Chandler subsequently won the Japanese round of the World Superbike series, at the Sugo circuit—a track he had never seen before.

I asked Rob Muzzy if Chandler is ready now to fulfill every roadracer's dream—to ride the Grand Prix circuit.

"If he'd finished all those races [on the Honda team, two years before], he'd be ready now. But no, I don't think he's ready yet."

Muzzy agreed that another year in U.S. Superbike would be pointless. What could Chandler do in 1991 that lies between U.S. racing and the Grand Prixs?

"World Superbike," Muzzy answered shortly. "If he were to go to Europe right now [in the Grand Prixs], he'd get a second-echelon ride, and you just might as well not do that at all. If you ride last year's bikes, like Bubba [Shobert] was supposed to do [in 1989], you'll be pretty near invisible."

I thought about that idea. A season in World Superbike would allow a rider the opportunity to learn the Grand Prix circuits and adapt to European life—without the super pressure of the Grand Prixs.

Muzzy's direct, economical manner is so authoritative that it discourages discussion. I pressed on. What qualities did Rainey and Lawson have when they were ready, that Chandler now lacks?

Muzzy's answer centered on Doug's one position at the top of U.S. racing. Without man-to-man competition, Chandler gets little opportunity for the cut-and-thrust of tactical racing. What will happen when he is confronted with what writer Michael Scott calls "the hard men of Europe" at full strength, plus the need to learn new circuits, plus the foreignness of it all?

Muzzy pointed out the pattern in the emergence of American road-racing talent. Each future great has had an opposite number, a nemesis, to act as a goad and a mirror for his developing talent. Lawson and Spencer had each other, as did Rainey and Schwantz, Chandler, like Kenny Roberts, has only himself.

Yet Chandler manages to grow, showing new turns of speed with each passing race. Almost as though the other riders weren't even there, he has risen through them and out of reach in a single season.

*Lee Klancher*

To become a factory Grand National dirt-tracker, Chandler has endured plenty of hard, elbow-to-elbow, man-against-man racing. His dirt track career began in 1972, as he made the local rounds from Monterey to Modesto, to the Lodi Cycle Bowl which helped shape many of today's stars. He became a four-time minibike champion and had a low-key rivalry with Chris Carr, now a Grand National superstar. In 1983, Chandler entered his first Expert race just after graduating from high school. Within a month, he won his first National at the Santa Fe short track, and went on to become Rookie of the Year.

"To me, mile racing's the best type of racing I've ever done," Chandler said. "In the past, it's always been at least six guys up in the front draft for the win. You get used to running side-by-side with a couple of guys lap after lap. A roadrace guy very seldom gets that many guys going for a win and it's new to them. They get in that situation and they kind of panic." When Chandler reaches a level of pavement racing at which he again has competitors, his background will help him cope.

And is there only one correct route to the top? Kenny Roberts and Freddie Spencer burst on the scene ready to win Grand Prixs. Lawson had to emerge from the shadow of Roberts and find his own way in Europe. Rainey departed America with his fire seemingly burned down to embers; confronted with the European challenge, he instantly and brilliantly reignited. Schwantz in his final U.S. Superbike season threw away the title trying to win corners and races rather than points. Yet now he is the most sought-after Grand Prix rider. Despite being contemporaries in U.S. racing, Lawson and Spencer ran few laps locked in man-to-man battles; for each of them it was the psychological presence of the other, and the lure of the Grand Prixs that stimulated learning.

The recent pace of Chandler's learning hasn't suffered from the absence of an external nemesis. Therefore a threat must be present—an internal threat. This year he has learned, among other things, to gauge the state of his tires as he rides, and to act on that knowledge to get the best result. He has learned how to quickly set up his bike so that it can slide controllably. Of what use is it to be tearingly fast if a rider's tires only last 10 laps? What good is skill if it must all be used up in simply maintaining marginal control of an unstable machine? "I'm really proud of myself," Chandler said. "In the past in my roadracing, we've always gotten hand-me-down bikes. It was always set up, so I really didn't have that much experience as far as bike settings, chassis settings. . . . Last year was my proving year of getting the bike, sorting the whole thing out to where you could win races. To me, that's where you can tell the good riders from the not-so-good riders."

Aside from the bare facts on the stopwatch, grace is what distinguishes Chandler's riding. He is not a muscle-over-machine rider like many others. He's not a "bust the tires loose and try to cope" improviser. Grace is the hard-to-define quality of economy of movement, of finding the natural course, of being always somehow in step with the machine. Grace cannot exist until the multitude of necessary tiny corrections in performance have dwindled into invisibility; only the performer remains aware of them. Because Chandler's speed steadily increases, he must be continually experimenting—making those little mistakes and corrections—but he manages to do so within invisible confines.

The traditional view ties grace, consistent lap times, and lack of pressure together. The buses run on schedule when times are easy. It is when the pressure is on, when another rider is aggressively sticking a wheel in, that a rider's experiments expand into gambles, and his mistakes grow into big variations on the watch. Muzzy is concerned about the lack of pressure, and what that may mean for Chandler's future, but I'm not sure this applies. His rate of learning has remained high, so the pressure must still be there. We can't see it. The pressure comes from within.

I spoke to Chandler in his garage at Mid-Ohio, where a lot of others were waiting for an autograph or a consultation. Eventually, I was next in line and was able to ask him, "Do you surprise yourself? Has your rate of growth in this sport surprised you as much as it has the rest of us?"

"No," he answered, in a quiet, matter-of-fact sort of way. "I always knew I had it in me. Even when I was doing that Honda business, I knew that once I got on bikes that were really good, bikes that would finish races, I would do it."

Most of the 1989 season must have seemed to him like more of the same, but as soon as the Kawasaki could finish races, Chandler won with it. Muzzy, when he hired Chandler for his team, had said, "I think you've got it in you, but right now you aren't riding as aggressively as you'll have to." Chandler had agreed, saying that he wasn't passing that one extra backmarker before shutting off for turns, not pushing instantly when opportunities winked. Seasons of non-finishes will do that to a rider. It's hard to develop your talent when you privately suspect you have little chance of finishing.

I asked how he uses practice. I described the Roberts/Baldwin system of running a few laps, then sitting down to mentally replay and study the results. I described also the intuitive Spencer approach: three laps on a new track, followed by a new lap record. I asked how he works.

He replied, "I like to run all the practice I can, and work with Merlyn [Plumlee, his mechanic] to get the bike working right. But if things don't go the way I'd like them to, it's no good my staying around the garage. Everyone there has a different idea about it, and it can get confusing. Then I have to get away somewhere to find out what I think—whatever the problem is."

I spoke to Muzzy separately, but on the same question. He said, "He gets moody. He gets moody when he's not the fastest. All the good ones are like that—they get moody if anyone's time is even close. It seems like they're moody, but really they're thinking. If there's anyone within a quarter or even a half-second of his best practice time, Doug's not happy. Then he goes off by himself to figure it out."

Keith Code, operator of the California Superbike School, is a frequent presence in Chandler's garage area. I asked Doug about him.

"He's the one who showed me that you could think about what you do on the track, and figure out how to go faster. We talk. He's helped me a lot."

Top riders are intelligent men and, being so, require something for their minds to do. Good minds need interesting problems. Between races, Chandler rides his motocrosser at least every other day, at various tracks so it doesn't become dull. He spends hours sliding around his father-in-law's personal short track, and on one of his own. In an interview before Daytona, Chandler said that once a rider wins the dirt track championship, the only thing he can do for an encore is win it again. In roadracing, he noted that as one level of competition is mastered, and one kind of equipment learned, there is another level above that—until the 500 Grand Prixs are reached, with equipment that is evolving at least as fast as any man's talents.

You can be sure that every Grand Prix team knows Doug Chandler's name and telephone number. Every top team is now asking itself, "Who is potentially capable of taking Wayne Rainey's 500 Grand Prix title, and won't demand three million dollars?" First-timers are not always forced to accept second-echelon rides; Schwantz didn't. There's been a lot of attrition this season, so someone new could look pretty good to a team whose only other choices may be experienced but battle-shocked men.

Whatever Doug Chandler does in roadracing next year, it will be worth watching.

# Forever Young:
# Gary Nixon

*Nixon is our hero.*

I turned the corner at the end of the garage and there was Gary Nixon, in a lawn chair as always, surrounded by bikes and activity. Nixon is 51 years old and looks entirely himself—no thicker or thinner than in his factory racer days, his hair and deeply creased face as distinctive as ever. He rose to greet me.

Behind Nixon were the many classic race bikes of Team Obsolete, the creation of lawyer and all-around controversial large person Robert Iannucci. There's a 500cc Manx Norton, two Matchless G50s, an AJS 7R, a BSA Rocket 3, all on fresh tires, many built from recently made parts supplied from the world's amazing classic-racing infrastructure. Need a Manx cambox complete? A firm in England will supply it in the original green-finished magnesium, at just under $4,000. Iannucci himself is a man who inspires strong feelings. Loyalists propose that he has single-handedly put classic racing on the U.S. motorsports map. Others paint him as a self-centered empire-builder. Both groups know he is highly intelligent and energetic, infuriating perhaps, but good company all the same.

I asked Nixon how things were going. "I wish Erv was here," he said through almost-closed teeth, his lips hardly moving. "Erv" is Erv Kanemoto, Nixon's tuner for most of the 1970s.

This is to be a weekend of vintage racing for Gary Nixon, Team Obsolete, and Robert Iannucci here at New Hampshire International Speedway. In the years before this track replaced the old 10-turn Loudon circuit, Nixon won nationals here on four different brands—Triumph (1967, 1970), Yamaha (1973, 1978), Kawasaki (1973) and Suzuki (1974).

Indeed, this is the weekend of the AMA national as well as the American Historic Racing Motorcycle Association (AHRMA) national; in the pits are lined up the tractor-trailer rigs of the major factory teams, and the shriek of inline-fours fills the air.

There are other familiar faces here. Talking with Nixon and his college-age daughters is David Aldana, who will ride the Team Obsolete BSA. Aldana won his first roadrace national, at Talladega in 1970, at the age of 19 on just such a factory triple. Busy with details on the 7R is permanent racer and globe-trotter David Roper, who now has an incredible number of hours on single-cylinder machines. Roper is a very talented rider in his own right, not just among vintage riders. He simply enjoys racing—of whatever sort. While Iannucci might like to expunge two-strokes from his version of history, Roper has a Kawasaki AIR that he rides for pleasure. The two men agree to disagree for their mutual benefit and amusement.

And maybe Iannucci isn't as historically doctrinaire as he is billed. On the workbench I see a tube of Yamabond case sealer. A hard-liner would surely use only Hylomar.

Why is Nixon here? Has he been drawn back by the promise of castor-oil fumes, vibration, and the opportunity to relive a halcyon past? Will we hear him fondly recount tales of races won on carefully crafted old-world machines whose like we'll never see again? No. Nixon is here because he is

*Lee Klancher*

being paid to be here. That's how racing works among professionals. Nixon is professional to the core.

Racing hasn't been all positive cash flow for Gary Nixon. Unlike today's roadrace stars, he had no manager, cutting deals and investing wisely in condos and tax-free bonds. When Nixon began racing, wealth meant having enough money to keep the bike running and get to the next race. As it is, he says he has enough money "to about last me, if I'm careful." Gary Nixon Enterprises, a racing-supplies business he ran for years, has now been supplanted by a radio-controlled-model store. Nixon gets by.

"I think I still got some Mikuni slides and needle jets—all the things that cost too much for anyone to buy—somewheres," he remarks, grinning suddenly, revealing his large white teeth.

Practice goes poorly, and Nixon is preoccupied by it. Racing is like that. The number one Matchless, the one descended from the work of legendary practical engineer Albert Gunter, won't start. No compression. Nixon gets stiffly off, just as I recall his doing from countless Kawasaki H2Rs, and returns to slump in the lawn chair. Somehow the cam drive on the big single has slipped. Iannucci is disgusted, issuing commands to his retainers. In time, the machine is put right, but with much head-shaking. It's hard to get a machine built as a race bike should be built without the solid foundation of a permanent rider-tuner relationship.

That's what Nixon had with the equally legendary Erv Kanemoto, with whom he had a 50/50 partnership, win or lose, from 1973 to 1978. Together they built an incredible string of wins, nearly including the 1976 World Formula 750 title. That one was politicked out from under them by peculating race officials in Venezuela.

The G50 is ready again. It starts this time, and Nixon rides out to practice. Shortly, he's back. The engine has seized. There are days like this. At Atlanta in 1973, Nixon went through engine after engine—one nearly cut itself in half—on the factory Kawasaki H2R . Kanemoto, using an upturned gas drum as a workbench, tried to keep up. Then they came back to win three nationals in a row.

This time it's the G50's scavenge oil pump, which has somehow got a chunk of aluminum in its teeth. The engine comes apart again and Nixon is given a Team Obsolete customer bike, a 1992 model. The G50 was built from 1958 to 1962, but so popular are the bikes for today's vintage racing scene that entire new bikes can now be ordered, built from modern repro-duction and substitute parts. The price is about $45,000, or what you might pay for a nicely restored original machine.

The failures at Loudon are a break in Team Obsolete's usually high equipment reliability. Roper, on Iannucci's singles, has won countless races at prestigious invitational vintage meetings all over the world. But there are days at the track when nothing goes right.

Nixon comes back in from practice, growling, half amused, half concerned: "I got a 12-lap race to ride and my wrist is giving up after 8!" He sat in the lawn chair, examining the wrist and planning out loud how to deal with it. Nixon builds sentences like a hyperactive bricklayer working on three walls. He spits out a few words on one subject, switches to another, returns to drop another couple of explanatory adjectives on the first sentence then starts another. There may be long pauses, but all the subjects remain open. Later, he stalks off to find the medical service, and returns with a wrist brace.

"I was having to . . ." He forms his left hand into a hook, showing how he pulled the clutch with his arm instead of his fingers. Such physical disabilities preoccupy him; he holds up the arm, looks ruefully at it, and grins, saying, "I gotta do a few exercises." At Daytona in 1976, when a hard practice left him breathless, he had said, "I gotta get in shape," and started jogging down pit lane. Then he'd stopped, wheezing, and called for his cigarettes. Exercise did not make Gary Nixon a national winner; strength of character and determination did that.

Whenever describing a tough situation, Nixon makes a characteristic face pulling his mouth out wide with his cheek muscles in a kind of wince, with a sharp intake of breath through the teeth. Both he and Erv Kanemoto make this face. Which is the original? Probably, like everything else in their 1970s racing program, it was 50/50. Today, he makes this face when I ask him if he's enjoying this kind of racing, whether he'll do more of it in future.

Nixon motioned towards the Matchless, which besides its engine maladies, had managed to leak a fair amount of its vital fluids. "Rode that one, the 'hot' one (he says this with an upward flick of the eyebrows) and stuff come out the side. Stuff come out the bottom. I don't know where it's gonna' come out next. I don't think very many people want to pay money to come see me wobble around in last place." Nixon fans remember this brand of painful honesty: "Gary, how come you didn't win that last one, man?" someone would ask. "Them other guys rode faster 'n me," he would answer.

Nixon's two daughters push him around in gentle, familial ways, grabbing his last french fries, bantering, making off with the van to get supplies. He's a lucky man to have such company, and he knows it.

Meanwhile, it's time for Thursday's AHRMA vintage-bike program. Races are running, and we all walked out along pit road to watch. A race countdown is at one minute when Aldana said, "Excuse me, I gotta see this." I stand aside as he looked with interest at the starter's technique with one-minute board and flag, "Okay, he gives it the slow turn. I know when I'm goin'!" Aldana remarked. Dirt-trackers pay close attention to starts.

Aldana's race is next up, and he is far back on the grid. When the flag drops, two men are away a close 1–2; local star Todd Henning from row one, and Aldana carving through from nowhere. It would be this way all weekend; Nixon and Aldana, the veteran dirt-trackers, consistently got rocket starts.

Aldana has his share of the weekend's bad luck, though. The five-speed gearbox in his Rocket 3 breaks a shift fork. As a Team Obsolete mechanic pulls the beefy internals out into a tray, Aldana starts telling BSA stories. He gets halfway into a second funny one when he stops, saying simply, "Aaagh, BSAs!"

That dismissive gesture defines a distance between vintage machines and the men who rode them. The machines are mute, and anyone can appoint himself their spokesman. Whether for the simple pleasure of ownership, or for financial speculation, the message is nostalgia. On the other hand, the heroes who rode these bikes know too much. Real life is real life whenever it was lived. For every intense moment in Turn Three or at the checkered flag, there was a balancing negative—for instance, to see the hot kid of the week get the smiles and good stuff from factory bosses, while an honored veteran gets hooked-over sprockets and a tired engine. Racing is a lot like life that way.

Gary Nixon never gave up racing. Every time his racing career appeared to be over—whether from injury, factory unfashionability, or personal matters—he would emerge as strong as ever, still winning races. When people would ask about his latest comeback, he'd reply, "What comeback? I was never away."

Any attempt to talk to this man about the nuts and bolts of racing is met with bland-disclaimers: "I don't know . . . never thought about it much." In 1976, at the original Loudon racetrack, he astonished everyone along pit lane by braking so powerfully for Turn 10 that his back wheel hovered three inches off the pavement all the way in, every lap, smoothly and predictably. Today, this is normal for riders in a great hurry; in 1976, no one had ever done it before.

"I never knew that was even happening . . . 'til someone showed me a photograph," was all Nixon had to say about it.

Nixon was once invited to teach a racing school. "What would I tell 'em?" he asked. "Watch the starter, try to get a good start, then when the race kinda' settles in, bike's runnin' halfway decent, start lappin' guys, and if everything goes right, you win the race."

Nothing to it. If you watched his riding closely, you'd never see him take the same line twice. "Them other guys, ridin' that 'Hailwood' line (again the special emphasis, the slightly mocking lift of eyebrows), you could get their attention pretty good if you come up the inside, lookin' like you're not gonna make it." That was the essence of the "inside stuff," the Nixon maneuver that pushed classicists off their wide line, then left them behind.

By 1977, Nixon and Kanemoto had left the Kawasaki camp and were re-equipped with the next-generation 750—the four-cylinder Yamaha TZ. Results escaped them with this bike. Each man went through a torment of self-examination, sure he alone was to blame. The bike was blindingly fast, but there were always problems—detonation, a bad day, a swelled O-ring. To keep the operation going, Kanemoto prepared bikes for younger riders; at first Randy Mamola, then for a young, fast Louisianian named Freddie Spencer. Nixon's bike was always ready for him every race, but after a while, the Nixon/Kanemoto partnership went onto a mutually agreed hold.

Fifteen years later, Nixon, frowning, stood in the Loudon garage and looked out. "I wish Erv was here," he said again. It's a cruel fact of racing that tuners' careers continue after riders must turn to other things. The relationship of rider and tuner can be very close, with the mere presence of the tuner coming to stand for reliability, security, good handling, good times. With that kind of support, it's easier to trust that the front tire will take the hard flick-in, lap after lap. For the tuner, a rider like Nixon, who genuinely gives all he can, is his only professional means of self-expression. When that relationship ends, it leaves a big emptiness on both sides. Nixon and Kanemoto are still close. Spencer and Kanemoto still spend time on the telephone. By saying, "I wish Erv was here," Nixon was saying, "I wish everything was all right. I wish I was having a better time."

Motorcycle racing enthusiasts who saw the contests of the late 1960s and 1970s remember starting grids full of strong characters like Nixon and Aldana—three-dimensional people with strong and evident likes and dislikes. Some say they find today's riders somehow lacking in these dimensions. This sounds like sour grapes nonsense, like old timers saying, "They don't make 'em like they used to." Of course, today's riders all have personalities; it's just that under today's conditions, they can't afford to play them at full volume.

Today's top riders are paid big money, and they know that this money paid makes them representatives of The Company. They are ambassadors of good clean fun and family values. To qualify for big money, they must not only perform well in races, but they must perform elsewhere in corporate-approved fashion. This is simply today's Yuppie contract, translated into racing terms. Give up your own personality in these listed respects, and assume instead our prosthetic personality—and we'll give you the money.

Gary Nixon missed the big money, but he had, and still has, his liberty. His exercise of freedom and independence—standing up to officials, speaking honestly and directly, and continuing to win international races long after factory team managers had dismissed him as history—these are the reasons we love him. We'd all like to be able to afford that kind of freedom.

Saturday at 12:45 was the hour scheduled for the grandly named Two-Wheel Greats Showdown, run as an appetizer to the AMA program, in which it was "hoped" out loud that the riders invited would create at least the appearance of a contest.

In the end, no one was pleased. The first displeasure is that vintage racing is not well-accepted by the AMA. The AMA is streamlining itself for television, while vintage racing hails itself as "the fastest-growing branch of motorsport." Both AMA and AHRMA need more space in the program, but there is neither room nor official tolerance for both. Anyone who saw the vast vintage pits at Daytona knows that vintage activities can no longer fit into one day. At Loudon, what formerly were several Sunday vintage events have been shrunk into five laps on Saturday. The final discontent was that while some of the two-wheeled greats produced the hoped-for contest, others streaked out ahead as racers will.

Never mind. It was great to see Gary Nixon at a national, neither reduced nor magnified by time's passage. After the racing, a plan was proposed to put Nixon back on the 750 Kawasaki he had ridden in late 1976. The machine now belongs to a collector who would love to have the great man ride it again. Would Nixon be willing to consider it?

Yes, he would. On a professional basis, of course.

# Ago: Giacomo Agnosti and MV Agusta

*Here's the story of all those championships. Did you know he
also had a career in B movies?*

Parents never know what may come of it when a child is given a
chemistry set, a baseball glove, or a small motorbike. In the early
1950s, Sr. Agostini, proprietor of a construction-and-transport business,
brought home a Vespa scooter to his son Giacomo. This act of parental
indulgence led to 15 motorcycle Grand Prix world championships and
over 130 Grand Prix wins—the highest totals ever achieved.

The step-through Vespa was a way to get a short-legged child riding
before he could get a leg over a motorcycle. And he did ride, quickly moving
on to a Bianchi moped, and in time a trials Parilla and a 175 Moto Guzzi.
Upon finishing school, he naturally began work at the family business,
but motorcycle racing had become too important to him. "If I wanted
a day off, I took it, and as I got more and more interested in racing, so I
took more and more time off until I stopped working for him (his father)
completely," Agostini has said.

He entered hill climbs and Italian races on a 175 Morini Single in
1960–61. His success earned the loan of a works Morini 175 Bialbero.
Entering his first big event at the park-like Monza track in 1963, Agostini
led the first lap by on-the-edge riding, while the experienced stars waited
for the usual beginner's mistake that would let them by safely to get on
with their race. Young Agostini soon put such mistakes behind him to

become the rider Morini had prayed for. Veteran Tarquinio Provini on the Morini 250 had nearly taken the championship from Honda in 1963. Morini signed Agostini for the 1964 season, and he did not disappoint them, taking the Italian 250 title from the great Provini, now on the Benelli four.

Eraldo Ferracci, today the U.S.-based team manager who took Ducati and Doug Polen to two World Superbike titles, was then a Benelli factory rider. Asked about young Ago, he replied, "In those days, he was an animal." The major Italian factories had agreed at the end of 1957 to quit racing, as the availability of low-priced cars like the Fiat 500/600 had killed bike sales. Unlike the others, MV Agusta didn't depend on motorcycles for survival; its major business was helicopters. Count Domenico Agusta, a son of the aircraft company's original founder, was a motor sportsman able to indulge his taste grandly. To win 500 and 350cc world championships, Agusta had imported foreign riders—Les Graham, John Surtees, Gary Hocking, and most recently, Mike Hailwood. When Agostini flashed into prominence, Count Agusta reached out and seized him.

Agostini's freshman year on a 500 was the ultimate racing education. For tutor, Mike Hailwood; for equipment, the multi-cylinder MVs. His world expanded from Italy to the grand racing venues of Europe and the world. Hailwood showed him the good line in practice then switched places to critique Ago's moves. It worked. Giacomo Agostini won his first Grand Prix that year, the 350 event at the German Nurbürgring.

Learning to ride the MVs was probably not difficult for Agostini, who had mastered the narrow power of the Morini. To make power despite limited revs, singles were tuned to use intake and exhaust resonances, effective only over a narrow speed band. By contrast, the MV fours made power through high rpm, and could be tuned more mildly. Hailwood described their having a "delightfully smooth and seemingly endless flow of power." Veteran tuner Nobby Clark points out that the MVs were, however, much less forgiving than the singles. A single could slide in control, but the MV fours would bite you.

Thus, Ago's early career was unique. Instead of scratching his way to success against a horde of identically equipped rivals, he learned out front, on machines that usually provided comfortable superiority. Countless racing miles let Agostini perfect smoothness and economy of action. Professional flying has been characterized as "years of boredom punctuated by moments of sheer terror," but Grand Prix racing in the 1960s, with its bad weather, oily surfaces, and unprotected guardrails, provided moments in plenty.

There were other contrasts. Nineteen sixties Grand Prix racing existed on two planes. On top were stars like Agostini and Hailwood, traveling in luxury. Below were the privateers. Today's Grand Prix paddock is filled with giant motor homes and transporters, but then it was a gypsy encampment. Privateers lived in small trailers, sharing space with machines and fuel. Wives and girlfriends washed and hung out clothes while riders schemed for meager starting money. Now, machines of top and bottom finishers are much the same, differing mainly in use of exotic materials and computers. In the 1960s, after the 500cc MV and Honda fours howled past, the rest of the field droned by on singles, 20 miles an hour down on top speed.

Despite this, Ago soon had his hands full. Hailwood was hired away by Honda after 1965 to ride the new four. In the 500 class, Honda desperately lacked what MV had: experience. Hailwood's Honda was not only unreliable, it was downright unstable. Agostini took the title from his mentor of the year before in alternating hard-fought races and Honda DNFs. At the Dutch TT in particular, Hailwood prevailed by 5 seconds, but was so exhausted at the end that he had to be assisted to the podium. Ago repeated the following year. His weapon was the compact and handy three-cylinder MV 500 that the autocratic Count Agusta had ordered built over his engineers' objections. Then Honda switched to auto racing.

The years rolled by, and Ago and his MVs amassed world titles. In 1971, New Zealander Ginger Molloy livened things up by finishing second to Ago on a private Kawasaki two-stroke H1-R—a portent of the future. Japanese development in the smaller classes was furious, as engines went from twins to fours, fives, and even sixes. For MV, still secure at the top, no such effort had ever been necessary. Sound engineering combined with conservative preparation and Agostini's fast, secure riding had always been enough.

At the end of 1972, Yamaha introduced its two-stroke, reed-valve OW-20 Grand Prix four. The brilliant Jarno Saarinen, who had challenged the 350 MV with Yamaha's two-stroke 350 twins in 1971, now brought factory two-stroke power to 500cc racing. For the moment, the MV remained the more powerful machine, but the motocross-stimulated suspension development undertaken by Yamaha made its bikes faster into and through turns, while the MV accelerated harder and had a top-speed margin.

A more important challenge to Agostini came from Phil Read, former Yamaha factory star. Read, a tough, experienced rider and an ambitious, highly competitive person, was hired by MV to team with Agostini. Too much was happening at once. Domenico Agusta, the force behind the team, had died in Milan in early 1971. Meanwhile, Gruppo Agusta had designed the A129 Mangusta antitank helicopter, and the Italian government wanted and took a 51 percent interest in the company. Without Agusta, the racing team shrank in importance. Just as intensive development was essential to counter the Japanese challenge, it became politically and financially impossible.

Phil Read knew factory racing politics. As the Yamaha improved, Ago became critical of the MVs, but Read understood the uses of action—and silence. After a professional lifetime with MV, Giacomo Agostini felt himself losing ground. Read, a hard man who had thrived on interpersonal rivalry, pushed on to become 500cc world champion in 1971 and '74.

Was Agostini the protected, insulated figure his critics described, able to calmly win countless titles only by having the fastest machine? Or was he a real champion who rode only as fast as necessary to win, as his admirers believed? Now was the time of trial. Yamaha needed a championship-quality rider to replace Saarinen, who had been killed at Monza. The choice fell upon Agostini.

His first ride for Yamaha came at Daytona, on the completely new TZ750A. With his characteristic calm and apparent disregard for racing's pressures, Agostini practiced competently but without distinction. In the race, he survived several challenges, often seemingly out of the results, but came through to win the 200-miler despite suffering terribly with the unusual heat.

In the Grand Prix season that followed, Ago rode well, but rapid machine development sometimes gets in the way of winning races. Read was champion, with his new MV teammate Franco Bonera second. Ago had to be content with the 350 title, won on the new liquid-cooled Yamaha twin over MV's new technology, 17,000-rpm, 16-valve four. The following year, Ago got what he wanted; Yamaha fielded a fast and reliable 500cc two-stroke, and Agostini pushed Read down into second place.

For 1976, Ago returned to MV, running the great machines under his own Team Agostini banner. But time had run out. Without serious development, the MV fours were now behind in all areas. The hoped-for new engines—a bulky Boxer four and a new *transversale* engine with FZR-like inclined cylinders—had not materialized. The final blow was Ago's test of a private Suzuki RG500 in mid-season; even it was clearly superior to the Italian machine. The future had ended for MV, which had failed not because the four-stroke principle had nothing more to give, but because the parent company had lost the means and will to continue the work.

Agostini formally retired the following year, but his name now had enormous value. Perhaps an entirely different career in film? Ago's handsome features did grace more than one B movie, but this hardly comported with the dignified figure he had cut in racing. Ago tried—like Surtees and Hailwood before him—to enter car racing, but the intensity that had put Ago on the factory Morini in 1964 was no longer available to him. He found a new role as team manager with his old benefactor, Marlboro and Yamaha, after 1983.

Ago as manager did not please everyone. Eddie Lawson, among others, had differences with him. A new name, "Ago-stingy," was coined. On the other hand, Kel Carruthers, who worked with Ago for five or six years, says the man was never other than correct in his dealings with him. He suggests that a contract is the proper basis for professional relationships, and that those who don't write their own contracts (this often includes riders) may miss what is required of them. Still, there are too many "Ago stories" to be entirely ignored. They consistently describe a man whose eagerness for financial gain has hurt him, cutting him off from opportunity, antagonizing potential allies. Fact, or just the railings of the envious?

Agostini has advised riders, "In the years when you are riding, that is no time to think about money. Just put it in the bank and concentrate on your riding. When you retire, there will be plenty of time for investment and management." Wise words. Better indeed, if possible, to put money out of mind and work on the crucial problem of how to go fast and finish races.

While Team Agostini/Marlboro/Yamaha operated out of Italy, the Kenny Roberts organization, as tightly focused on racing success as KR himself had been, came to full strength. The Roberts team eventually assumed the dominant role as the major Yamaha team in Grand Prix racing. Team Agostini/Marlboro faded away. Today, Agostini manages Cagiva's promising Grand Prix team, handling the business side while Kel Carruthers and Firenzo Fanali manage the engineering for riders Doug Chandler and John Kocinski.

What can we say in sum? Here is a man from a family in commerce, who rose by his own quality and by opportunities taken, to become an Italian national icon and a world sports figure. When success became easy, he enjoyed it. When a challenge was presented, as by the mighty Hailwood in 1966–67, and by the aggressive Phil Read in 1972–74, he was equal to the struggle. Yet, as we all do, he has limits. If critics suggest that money may mean too much to him, or that he always plays to the audience and the cameras like a film star, can we accept this possibility? We must, or we set the scene for our own disillusionment. We are fatally tempted to hold our heroes to impossible standards, and we shouldn't. Anyone with direct knowledge of riders knows that the competitive, "me-first" personality that wins races, does not operate solely on the racetrack, and does not cease to exist when the helmet is zippered into its bag for the last time. It simply takes on new forms and continues its life. Giacomo Agostini, winner of more Grand Prix titles and races than any other rider before or since, is a man like other men, with a man's contradictory and fascinating mixture of strengths and weaknesses, wisdom and foolishness.

That mixture has earned him his place in the history of motorcycling.

*May 2000*

# History at Speed: 20 years of Honda Superbikes

*Even mighty Honda had to put their name on good old-time homebuilding from time to time. This was life at Honda, back in the 1,025cc sit-up Superbike days.*

American Honda has now raced 20 seasons in AMA Superbike, beginning in 1980 with a 1,011cc version of its air-cooled inline-four CB900F, continuing with the V45 Interceptor, VFR750, RC30, and RC45. Honda's Superbike team is now preparing for the 2000 season with its brand-new RC51 999cc V-twin.

To celebrate these two decades, Honda invited the legendary Freddie Spencer to California's Willow Springs Raceway to ride the bikes that book-end this era. The first was the type on which Freddie began his relationship with Honda—the 900F-based Superbike, last ridden by teammate Mike Baldwin to victory in 1982 at Miami. The second was the new RC51 racer, at Willow for its final shakedown before Daytona.

As I drove the last miles to the track, I could see the Mojave's mountains rising up to blend with wide brushstrokes of dark cloud, from which descended a shaft of rainbow. As the day unfolded, photographers ran to use the occasional shafts of sunlight then sought cover from misting rain. Race transporters from Team Honda and Erion Racing were on hand, with 600 Supersport CBRs and two just-built RC51 Superbikes, one for veteran Miguel Duhamel, one for *wunderkind* Nicky Hayden.

Honda was not always a pillar of U.S. roadracing. After the flash of Dick Mann's 1970 Daytona win on a race-prepared single-cam CB750,

Honda reverted for the rest of the 1970s to a General Motors–like aloofness toward motorsport. With more than 50 percent of market share, who needed racing? Then came Yamaha's challenge in the late 1970s. Part of Honda's response was a crash U.S. roadracing program, beginning 1980. Because no Honda race equipment met AMA Superbike rules, a combination of factory help and imaginative homebuilding was necessary. The basis would be the CB900F, an enlargement of the twin-cam, inline 750F, which had in turn evolved from an endurance-racing design into a street bike. Endurance-racer parts, improvisation, and a lot of human hands produced the 1980–82 Honda Superbikes.

The example that Freddie would ride at Willow now belongs to Rollin Lofdahl, and is from the 1982 season. Its stroke is actually longer than that of the current RC51 twin, showing how much engine design has changed over two decades. Bore/stroke ratio of the 1982 bike is .99 (68.3 x 69.0mm), while that of the RC51 is 1.57 (100.0 x 63.6mm). Where a weak point of that early four was its chain cam drive, the cams of the new RC51 are actuated by geartrains. Continuing the comparison, the 900F racer is air-cooled and carbureted, while the 51 is liquid-cooled and fuel-injected. The 900 is also a classic "standard," a naked bike, while the 51 is closely faired (and almost two inches narrower than the RC45 V-4 that preceded it).

The machines fielded by American Honda in 1980 combined parts from the endurance-racing program—the dry clutch and dry-sump oiling system, for example—with cylinder-head preparation from the U.S. side. Heads were sent out to all prominent airflow shops. Everything would be dynoed and the best components chosen. The professionally outrageous former racer Steve McLaughlin was made team manager; ex–Butler & Smith BMW engine builder Udo Gietl became his crew chief; and extensive fabrication was directed by the massively genial Todd Schuster. As legend has it, when Gietl proposed testing Del West titanium valves, McLaughlin grandly wrote an order for $12,000 worth. Everything was done with a flourish (to this day McLaughlin, no longer associated with Honda, arrives by limousine for business meetings in a white suit and Borsalino hat). A huge amount of work was accomplished, machines were built and raced, and Honda was back on the U.S. competition scene with a crew that knew its business.

Nothing this unconventional could long co-exist with responsible accounting practice. Ron Murakami replaced McLaughlin as team manager and set about making Honda racing sustainable. The weak RSC ignition was replaced by a reliable German-made Kröber. When Freddie dragged this ignition on the ground at Laguna Seca, Gietl moved it to where you see it on this machine, safely above the gearbox on the right side, driven by a cog-belt. The formed-aluminum front fender bracket is one of many made by Schuster—he hand-fabbed the first one at Daytona. Once proven, trick, hand-built parts like this were replaced by accelerating flows of series-produced hardware. The machines became maintainable, and mechanics ceased having to do engineering after midnight.

For the first go at Daytona, 1980, Mr. Aika, famed manager of Honda's 1960s Grand Prix team, was present. Although he guaranteed the durability of the 1,011cc engines, the team soon found ways to break them. Can mild endurance cams win sprint races? No, and sprint cams with tall, pointed lobes break the best of camchains, even with light titanium valves. At Daytona 1981, all available fresh engines were wrecked by Tuesday p.m., and the crew spent Wednesday building new ones from parts. Reliability is always made from broken parts, and in this rush program, there was no time to break them in secret. It all happened in broad daylight, just like the early U.S. space program.

*Lee Klancher*

For the 1983 season, the AMA cut Superbike displacement from 1,025 to 750cc. Honda's new V-4 750 Interceptor was ready. Intended only as a homologation special estimated to have low sales prospects, this model stunned its creators by selling out on the strength of its excellent handling. Up to that time, bikes were sold on appearance and "numbers"—quarter-mile time and top speed. The Interceptor not only redefined the sports motorcycle, in 1984 it brought Honda its first Superbike title, with rider

Fred Merkel. Merkel repeated in 1985 on the Interceptor, and again in 1986 on the new VFR750. Wayne Rainey and Bubba Shobert likewise took Superbike titles on VFRs in 1987 and 1988.

Meanwhile, Freddie Spencer would win the Daytona Superbike race four times in a row, beginning in 1982. In 1985, he won all three classes at Daytona—the 200-mile Superbike race, Formula 1 and Formula 2, then went on to win both the 250 and 500cc world championships—something that has not been achieved since. They say that time is what keeps everything from happening at once, but Freddie rode as if time didn't exist. For him, it *did* all happen at once. Of that season, Mike Baldwin (Freddie's teammate in 1981–82, and himself a former Grand Prix racer) said, "If you didn't see it, if you weren't there to see him get off the 250 and go straight out and win the 500 race like it was the easiest thing in the world, you just wouldn't know. He was brilliant."

For the 1990 season, new AMA PRO Competition Director Ron Zimmerman pushed through equipment rules allowing World Superbike-derived machines like Honda's limited-production RC30 to run in AMA Superbike. Duhamel won the 1991 Daytona with one, but the RC30 never took a U.S. title.

In 1994, three years later than planned, the RC30's replacement arrived in America: the RC45. This slow-developing machine would win two AMA Superbike titles for Honda—in 1995 (Duhamel) and 1998 (Ben Bostrom). Today, all RC45 V-4s have been retired, and both AMA and World Superbike teams will race only the new RC51 V-twin. In early testing, the twin set the quickest times at WSB practice in Australia. This move from four to two cylinders is a big step for Honda, whose name has been associated with four-cylinder racers ever since the first 250 fours, 41 years ago.

Now my attention switched to the 1982 bike. Owner Lofdahl and a volunteer crew were trying to push-start it, and it was responding by dragging its back tire, chattering, and popping. At length, it started and ran. The engine has Keihin CR carbs on it now, even though the bike still has period Qwik Silver stickers showing. It warmed up on a high, fluttery idle that Baldwin says was a CR characteristic. With the much bigger Qwik Silver carbs (good for a rumored extra 30 bhp), the bike had to be set up to "idle" at 3,500. The reason for this was two-fold: First, high idle softens wheel hop on big four-strokes during deceleration. Second, the throttle gates on the Qwik Silvers had so much stiction that idle vacuum made the throttle stick shut, impossible to lift smoothly.

"Getting that bike on-throttle was like pulling the cork out of a wine bottle." Baldwin explained. "There's this big effort, then *pop!* and you get a big surge from the engine."

Baldwin and tuner Ray Plumb tackled the on-throttle problem by hacksawing "vacuum-breaker" slots in the throttle gates. This made throttle-up much easier and smoother.

What about powerband? "The cam chain would break at 10,000 rpm, but it would pull from as low as 3,000," remembered Baldwin.

Now the 18-year-old bike was warmed-up and ready so Freddie suited up and went out on it. At first he went slowly, appropriate on a historic machine in unknown mechanical condition. Later, he rode it harder and Plumb (still with Honda after 19 years) reminded him, "Remember, they blow up at 10,000."

"That's why I'm only revving it to 9,800," was Freddie's affable reply.

This was a long bike—the wheelbase is 58.5 inches. To avoid glacial handling, the team put a quick-turning 16-inch front wheel in place of the stock 19-inch "flywheel." As Baldwin told me recently, "That dropped it down a couple of inches in front. Then, they kicked the steering head in another inch. So it (the steering-head angle) was really steep. It was the weirdest thing: Hard on the brakes, with the front end all the way down and the rear end all the way up, you could get the front end 'over center'— like negative trail. If it turned the slightest bit to either side, it would try to turn even more, and if it tucked, it was gone! It even got Freddie once. It was right on the edge."

In effect, then, this bike had the quick steering of a 250 Grand Prix bike, joined to a bus's wheelbase. "It didn't feel like it was 58 inches," Baldwin said. "But being so long (and therefore light at the rear), you could light up the back tire and slide it." This lack of rear grip would be crucial at the wet start of the pivotal Seattle Superbike race in 1981. The Hondas went up in wheelspin off the line, while Kawasaki's Eddie Lawson got the drive and a commanding lead he held to the flag.

Crude equipment? Maybe, but those do-it-yourself experiments were the foundation of Superbike's current sophistication. They were the school that educated essential men like Ray Plumb and Merlyn Plumlee—both at Willow on this day, looking after the new RC51s.

Want numbers? On a good day, this old bike might have made 145 horsepower at 9,800 rpm and Superbikes of that era pushed close to 160 mph at Daytona.

After a couple of sessions on the old air-cooled F, Spencer threw a leg over Duhamel's RC. To eliminate the complication of starting rollers, these bikes sensibly have retained the street bike's electric starter. Freddie hit the button and he was off. Like the RSV Aprilia, the 51 makes a lot of valve noise because its geared cam drive has to overcome all that valve-spring pressure, pushing the cams first this way, then the other. The exhaust sound is like that of the Ducati 996, but perhaps a bit less breathy, the individual pulses a little sharper. Instead of the side radiators of the street bike, there is a top rad mounted conventionally, another mounted vertically in the left of the fairing opening, and an oil cooler in the mirror-image position—all safe from crashes. As with all twins, total radiator area is small.

The exhaust system begins with two tapered headers in titanium, snaking all over the machine to join under the rider's right foot, then splitting into two pipes serving the two mufflers. The titanium welding rivals the splendors of Tutankhamun's treasures—wonderful!

Plumlee says of the heads, "It was kind of a shock. They look so plain inside, so much like . . . street parts. That's because they lack all the massage that's been necessary over the years to make the RC45 what it was." Honda engineers in Japan say this bike is "a much better platform than the RC45 was at its introduction." The good lap times run at Phillip Island and Daytona tire tests show how close to right this bike is.

"The first thing I noticed was how well the RC51 changed directions, that initial movement off-center," Spencer explained. "Going from left to right, through turns three and four, it turned a lot better. Right off the bat, it was much better than the RC45. It's smaller and more compact, but more comfortable and rider-friendly. I felt in control."

Duhamel concurred, saying that the RC's front end has a feel that the 45 never had. Power range? "It comes on at 7,500–7,800, and runs to 11,000–11,400. It'll pull at six, but you aren't going to win any races down there," noted the sage-like Miguel.

Lofdahl summed up the day best by saying, "When you look at all the progress there's been from 1980 until now, it makes you wonder what we'll think of today's bikes in another 20 years—what the breakthroughs will be that we'll take for granted then."

I hope to see it.

# Behind the Barrier:
# John Kocinski

*It didn't work out. Riders learn their skills on machines and tires that evolve steadily. Riders work to make these evolved machines handle and respond like the machines they began their careers with. That works for a while, but eventually the bikes and tires have changed so much it stops working. They can no longer be made to feel as the rider needs them to. Younger riders don't have this problem—yet—so they become faster. It can be puzzling and frustrating.*

I make people nervous," John Kocinski says, staring earnestly into my face. "I radiate energy. People can feel it."

Kocinski has just emerged from semi-retirement. Having not ridden a motorcycle in the nine months since his 1999 Grand Prix season finale on a Team Kanemoto Honda NSR500, he was "called up" to ride the Vance & Hines Ducati 996 in the AMA Superbike series. He replaces Troy Bayliss, who has taken Carl Fogarty's place on Ducati's World Superbike team. We were talking in the hushed, cool lounge of the V&H transporter at Elkhart Lake, Wisconsin. At the Road Atlanta round, one week before, John had begun by finishing seventh in the first race and fourth in the second.

Kocinski is not like other riders. His intensity is painful. He *does* make people nervous, because his emotions are on the outside, not the inside. He is mysterious and unpredictable, but he is also emotionally naked. Whatever he feels, you feel.

When I asked him if there was a time when I could speak to him at length, he was sitting at trackside, race face installed, waiting to go out to practice. His answer? "Next year." Then he said, "After the race. Come to the truck." I left him with his responsibilities.

Elkhart now runs a two-race format. There would be races on Saturday and Sunday, with very little practice time. In Saturday's race, there was a red flag on lap one. V&H teammate Steve Rapp touched the back of John's bike with his brake lever entering turn one. Rapp's bike flipped, bounding off the track, breaking into pieces. Rapp was unhurt.

Kocinski led off the line at the restart, smoothly pulling away from the top AMA stars, and for seven laps thereafter. Then he slowed back—sliding to a fourth-place finish, with his bike overheating badly in the final three laps. I went to the truck, but no John. Shortly team owner Terry Vance emerged, on his way somewhere. I told him I'd come to talk to John.

"I don't think so!" he replied. "He's hopping mad because the bike let him down, and he's in his motorhome at the top of the hill. You can go knock on the door if you like."

I walked up there and found the address revealed by the red V&H pit-scooter parked in front. Tossed on the pavement were John's leathers and boots. Bad time! That morning, I had talked to people who had dinner with John the night before. Their impression was that he was just doing this gig for fun, that he was above life's little struggles now. A senior figure. Ha! Don't bet on it. I returned to the truck. When I described the tossed leather and boots to V&H crew chief Jim Leonard, he replied with characteristic understatement: "He wants to do good."

In time Kocinski appeared, and he was gracious, making sure to thank each of his mechanics, then getting me a drink and excusing himself to go talk tires "for 10 minutes" with Dunlop technician Jim Allen. This was fine with me—I'd rather tell my editor there was no story than get in the way.

On his return, John marched back into his post-race debriefing, announcing first that he'd gotten another tire—one that was supposedly unavailable—for Sunday's race. Looking around at everyone, he repeated the words, "The power of negotiation," twice for emphasis. Then, he launched straight into his mental do list, beginning with a cryptic query about rear-rim width, "Five-seven-five?"

"That's little," replied Leonard.

"Yeah, but I always burn up the tire on those wide rims. Anyway, Kevin's here to talk to me. He doesn't want to hear this stuff."

"He loves it," said Jim, arranging the papers on his clipboard.

And so, standing in the doorway of the little gray corduroy cool-room, I got to hear these super-professionals go through their business. For them, it's routine—the bricks and mortar of their days. For me, it was a wonderful snapshot—John and Jim proposing and disposing, with both an Italian and an American mechanic contributing and Vance silently taking it all in. I was the fly on the wall.

"Can I get some wheelbase?"

"No. Not unless you can stand a tooth off the back."

The Ducati, with its swingarm pivot a part of the engine cases, its chain tension adjustment on an eccentric and its short swingarm length, is one of the most tightly compromised designs in Superbike racing. Changing one thing means changing everything.

"One tooth," Leonard continued. "If you're not revving it real hard you might get away with it."

"How much more?"

"Three hundred rpm."

"Can you change the internal ratios to get it back?"

"Nope."

Extra wheelbase would slightly increase front-wheel load—and might make steering on the front wheel more practical.

Earlier, rear spring rate came up: "The back of the bike's wallowing up and down," John said, making the motions with his hands. "What's that?"

"Too stiff," offered the Italian.

"Can we go lighter? Ten-eight (spring)? Anyway, I don't care if it's wobbling around, as long as it's turning. It can wobble all it wants—I need it to turn."

Kocinski's style has always been to steer with the front wheel—as he learned to do so—so brilliantly in his early years on Bud Aksland's Yamaha TZ250s. But the acceleration of big bikes unweights their front tires, making front-steer difficult. Therefore, most successful 500cc Grand Prix and Superbike riders steer with the throttle, through controlled wheelspin. This is not John's style—although he did it when necessary en route to winning the 1997 WSB title on the Castrol Honda RC45.

Jim said, "Did you look at your tire? It's not nearly shagged."

This means: You can use it harder. Spin it, even. I couldn't resist saying, "The tuner tunes the bike, the rider tunes the tuner, and around it all goes."

"Kevin has some pretty weird ideas," John said to the ceiling.

"John's pretty weird himself," Jim put in, passing on the ribbing. "His mind is a strange little room."

As the discussion continued, each point covered revealed more clearly that John wanted the machine to steer his way, and Jim wanted John to accept that Ducatis don't make that easy. The Ducati, with one of its two 90-degree cylinders horizontal, has its engine mass significantly farther back in the chassis than does an inline-four. Finally, both men ran out of words, and simply stared at each other across the small space, each one silently radiating his own thoughts. I thought of an earlier cryptic remark of John's: "I have to be able to see through steel."

Later, talking to Jim alone, I asked if he thought the Ducati could only be steered Anthony Gobert's way, on the throttle.

"No, I keep an open mind. We'll get it. It'll just take time."

The week before, in Atlanta, practice had been a madhouse of rapid-fire changes to get the riding position—pegs and bars and seat—to where John needed it. Ducatis steer as well as they do because their powerband has been smoothed to eliminate torque surges that could upset the front tire's grip. Ex-Ducati rider Pier-Francesco Chili, now with Suzuki, used high corner speed to make acceleration less necessary, but it is speed onto the next straight that's needed. Speed at the apex is not the same as speed off the corner. The coming of the Honda RC51, which is like an intensified Ducati, is magnifying the faults of the original—one of which is touchy front grip.

Speaking of the two-race format, Vance said, "The pace is too quick. We'll get something here (in terms of a useful setup), but next weekend at Loudon, we won't have anything, and we'll have to do it all over again. Did you see John's race? He's so smooth, he doesn't even look like he's going fast." The discussion in the transporter continued.

"Ten-five," Kocinski said. "That's what it's gotta' be tomorrow (the lap time–2:10.5). A lot of things have to change to make that happen."

"The leader's average lap was 2:11.7," commented Leonard. Big difference.

"That bike I rode today isn't going to do it. We have to find something that'll work."

When the invisible checklist was finished, John and I were left alone.

"Well, what do you want to ask me?" John began.

I told him that our readers' letters and e-mails show that they regard him as the misunderstood genius of roadracing. How does the misunderstanding happen?

"Neil Tuxworth [the Castrol Honda team manager] knows how to run a race team," he began. "He knows that riders need certain things to go fast. He either sees to it that they get what they need, or he makes a sincere effort. A visible, sincere effort. He does things right. They have the people."

How about the Spanish team? (Kocinski rode Sito Pons' Movistar Honda NSR500 in 1998, and somehow never hooked up—despite the fact that he made it clear that getting back on a 500cc Grand Prix bike was his real goal.)

"I speak English. I need to work with a team that speaks English—like the Castrol team."

How about Erv? (Last year, Kocinski rode Kanemoto's NSR, again with disappointing results.)

"I still have his sticker on my helmet. I ride with it. I called him up, said I was going racing again."

But was there a specific problem?

"Money. There was never enough money." Kocinski said this with clear regret—he obviously respects Erv very much. No money means no parts, no test dates—maybe even no results. Erv's teams are like promising little colleges with great professors and no endowment.

An Arai helmet technician poked his head in the door, offering a freshly painted helmet with duct-tape-tabbed tear-offs already in place. After a brief exchange over this, John turned to me and said, "That's what I like. Things that are done exactly right. This helmet is perfect. Perfect."

He was silent for a moment then said, "I need to work with people who believe in me. I expect help. When I say there's something wrong with the motorcycle, there's something wrong with it. When that gets fixed, I go faster. I have to work with people who believe in me."

"Then once a rider finds the right engineer or crew chief to work with, he should take that person with him wherever he rides?" I asked.

"Yes! Because once they stop believing in you . . ."

Kocinski clearly wasn't in that situation at the moment—Vance and Leonard both say they believe John will pull away once they work through to a setup for him. But the not-believing situation is one I've seen more than once, and John knows how quickly confidence turns into its opposite.

"I can ride a motorcycle. I haven't reached that point [of declining skills]. I ask a lot from myself, and I expect a lot from the people around me. If I'm working out, getting in shape, and somebody on my team comes up and says, 'Hey, you've gotta work harder,' that's okay, my feelings aren't hurt—I've gotta work harder. So if I say the same thing to people on my team, it's just the truth. I don't want to hurt anybody's feelings, but if something's wrong, I want somebody to know it."

Sunday morning would give only 10 laps of practice time. Of this, 3 laps would be needed to check out the replacement engine freshly installed in the Saturday bike. To get maximum test time, a second bike, with new experimental settings, would be warmed up and waiting at the pit wall.

If this were a novel, the experiments would solve everything and lead to a spectacular win on Sunday. After all, Ducatis have won this event the past four times. But making a fresh marriage of a man and machine is not a literary problem.

Here is a worst-case scenario: When a new rider replaces a departed champion—as Daryl Beattie did at Suzuki when Kevin Schwantz retired—he tests the machine and requests changes in its setup. Team engineers look at each other knowingly. Change perfection? No way—they know the answers. Therefore, the new man's requests are either ignored or only partly answered. Unable to make the lap times, the new rider does the only thing he can do—he rides harder. On an unfamiliar bike, which responds to him in strange ways, this is risky. He crashes.

This scenario isn't happening to John Kocinski, but he knows it can. It's not happening here because of the professionalism of Jim Leonard, and because John makes the bike go faster when specific problems are fixed. As he said, racing success is about people.

In Sunday's race, series points leader Mat Mladin, his Yoshimura Suzuki teammate Aaron Yates, and eventual winner, Honda-mounted Nickey Hayden, had a frighteningly intense battle, while Miguel Duhamel and Kocinski, who again led briefly, ran nose-to-tail some distance back for fourth and fifth. Kocinski was running his bike right to the edges of the track (even posting the quickest lap of the race, a 2:10.071) but was unable to launch himself past Duhamel to move ahead. The power is there. The turning, so far, is not.

Leonard's comment was, "If you can't get onto the straightaway here, you're done." That means making the bike turn while accelerating hard—something that's not possible with the current setup. Progress requires testing, and testing is scarce mid-season.

Leonard continued, "We talked about going with something new (on Sunday). I couldn't say it'd be better for sure, but I was pretty sure. So in the end, we went with the conservative choice (basically, Saturday's known setup). We've made progress. It doesn't show in the results, but it's real. This is a completely different motorcycle from what we started with in Atlanta."

Reality is more interesting than a novel. Racers must above all be conservative, because the job is to get points. That means finishing races with the best-known setup, not gambling on novelties and then either having to override the problems or running slow. Yes, the experimental setup might have been better, but the risk of its not being better made it a bad play. Some programs "come good" very quickly, as Honda's RC51 has done. Others take months or years—as Suzuki's recent GSX-Rs or Honda's RC45 did. Setup is about rider confidence, and it's the hardest problem in motorcycle roadracing. To jump into a war fought by factory teams absolutely cold and get seventh-, fourth-, and fifth-place finishes is a high achievement. In the weeks to come, Kocinski and his Vance & Hines crew will work hard to make the bike work for him. Like others before them, they will either succeed or fail.

# Farewell, 500s

*Change did come to sweep away all our old certitudes. And despite a certain pro-two-stroke partisanship, I have to admit that in retrospect the 500s now look like what they were—crude, explosive devices. Despite that, we learned a lot from them.*

Two-stroke 500cc Grand Prix bikes have been motorcycling's pinnacle for a quarter-century. Now, they are to be laid low by the FIM's administrative act of writing 990ccc four-strokes into racing's top class and renaming it MotoGP. The 500s stuffed 190 horsepower into a 286-pound package that accelerated like nothing else. Riding these machines was racing's supreme art. Even masters of four-stroke Superbikes of nearly equal power often failed to come to grips with the two-stroke's explosive qualities. The management of these qualities in 500 racing has yielded a rich technological harvest, for the capable chassis, brakes, and suspension of today's production bikes are the direct result of 500cc development.

The first East German MZ two-strokes in Grand Prix racing caused no comment in the middle-1950s. Two-strokes were a poor man's engine—slow, smoky, and unreliable. When MZ's Dr. Walter Kaaden put resonant exhaust pipes to work, pumping air into these simple machines, they began to win races. First Suzuki and then Yamaha applied Kaaden's ideas to their own bikes, and an unstoppable process was begun. Suzuki took the 50cc championship in 1962 and the 125cc title the next year. Then in 1964, Yamaha was 250cc champion. A decade later, Yamaha was just a step away from its first 500cc title.

On a grass-roots level, the two-stroke meant a person with ideas, a bent file, tin snips, and a gas torch could make his own simple machine faster than any 20,000-rpm complexity of gears, cams, and valves. This has remained the great strength of two-stroke racing—that development does not cost the Earth.

This past season was the 52nd and final in which Grand Prix two-strokes and four-strokes were mandated to run at the same 500cc displacement, though no four-strokes have taken to the grid since Honda's ill-fated NR500 of 1982.

The 2001 contest began as yet another triumph-in-the-making for 22-year-old Valentino Rossi, who moved up to 500s the previous season. Prior to this, he had won both the 125 and 250cc titles, each after only a year of study. Winning the first three Grand Prixs of the 2001 season, he seemed set to sweep to yet another success. Max Biaggi, the man everyone expected to be his principal rival, was struggling, his Yamaha YZR500 off the pace.

Reigning World Champion Kenny Roberts Jr. found his Suzuki even further behind than a year ago. The year he won his championship, he could lead off the start, block his rivals as tires aged, and win or finish well. This year, the Suzuki's powerband still overtaxed the rear tire, while his rivals' machines were improved more than his own. This left him unable to defend the early leads he so brilliantly achieved. One by one, rivals passed his grip-impoverished bike, leaving him to finish well back.

Soon, Biaggi's Yamaha YZR500 received a fresh setup more to his liking. He suddenly set pole and won the French Grand Prix while Rossi managed only a third. Then at Mugello, Italy, Rossi crashed out, while a third place by Biaggi pulled him to within 21 points. Which man could summon the resources to win a straining season-long arm-wrestle?

At Spain's Catalunya circuit, Rossi perfected the method that would work so well the rest of the season—waiting until everyone's tires had fatigued to the point that his Honda's exceptionally smooth torque curve could make best use of the remaining grip. Hard words and even blows between the two camps had by now expanded the Rossi/Biaggi rivalry beyond racing. Life and racing are an amusement for Rossi. His sense of humor and intelligence are always evident, whether he is making witty, two-edged comments about his rival or parading zany inflatable theme dolls on his victory laps. His race management shows that he has the processing power to simultaneously race and plan strategic problems for his opponents.

Biaggi, by contrast, seems a lonely, even desperate figure for whom winning is painfully important. His machine control is wonderful, but he trusts no one—sometimes not even his own crew. This has in the past compromised his machine setup, forcing him to ride harder to compensate.

Rossi's best performances were full of assurance, planning, and control. Biaggi's rides were brilliant—but with a brittle element. Riding as close to the edge as he must, even a small mistake means a crash.

For Jurgen van den Goorbergh and the Kenny Roberts KR3 Proton Triple, lack of resources made 2001 frustrating. After seasons wasted in vibration and failure, this breakaway design finally seemed ready to prove its original thesis—that a lighter, narrower, handier bike could match lap times with the power-laden fours. Promising speed at certain tracks was negated by nuisances—clutch grabbing, surprise tire chatter, mysterious power drops, and crank torsional vibration. What for Proton next year? For economic reasons, the two-stroke triple may soldier on in place of a rumored four-stroke.

Late in the season, Biaggi began to crash. His idea of the cause was "machine imbalance." Whatever the reason, Rossi pulled away from his rival, while Biaggi in two events remounted after crashing to salvage points. By the Australian Phillip Island race, Rossi had only to finish eighth or better to become the last-ever 500cc world champion. He did better, winning the most exciting race of the year over Biaggi in pass after pass with as many as six other riders—and sealing the 500cc title—by a powerful, yet miniscule, 0.013 of a second. Rossi's comment on the win? "Trying to finish eighth would have been more risky."

Thus 500cc two-stroke racing ends at its peak—as a tense, seesaw struggle between two great and contrasting talents and motorcycle brands, building to a climax, against a background of other able riders.

Even those who vividly remember the ascending scales sung by the megaphoned four-strokes of the 1950s and 1960s must admit that we have been treated to a golden, multi-brand age of 500cc competition over the past 25 years.

Since the first two-stroke 500cc title in 1975, we have witnessed continuous chassis, suspension, engine, and tire development. Long-travel suspension, gas-pressurized dampers, and high-stiffness aluminum chassis have been part of the achievement. Tires advanced from narrow, hard-compound patterned-tread "triangulars" to wide, round-contour belted semi-slicks, and finally Michelin's pioneering work advanced the art to radial belted tires. These run so cool that rubber compounds formerly usable only in rain can now be run in the dry. Engine power has not only doubled in this period, but has been smoothed and civilized to a degree no one would have believed possible even as recently as 1988.

Yamaha's 90-bhp reed engines gave way to Suzuki's disc valves. Kenny Roberts in 1978–80 put 125-bhp Yamaha piston-port engines on top, only to yield to another generation of 135-bhp Suzuki disc-valve engines in 1981–82. Then came Honda with motocross-inspired reed valves, and everyone had to follow suit, leading to the closest-ever competition among supermen such as Rainey, Gardner, Lawson, Schwantz, and then-mighty Mick Doohan. After 1991, lap times stagnated while innovation continued with 190-bhp big bang engines, torque controls and computer data acquisition. Doohan, despite his injuries and through dogged recoveries, reigned supreme with five world championships.

Most recently, the maturing of a new crop of riders like Biaggi, Rossi, and Roberts Jr. has revitalized the action. After 52 seasons of 500 racing, this is the end—and a new beginning. Everything stops for the leap to four-stroke MotoGP.

How will four-strokes change racing? Their great strength is smoothness in coming on-throttle. Two-stroke 500 riders must try to get away first, block their four-stroke rivals' smooth early acceleration in mid-corner, then use the speed arising from superior set-up experience to stay ahead. As four-stroke teams and riders gain experience, their big-inch horsepower and early throttle smoothness will win the day for them. As they say in boxing, "A good big man will always beat a good little man."

At first, only Honda's RC211V and Yamaha's YZR-M1 four-strokes will join the existing two-strokes on starting grids, but change is coming to sweep away all our old certitudes.

# Grip, Gripe, Grip

*The motorcycle set-up problem is never solved—just elevated to a higher level of performance.*

As you watch the early laps of MotoGP races—whether on TV, on DVD, or in person—you see a colorful, high-speed parade of sophisticated machinery snaking around racetracks all over the world. Watching for more than a few minutes, however, reveals that not all are fast for long, and that some are not fast to begin with. Usually, one or two machines come to the front while the rest fade. And occasionally, a rider will move up as the race continues.

So, what sorts the fast from the slow?

For some of the slower riders, a common post-race explanation is, "I picked the wrong tire." But can it be that simple? Tire makers provide good advice, and strong teams have an excellent understanding of their tire choices as a result of full-length race simulations during testing. More likely, the team in question was unable in the time available to get further than a "one-lap set-up," and some teams struggle at this stage through a whole season. A one-lap set-up may be fast, but it destroys tire properties too rapidly to be competitive throughout the entire distance of the race.

Other riders are clearly struggling to keep the pace, spinning and sliding off corners or tail-wagging threateningly during braking. In general, the more hero saves a rider makes, the less likely he is to finish the race, for there are limits to the concentration and endurance of even the most able riders. When this is the only way a top rider can be competitive, something is very wrong with the machine.

Here's an example of the kind of thing that can result in a one-lap set-up. The bike in question has poor swingarm geometry, such that during off-corner acceleration, weight shifts to the rear, causing squat. This squat takes load off the front tire, reducing its ability to steer, thereby making the machine run wide off turns. If the swingarm pivot is cast into the back of the gearcase, its height can't be changed to create more chain-derived lift force to counter this weight shift. In this case, the Band-Aid for acceleration squat is a stiff rear spring. That allows the rider to go fast for a short time, but the excessive firmness of the rear suspension beats up the tire. The tire goes away in 5–10 laps, and so the rider—despite knee-saves that make the crowd roar—fades from the top five.

Motorcycle suspension adopted long wheel travel from motocross in the mid-1970s, and riders using it reported they could keep the power on across rough pavement that had previously required them to roll off the throttle. But at the same time, disc brakes and slick tires had just hit the scene, and their combined power caused rapid front-end dive as brakes were applied. Long travel allowed the chassis to acquire rotary momentum as it pitched forward, and as the suspension stopped the motion, this momentum picked the rear wheel up off the track.

Between 1978 and 1982, the response to this condition was mechanical and hydraulic antidive devices. Meanwhile, much-improved dampers were developed (derived, like long-travel suspension, from motocross experience), and their ability to package more control into each inch of suspension stroke began to drive a trend back toward shorter suspension travel. That, in turn, ended interest in antidive. Teams and riders also realized that dive can be desirable, for as a machine dives, its *CG* is lowered, permitting harder braking.

What remains of these changes today are two competing modes of suspension setup. One seeks to isolate the machine from the upsetting effects of pavement roughness through use of the lowest practicable spring rates—really, the classic 1950's automotive concept. Extra support to prevent suspension bottoming is obtained by careful use of low-speed compression damping (a technology developed around 1980).

The other mode considers the suspension less as a means of de-coupling the chassis from the bumps than as a means of managing acceleration and braking forces controllably. By using stiffer-rate springs and correspondingly less compression damping, this method limits the forward rotation of the chassis as the brakes are applied, and is therefore less likely to pick up the rear tire as braking begins. The stiffer springs work the tires harder,

*Lee Klancher*

but that must be considered against the gains from improved braking stability.

In the first two years of MotoGP, braking instability was a big issue. Powerful carbon-carbon brakes and wide front tires have the power to lift the rear wheel at will, and this, combined with then-unsolved engine braking forces, conspired to destroy the rear tire's directional stability. Instead of giving two or three Ben Bostrom–style side-to-side shakes during hard braking, the rear ends of some MotoGP bikes were building up into a violent oscillation, resulting in quite a few get-offs. More than likely, a combination of extended wheelbase and improved engine-braking behavior are the factors that have brought braking instability under control.

In corners, suspension becomes increasingly irrelevant. With the bike leaned over at a 60-degree angle to the vertical, a one-inch-high bump would require a perfectly compliant suspension to move two inches (draw the triangle and do the trig). This geometric effect makes leaned-over suspension act twice as stiff as when upright.

It gets worse. With only about four inches of travel to begin with, of which an inch is sag with another couple of inches used to support cornering force, there's little travel left. How do we handle bumps with no travel, especially with the above-described stiffening effect?

Well, with chassis that are very stiff laterally, as developed for 500cc two-strokes, you don't. The result was, in Wayne Rainey's words, "Chatter, hop and skating." The over-stiff, nearly bottomed suspension, combined with a stiff chassis, caused the tires to spend much of their time in the air, skipping along the tops of pavement ripples.

The ad-hoc "answer" has been to put back some of the lateral flexibility possessed by the tubular steel chassis of the past. Swingarms are now built with beams that are very tall vertically, making them strongly resist tilting of the rear wheel, but fairly thin laterally, allowing the rear wheel to move side-to-side to accommodate small in-corner bumpiness.

Racing four-strokes originally bolted the steering head to the nearest solid object: the cylinder head. This made for a very stiff assembly. But nowadays, to provide some lateral flexure, longer and laterally more flexible struts go from the steering head all the way down to the crankcase and are bolted there. Although the notion of the entire front wheel, fork, and steering-head moving sideways to accommodate small bumps seems cumbersome, it appears to have some desirable effect. Surely, something better—providing the necessary flexure closer to the road surface—will emerge from the R&D shops soon.

But have a care! Uncontrolled structural flex also leads to chatter, that most disturbing phenomenon. In chatter, a heavily loaded tire, cornering on high-grip pavement, is driven to its traction limit and lets go. It slides for an instant, then grips. The kinetic energy acquired in that instant of sliding acts to compress the tire as it grips again, and the elasticity of the tire causes this compression to rebound, causing the tire to let go again, repeating the cycle rapidly. The tire itself, and/or the suspension damper, may take sufficient energy out of this cycle to slow or stop it; but if the cyclic motion happens to be nearly in step with the natural frequency of some part of the chassis (for example, the longitudinal bending frequency of the front fork, or the twist frequency of the steering head), it may build up to an amplitude large enough to make the affected tire go hopping toward the outside. In this worst form of chatter, the rider's attempts to throttle-up while accelerating out of a turn just increase the chatter, making it impossible to hold line.

A prime antichatter tool has been the higher stiffness of male-slider forks. This raises their natural bending frequency high enough that it can no longer fall into step with tire bounce and thereby foster chatter. But there seems to be a general increase in the frequency of chatter as tires and chassis have developed. Formerly, the chatter frequency was in a range of 18–22 cycles per second (NASA research calls this the "seeing double" range), but now it has moved up towards 25 cycles. Fork dampers, marginal at the old frequency, were generally unable to handle these higher numbers. Traditional fork dampers operate at atmospheric pressure, which means that as the damper's cylinder refills, only the 14.7 psi of the atmosphere is available to push oil into the cylinder through its recuperator valving. As the damper strokes more and more rapidly, the valves must either be made larger or must lift farther in order for the flow to keep up. This means that more of the damper's stroke is used up in the process of opening and closing the valves, which now flutter indecisively.

It is to deal with this problem that Öhlins has developed its current pressurized fork dampers, which have distinctive, pressurized accumulator cylinders in front of each bottom tube. With 10 or more times atmospheric pressure now available to refill fast-stroking dampers, valve lift can be made smaller and faster-acting. The result is that damping can again keep up with the chatter frequency. Gas-pressurized fork dampers will soon be the new orthodoxy.

As noted by Valentino Rossi, engine power delivery is a decisive component of handling. As the rider begins acceleration in mid-corner, the power must begin very smoothly or the tire—already giving almost all it can as cornering force—will break loose and slide. As acceleration continues, any sudden peaks or dips in torque output can have the same effect. Attempts by the rider to compensate by rapid and artful throttle movements will take his attention from equally important concerns.

Yet as Rossi's engineer, Jeremy Burgess, says, "We can only shave off the peaks of the torque curve; we can't fill in the valleys," so smoothing the power delivery will involve some loss of power. A feature of top teams is trackside engine mapping, not pleading for action from the home office. An engine with such smoothed power gains ground off every turn by not wasting time in wheelspin and constant corrections. In the 2005 season, the game will be to somehow combine controlled power delivery with higher performance. In 2004, Honda and Ducati gambled that they could do this electronically, but the necessary smoothness eluded them.

Tires can lack off-corner smoothness just as engines can. Tire engineers try to give riders what they ask for; and if they ask for more grip at middling lean angles, the engineers can provide it. So then, when leaned way over in a corner, the rider gasses it up, which pushes the tire smoothly sideways as part of the steering process; but as the bike rolls more upright, it hits this new "traction enhanced" region of the tire. The result? The bike stops throttle-steering, so it runs wide. The rider, seeing this, concludes that the tire lacks grip. Development time is subsequently wasted in providing even more grip, and then discovering that it only makes the problem worse. For reasons such as this, sorting out handling requires thought, not action on the first idea that comes to mind.

This raises the question of just what it is that riders cue on. The rider in the previous paragraph is watching his corner line, not measuring lateral G-force (aviation studies show that humans cannot sense acceleration to greater than 20 percent accuracy). If the tire engineer uncritically accepts the rider's view that the tire lacks grip, he goes up a dead-end street. Therefore, the engineer must always consider how the physics of the situation is being filtered through the rider's perceptions.

Another example is the rider who complained of excessive braking distances. Close investigation revealed that over-rapid forward pitch was picking up the back tire prematurely, sending the rider a "that's enough!" signal. Once the rapid pitch motion was eliminated, the rider felt free to brake much harder.

In another case, a rider's rate of brake application had to be considered. On a bike with a desirably low CG height, weight transfer to the front wasn't fast enough to keep up with the rider's rate of brake application. This made the tire feel "loose." Raising the CG height—which, in physical terms, is counterproductive because it makes a stoppie occur at a lower rate of deceleration—transferred weight forward faster, in step with this rider's style. This made him *feel* it was safe to brake harder.

Since 1980, suspension tuning has become a mature art. If a team can't handle a given situation "on the clickers," the damper is taken to the Öhlins or Showa truck where it is depressurized and disassembled. Then its internal damping-control washers are restacked to change the damping in the desired direction. The process has become quite refined, and teams pay an annual fee that covers a certain number of such rebuilds per meeting.

Yet, damper engineers know this is all a big mistake. Specific problem frequencies must be damped—such as the chatter frequency, the chassis pitch frequency, suspension frequencies, etc. But for all other frequencies, damping is just a friction force slowing suspension movement, interfering with its ability to track road irregularities freely. The trouble is that there is no convenient, non-electronic way to build a damper that can damp specific frequencies selectively. The Öhlins CES electronic damping control system of the 1990 period was a step in the right direction, and a further-developed version may soon be seen. For the moment, dampers crudely damp all movement, and riders must make the best of it.

A controversy of this past season was the proper extent of chassis adjustability. Common sense tells us that the more chassis adjustments a bike has, the more tools there are available for addressing problems. On the other hand, more adjustments also invite a team to get lost in a maze of choices (yes, this does happen!). Honda came to MotoGP with a mature machine, the result of a great deal of development, and so its chassis featured a minimum of adjustments. Like Honda, Ducati chose to cast its swingarm pivot into the back of its engine/gearbox unit. In either case, this is the act of a team sure of its conclusions as a result of thorough testing.

Along came the new Yamaha-Rossi-Burgess team for 2004, with a very different approach. In the past, Yamaha had tried to please each of its riders individually, building many chassis, swingarms, and engine characteristics. Burgess's view is different: His goal was to build one machine that every rider would want to ride. Consequently, *everything* was made adjustable. Later in the season, this provoked Honda's Colin Edwards to say that Michelin tires were optimized for the Yamaha because only the Yamaha had the adjustability to properly exploit the possible advantages of tire development. Whatever the truth, the Yamaha quickly converged on a workable setup and did seem to exploit its Michelin tires well.

Full adjustability means that steering stems can be moved forward and back within the headstock, and that rake angle can be altered in small increments, all by means of variously machined bearing carriers. Swingarm pivots can be raised and lowered. A fixed pivot, its optimum position determined by testing, would provide a stiffer connection between swingarm and chassis. But what if tires evolve during the season? What if, as appears to have happened in Honda's case, the chassis is developed for one set of tire choices, and something new (in this case, the larger 2004 Michelin rear) appears just as the season begins?

As a vehicle accelerates, thrust is generated at ground level. Because the center-of-mass of machine and rider is 20 to 24 inches above that, a leverage is created that tends to extend the front suspension and compress (squat) the rear during acceleration. When this happens as the bike is leaned over and accelerating out of a corner, it has the effect of unloading the front tire, reducing its grip, and causing the machine to "push," or run wide. This is the classic "squat and push" problem. To correct it, the swingarm pivot height and swingarm droop angle are chosen to cause chain pull to generate a lift force that cancels this rearward weight shift to any desired degree. (Note: Making the engine sprocket concentric with the swingarm pivot axis does *not* accomplish this.) It is for this reason that rear suspension is often seen to extend rather than compress during lower-gear acceleration. But if rear-tire development increases grip during the season, this cancellation effect will change with it—and so will handling. If the pivot height cannot be changed, swingarm droop angle can be adjusted to get a similar effect; but this changes the machine's ride height, which is not always a desirable outcome.

Chassis non-adjustability reeks of self-confidence, which, in Honda's case, was justified until 2004. It must feel grand to wheel out a beautifully finished machine—one that closely resembles a production bike—that wins races without timid reliance on a lot of cover-your-bets adjustments; that's just Honda's cup of tea. On the other hand, Yamaha has now raised the pace of development and is prepared to respond instantly to changes in tire technology. Can Honda afford to do less?

Motorcycle chassis and suspension appear to present a complex physical problem—and so they do. But since riders cannot give their best unless they believe themselves reasonably safe in doing so, the rider-machine interface and reality as perceived by the rider have quietly become a hot area of development. More engineers and faster computers may not accomplish much here. Because as always, the rider is the most critical part of the equation.

# Index